7 day.

Scare Quotes from Shakespeare

Scare Quotes from Shakespeare

Marx, Keynes, and the
Language of Reenchantment

Martin Harries

STANFORD UNIVERSITY PRESS
STANFORD, CALIFORNIA 2000

Stanford University Press
Stanford, California
© 2000 by the Board of Trustees of the
Leland Stanford Junior University
Printed in the United States of America

Library of Congress Cataloging-in-Publication Data

Harries, Martin
    Scare quotes from Shakespeare : Marx, Keynes, and the language of
reenchantment / Martin Harries.
        p.   cm.
    Includes bibliographical references and index.
    ISBN 0-8047-3621-9 (alk. paper)
    1. Marx, Karl, 1818–1883.   2. Keynes, John Maynard, 1883–1946.
3. Shakespeare, William, 1564–1616—Influence.   I. Title.

B3305.M74 H333   2000
001.1—dc21   00-020696

This book is printed on acid-free, archival-quality paper.

Original printing 2000

Last figure below indicates year of this printing:
09   08   07   06   05   04   03   02   01   00

Designed and typeset in 11/13 Garamond by John Feneron

Acknowledgments

'SCARE QUOTES' IS in part about ways we can be unconscious of our debts. I finish it, nevertheless, believing I know many of the debts I have collected while writing it. I also know that there are some who have influenced this book in ways I no longer know how to acknowledge, and I fear that there might be other debts I have simply forgotten. I am also acutely conscious of the difficulties of expressing thanks as I would like in a short note such as this. I hope no one will mistake the spare form of a list for a lack of gratitude. First, I thank David Marshall and Jennifer Wicke, who advised me during the writing of the dissertation out of which this book grew; I owe much to their careful, constructive readings and support. Laurie Edelstein gave this book her careful attention over what now seem perhaps too many years. Cassandra Cleghorn, John Kleiner, and Shawn Rosenheim read drafts with unusual care and offered especially valuable criticism. Larry Danson, Maria DiBattista, Michael Holquist, Michael Levine, and David Quint all generously evaluated drafts at different stages along the way. Over more years than I care to count, friends and colleagues, sometimes quite deliberately, sometimes without knowing it, helped me learn what I was writing about. My thanks go to Elizabeth Abrams, Oliver Arnold, Jessica Branch,

Margaret Bruzelius, Lisa Cohen, Barbara Desmond, Adrienne Donald, Jonathan Freedman, Jeff Hilson, Kiaran Honderich, Nico Israel, Virginia Jackson, Hilary Jewett, David Moss, Jeff Nunokawa, Edgar Pankow, Joanna Picciotto, Henry Pickford, Danielle Rose, Laura Saltz, Natalia Sucre, Michael Wood, and Rishona Zimring. Richard Halpern and an anonymous reader were the ideal respondents to a manuscript. At Stanford University Press, I am grateful to Helen Tartar for her dedication to this book, and to John Feneron for his exemplary care in seeing the manuscript to publication.

A year of support from the Mellon Foundation was crucial to completing the dissertation, and a grant from Princeton allowed me to delve into the career of Henry Dircks in London. I am grateful to George Speaight and Don Wilmeth for their responses to queries about Dircks, and to the staffs of the Henry Price Collection of the University of London, the Theater Museum, and the Hackney Archives. An earlier version of chapter two appeared in *New German Critique* 66.

For support in good times and in bad, I thank my family and I thank my friends, who know who they are. I dedicate this book to my mother and father. I owe more of my education to them than I can know.

                                                                    M.H.

Contents

But nature is a stranger yet;
The ones that cite her most
Have never passed her haunted house,
Nor simplified her ghost.
                    Emily Dickinson

Man is changed by his living; but not fast enough.
His concern to-day is for that which yesterday did not occur.
In the hour of the Blue Bird and the Bristol Bomber,
    his thoughts are appropriate to the years of the Penny Farthing:
He tosses at night who at noonday found no truth.
                    W. H. Auden and Christopher Isherwood,
                    The Dog Beneath the Skin or Where Is Francis?

In the end, one always finds new tunnels to burrow, old mole
that one is.
                    Franz Kafka, *Letters to Milena*

Introduction

NOT ONLY THE sleep of reason, but its occasional waking hour, breeds monsters. This perseverance or return of the supernatural where modernity flatters itself culture has become disenchanted forms the largest frame for this study. What interests me most is not those literary or aesthetic forms in which the supernatural has found its recognized haunts and homes away from home—the Gothic, the horror story, the literature of the fantastic—but the surprising traces of the supernatural in works of political economy and social thought. I began this study by pondering the famous moment in *The Eighteenth Brumaire* where Marx alludes to *Hamlet*, where Hamlet's praise for the Ghost in the cellarage, "Well said, old mole!," becomes Marx's greeting to the revolution, "Well grubbed, old mole!" The language of Shakespeare's supernatural scenes forms a touchstone throughout. I argue that Shakespeare provides a privileged language for the apprehension of the supernatural—what I call reenchantment—in works by Marx, John Maynard Keynes, and others.

That Shakespeare, more than any other figure, shaped the English language and the forms of Anglo-American thought is, I take it, so dull a claim as hardly to amount to a truism. Jane Austen's *Mansfield Park* provides a pointed example of this shaping force. Henry Crawford reads beautifully from *Henry VIII*, even though he does not think he has so much as held "a volume of Shakespeare" since he was fifteen. Crawford explains this surprising aptitude:

> I once saw Henry the 8th acted.—Or I have heard of it from somebody who did—I am not certain which. But Shakespeare one gets acquainted with without knowing how. It is a part of an Englishman's constitution. His thoughts and beauties are so spread abroad that one touches them every where, one is intimate with him by instinct . . .[1]

Crawford's instinctual intimacy, his getting "acquainted" with Shakespeare "without knowing how" and reading beautifully from *Henry VIII* even though he has forgotten whether he has seen a production of the play or only heard about one, gives Shakespeare the status of common knowledge. The reader cannot know whether Crawford, the skillful and duplicitous performer, is telling the truth about his acquaintance—he might have been rehearsing all along—but he lies like truth, and he almost seduces even the novel's anti-theatrical heroine, Fanny, with his impressive recitation.

There are, as Gary Taylor notes, political—and politically conservative—nuances in the passage from *Mansfield Park*: Taylor links Crawford's speech to the charged issue of the "Englishman's political constitution":

> that mystical entity existed somehow, one had to believe, as an effusion of the whole. "Organic" was the adjective Coleridge used to define and defend both the English class system and Shakespeare's poetry. Shakespeare's plays were broken down into fragments and then disseminated through the bloodstream of English society, droplets of poetry suspended in a stable cultural solution. By the end of the eighteenth century, Shakespeare had become part of the English constitution.[2]

---

[1] Jane Austen, *Mansfield Park*, p. 335.

[2] Gary Taylor, *Reinventing Shakespeare*, p. 111. For discussion of how caricature used Shakespeare in ironic ways when Shakespeare was becoming "part of an Englishman's constitution," see Jonathan Bate, *Shakespearean Constitutions*. Bate takes his title from Austen; his prologue is an especially valuable discussion of the appropriation of Shakespeare.

Taylor echoes Austen: her sense of Shakespeare's words being "spread abroad," broadcast like seeds, leads to his description of the breaking down of Shakespeare's plays and their dissemination through the bloodstream. In Taylor's picture, quotation from Shakespeare invokes a more or less unquestioned authority. Shakespeare becomes a god, or beneficent demon, and quotation follows as a reassuring sublimate, "suspended in a stable cultural solution." Quotations become part of the body and part of the established body politic. Such quotation is then open to Guy Debord's critique that the "theoretical authority" of the quotation "is always falsified by the mere fate of having become a quotation—a fragment torn from its context, from its movement, and ultimately from the global framework of its epoch and from the precise choice, whether exactly recognized or erroneous, which it was in this framework."[3] This sort of quotation has its power precisely because people ignore the context to which the fragment belongs.

Another reason I begin with this quotation from Austen is that it firmly imagines Shakespeare as part of nature. Or, that is, it shows the process of making Shakespeare "natural" at work. The potentially insincere protestations of Crawford show how the assertion of the naturalness of Shakespeare may disguise a strategy. A distinction that drives this project is that between the authoritative quotation that disguises what is *made* under the guise of the natural, and what I call the "scare quote," which estranges this appearance of the natural. The category of second nature, the solid shell of tradition, custom, habit, and ideology that allows us to mistake what has been made as part of the "first" natural world, is important to much of this book.[4] I

[3] Guy Debord, *The Society of the Spectacle*, sec. 208.
[4] Susan Buck-Morss, paraphrasing Adorno, calls second nature "a negating, critical concept which referred to the false, mythical appearance of given reality as ahistorical and absolute." Buck-Morss, *The Origin of Negative Dialectics*, p.55; this quotation comes from a chapter that traces the concept of second nature from Hegel through Lukács's *The Theory of the Novel* and Benjamin's *Trauerspiel* study to Adorno's early essay, "The Idea of Natural History." Edmund Burke also quickly and suggestively sketches a rather different theory of second nature in *Reflections on the Revolution in France*, p. 299: "The legislators who framed the antient republics knew that their business was too arduous to be accomplished with no better appa-

do not question that one effect of quotation from Shakespeare has been that Shakespearean language has become part of official speech, and that his plays, especially but by no means only in Britain, have become part of a stolid, official culture. The focus of this study, however, falls on a different Shakespeare. Shakespeare may be part of a nearly impermeable second nature. Once in a while, however, that easy order of things goes awry, and Shakespearean language that at other times might fertilize second nature becomes a symptom of faults in its carapace. Shakespeare becomes a potentially eerie thing in Crawford's description—*Hic et ubique*, here and everywhere, as Hamlet describes the Ghost of his father—and this eeriness indicates how turning Shakespeare into part of the English "constitution" also means imagining him as an omnipresent spirit, or demon. Scare quotes are exceptions to Debord's description of quotation. Quotation and allusion, I argue, can be telling clusters in a social constellation; they can illuminate the "framework" from which they have been torn. Coleridge's invocation of the "organic" provides a precise way to understand why few quotations from Shakespeare are scare quotes. Scare quotes defamiliarize the supposedly solid structures of second nature. They are, to rewrite Taylor, shards of poetry that reveal faultlines in a cultural solution that is only apparently stable.[5]

---

ratus than the metaphysics of an under-graduate, and the mathematics and arithmetic of an exciseman. They had to do with men, and they were obliged to study human nature. They had to do with citizens, and they were obliged to study the effects of those habits which are communicated by the circumstances of civil life. They were sensible that the operation of this second nature on the first produced a new combination; and thence arose many diversities among men . . ." Burke's theory of second nature describes how different habits produce distinctions among people, and he defends the propriety of these distinctions. Burke does not, however, offer a naive defense of second nature. Like the later theorists of the Frankfurt School, he urges legislators and political thinkers to become conscious of this accretion of habit, and he realizes that the process by which that habit becomes second nature is not timeless, but the result of a slow historical process. Unlike Adorno or Benjamin, Burke champions this tradition.

[5] I do not claim to offer some general theory of intertextuality here. While works including Harold Bloom's *The Anxiety of Influence* and Jacques Derrida's *Limited Inc.* have influenced my understanding of allusion and quotation, my interest is in a more local phenomenon. I have found intriguing comments about allusion and quotation scattered across the work of Walter Benjamin, especially in

Despite my emphasis, I do not mean to suggest that understanding most quotations from Shakespeare as more or less unquestioning invocations of his authority is mistaken. Scare quotes are, I think, exceptions to the rule of the stabilizing and reinforcing quotation. Some quotations are what I call scare quotes; most are not. This study considers a mode of intertextuality that belongs to a particular period, roughly from the mid-nineteenth century to the mid-twentieth. As I suggest in my conclusion, the conditions that allowed for this mode may be dying out in their uneven way. Any transhistorical theory of intertextuality I might offer would then deny the historical specificity of the "scare quote."[6]

What people now commonly call a scare quote, a word or phrase put in skeptical quotation marks, follows from a strategy that at once acknowledges and distances. Writers (or speakers, with fingers mimicking quotation marks) put distance between themselves and a word or phrase. This word or phrase, however objectionable or outworn,

his essays, "Edward Fuchs, Collector and Historian," and "Karl Kraus." For discussions of Benjamin's understanding of quotation, see James L. Rolleston, "The Politics of Quotation"; Ian Balfour, "Reversal, Quotation (Benjamin's History)"; Bettine Menke, "Das Nach-Leben im Zitat"; and Eduardo Cadava, *Words of Light*. Without the example of Benjamin's work this book would certainly have taken a very different shape. Another figure important to the early stages of this work in untraceable ways is Kenneth Burke; the example of his *A Rhetoric of Motives* is especially important to me.

[6] A genealogy of scare quotes might also begin in "the end of the eighteenth century, [when] Shakespeare had become part of the English constitution"; Bate's study of caricature traces something like what I have in mind. The Gothic, too, might offer a sort of counter-history to the "stable cultural solution" in which Shakespeare's disseminated words hang. Indeed, the inaugural novel in the English Gothic tradition, Walpole's *The Castle of Otranto*, seems to me to be built around the elaboration of a Shakespearean pun: the *helmet* that rises from beneath the castle has an ancestor in the *Hamlet* that spooks the Prince from the cellarage. Walpole, indeed, claims his authority from Shakespeare. Defending his representation of the "deportment of the domestics," Walpole writes in his preface to the second edition, "My rule was nature." But he goes on: "That great master of nature, Shakespeare, was the model I copied." Walpole, *The Castle of Otranto*, p. 20. The shape of this possible debt to *Hamlet* first occurred to me in a seminar led by David Marshall. For *Hamlet*'s relationship to the Gothic, see Jonathan Arac's incisive comments in "Hamlet, *Little Dorrit*, and the History of Character," especially pp. 89–92.

remains necessary. The writer insinuates that the word or phrase is just what quotation marks imply—that is, a quotation, words belonging to another context, or to someone else—and also implies that this word or phrase carries values, which the writer partially or wholly rejects. By using scare quotes, one attributes a phrase to someone absent—to a ghost, one might say. One writes "spirit," or "supernatural," or "enlightenment," and assumes that by the typographical feint of quotation marks one has managed to demonstrate skepticism and critical apprehension of the many problems surrounding these terms and, at the same time, grudging acknowledgement that they must remain part of our vocabulary.

As I use the term throughout this book, the "scare quote" refers to something more particular, although the uneasiness of the simultaneous distancing and acknowledgment of a term in the everyday scare quote will be a concern throughout. The "scare quote" refers both to ways writers use, rewrite, and are influenced by their supernatural sources, and to the nature of the material they borrow. This study examines two groups of texts in light of these scare quotes. Two of Shakespeare's tragedies with supernatural concerns, *Hamlet* and *Macbeth*, form one group. Works with the common trait of significant allusions to the supernatural in Shakespeare—centrally, Marx's *The Eighteenth Brumaire of Louis Bonaparte* and John Maynard Keynes's *The Economic Consequences of the Peace*—form a second. Both Marx and Keynes allude to the supernatural in Shakespeare where they encounter blind spots in their analyses of critical moments in European history. Marx finds a contradictory image for what usually falls under the taboo like that against graven images— the revolution—in *Hamlet*'s old mole. Keynes pictures the forces that led to the destructive treaty of Versailles in *Macbeth*'s witches.

I use the "supernatural" as a general term. It covers phenomena, such as the Ghost of Hamlet and the witches in *Macbeth*, which are represented as alien or foreign to the "normal" order of things, yet to which the plays assign important agency within that order. The Ghost and the witches are in many ways different: different traditions lie behind them, and they have varying functions in the plays in which they appear. Nevertheless, they belong neither to "nature" nor to "culture," but to something else. This problem of their classification is not merely a problem for the later critic, dweller in a "disenchanted" world. The plays themselves represent these supernatural elements as contested, as shifting, as subject to interpretation and revision. Spirit of health or goblin damned; hags or prophets: the plays themselves stage debates about these unsettled, unsettling elements. An interest in the plays themselves led me to wonder about the function of the supernatural in them, and this book also includes chapters on *Hamlet* and *Macbeth*. My experience was that reading Marx and Keynes led me to read Shakespeare differently, and this book recapitulates the order of that experience, moving backwards from Marx to *Hamlet* and from Keynes to *Macbeth*, following the movement of quotations and allusions back to their sources.

I consider the supernatural, in Shakespeare as in the later writers, as part of a social constellation. To paraphrase Marx and Engels, the supernatural has as little an independent history as ideology.[7] In certain instances—this is sometimes true, for instance, in *The Eighteenth Brumaire*—the supernatural survives as a figure for ideology. As such, Marx does not simply exorcise and translate it into a more obviously "materialist" discourse. Such translation would distort the social forces Marx makes his subject. To represent the ruses of rationalization as rational would be misleadingly to follow rationalization, which disguises the subterranean and supernatural authorization from which it draws much of its legitimacy. The supernatural, then, figures the endurance of what Slavoj Žižek calls the *"fantasy which is at work in the midst of social reality itself"* and the resistance of this fantasy to straightforward translation.[8] For Keynes, too, the supernatural is not an ornamental or accidental discourse, but a necessary one: the supernatural has become an inescapable attribute of history; figuring it does not ward it off, identifying its political influ-

---

[7] Cf. Karl Marx and Friedrich Engels, *The German Ideology: Part One*, p. 81: "It must not be forgotten that law has just as little an independent history as religion." See also Louis Althusser's discussion of Marx's contention that ideology, like religion, has no independent history in "Ideology and Ideological State Apparatuses," pp. 159–62.

[8] Slavoj Žižek, *The Sublime Object of Ideology*, p. 36. Žižek's emphasis.

ence does not disenchant it. For Marx and Keynes, there is no easy reduction or dismissal of the supernatural, and this is, I argue, not only a rhetorical issue. It is an aspect of their recognition of and grappling with material effects of the unreal and irrational, effects that resist the political economists' efforts to legislate or prophesize. They register this resistance with the scare quote.

The supernatural comes as a shock in the work of Marx and Engels, and I suppose that that is how they experienced what they were trying to name with reference to Shakespeare. Where they and others expect disenchantment, they encounter reenchantment, a word I have borrowed from a passage in Susan Buck-Morss's book on Walter Benjamin's Arcades project, *The Dialectics of Seeing*:

> Based on the writings of Max Weber, it has become a shibboleth in so-cial theory that the essence of modernity is the demythification and dis-enchantment of the social world. In contrast, . . . Benjamin's central ar-gument in the *Passagen-Werk* was that under conditions of capitalism, industrialization had brought about a *re*enchantment of the social world . . . and through it, . . . a "reactivation of mythic powers."[9]

[9] Susan Buck-Morss, *The Dialectics of Seeing*, pp. 253–54. These pages have also influenced my discussion of Weber below. Heidegger, too, an odd companion for Benjamin, wrote against Weber's notion of disenchantment in the 1930s. Otto Pöggeler writes of what he calls Heidegger's "main work" (!), *Contributions in Philosophy*: "Heidegger . . . begins to develop his later opinion that the universal technology of our time is only the end of the metaphysical attempt to grasp the being of all beings. Heidegger regards Max Weber's disenchantment (*Entzauber-ung*) with the European form of rationalization as itself a great enchantment (*Ver-zauberung*); but for Heidegger it is only the enchantment of metaphysics, the European tradition that had remained unchanged ever since Plato's theory of ideas." Pöggeler, "Heidegger, Nietzsche, and Politics," p.134. Already in 1930, Ben-jamin predicted in a letter to Gershom Scholem that the Arcades project would include "a theory of the consciousness of history. It is there that I will find Hei-degger in my path, and I expect something scintillating from the connecting shock between our two very different ways of envisioning history." Buck-Morss, *Dialec-tics of Seeing*, 376n4. One of the ways to understand this "shock" is clear in the difference between Benjamin's sense of the specificity of the historical moment of reenchantment and Heidegger's notion that the twentieth century is only a sort of hypertrophy of the long and destructive enchantment—*Verzauberung*—that be-gins with Plato.

I read *The Eighteenth Brumaire* and *The Economic Consequences of the Peace* as responses to the "reenchantment of the social world." But these texts are not merely transcriptions of a magic at work in second nature; by representing this enchantment *as* enchantment and the magic practices that manipulate it *as* magic, they defamiliarize aspects of what makes second nature seem so "natural." The argument of this book is that supernatural moments in Shakespeare provide a privileged language for the perception of reenchantment. The question then arises: What is the relationship between the time of these appropriations and early modernity? If Marx, Keynes, and others struggle with a *re*enchanted world, is Shakespeare simply enchanted? That modernity finds versions of itself in Shakespeare is hardly news; such a work as Taylor's *Reinventing Shakespeare*, for example, is in part a compendium of such Shakespearean images of modernity. I argue that a particular aspect of modernity, reenchantment, discovers its image in appropriations of supernatural aspects in Shakespeare's plays. This book, then, self-consciously takes part in the tradition of reading Shakespeare that Richard Halpern has called "historical allegory." Halpern distinguishes historical allegory from anachronism:

> Like anachronism, it involves a direct mapping of the past onto the present. Unlike anachronism, however, this mapping takes place against an awareness of historical difference. While anachronism naively collapses two different historical periods one into the other, historical allegory willfully violates distinctions without obliterating them.[10]

I have taken scare quotes as containing within them the seeds of such historical allegories. The writers I study do not themselves fully work out these historical allegories, but these allegories are implicit in the webs of quotation I investigate. If the sort of quotation described by Debord would be merely what Halpern calls anachronism, the scare quote invites one to read the historical allegory of reenchantment.

The word "reenchantment," with its prefix, implies that a disenchanted time has come and gone, and that history has returned to

[10] Richard Halpern, *Shakespeare Among the Moderns*, p. 4.

haunted territories we all thought we had left behind.[11] To some extent, this narrative of return is illuminating: the work of allusion provides a microcosm of the move backwards, from a putatively disenchanted modernity to an enchanted early modernity. Whether such a narrative is historically accurate, whether 1600 was in any measurable way more "enchanted" or more haunted than 1900, is an enormous question.[12] What is important here is the evidence of felt affinities offered by the allusions I focus on. What does, I think, differentiate 1900 from 1600 is the more widespread *expectation* of disenchantment: modernity imagines itself as coming after the disenchantment of the world, after the decline of magic, after witch crazes, night battles and ecstasies. The surprising presence of allusions to the supernatural in Shakespeare in the works of Marx and Keynes, then, figures a much larger surprise: the surprise of reenchantment, of a recrudescence of magical practices, of a new age of witch hunts.[13]

A larger thesis, then, connects these chapters. Beside those features for which the period from 1848 to 1914 in Europe is most notable—

[11] There is a danger here of simply recapitulating, if with a spin, a standard historical narrative, aligning early modernity with enchantment, the Enlightenment with disenchantment, and modernity with reenchantment. I offer this scheme as a useful generalization nevertheless, also aware that insofar as the early modern period thought of itself as a "renaissance," it distanced itself from what it perceived as the enchantment or "darkness" typical of the Middle Ages. Crucial to my thinking about the complexities of this problem are Horkheimer and Adorno's *Dialectic of Enlightenment* and Jürgen Habermas's chapter criticizing their book, "The Entwinement of Myth and Enlightenment."

[12] In discussion following a paper given at Princeton in December 1995, "Magical Effects: The Cultural Work of Sleights, Tricks and Illusions 1720–1780," Simon During ventured the possibility that more people in Britain may have believed in ghosts in 1820 than in 1620. This puts the question starkly.

[13] I refer in the last two sentences to a number of works that have shaped my sense both of the arguments about the nature of disenchanted modernity and of enchanted early modernity. Inevitably central is Max Weber's *The Protestant Ethic and the Spirit of Capitalism*; I have also benefited from R. H. Tawney's response to Weber, *Religion and the Rise of Capitalism*. On supernatural beliefs in the early modern period, most important to me have been Keith Thomas's *Religion and the Decline of Magic* and the work of Carlo Ginzburg, especially *The Night Battles* and *Ecstasies*. Continually perturbing and provocative is the title essay in H. R. Trevor-Roper's *The European Witch-Craze*.

the consolidation of the hegemony of the middle class, the entrenchment of industrial capitalism, the expansion of imperialism—arises a supernatural second nature often lost in accounts of disenchantment and rationalization. Many have recognized World War I as a decisive break, after which European observers again became alert to irrational or supernatural forces in culture; the development of Freud's metapsychology in the years after 1919 is a familiar case.[14] But this account tends to misrepresent the Great War; its causes were not supernatural. Keynes writes in 1919:

> Very few of us realize with conviction the intensely unusual, unstable, complicated, unreliable, temporary nature of the economic organization by which Western Europe has lived for the last half century. We assume some of the most peculiar and temporary of our late advantages as natural, permanent, and to be depended on, and we lay our plans accordingly.[15]

This study concentrates on two political economists who, with all their differences, were acutely sensitive to the qualities suggested by Keynes's adjectives: "intensely unusual, unstable, complicated, unreliable, temporary . . ." One might even offer "supernatural" as the name for the contradictions in capitalism Marx described.[16] *The Eighteenth Brumaire*, indeed, ushers in a period of haunted instability; its supernatural rhetoric provides a model for the forms taken by an era's partly repressed sense of mutability. Certainly intimations of the transience of those "late advantages" assumed to be permanent

[14] For a useful survey of the relationship of Freud's metapsychological works to World War I, see Louise Hoffmann, "War, Revolution, and Psychoanalysis." In this project I by and large bracket a term other literary readers of "supernatural" phenomena, allusion included, have found useful: the uncanny. By positing a psychic mechanism that reproduces supernatural effects, Freud, I believe, rationalized reenchantment, making it a physiological if not a social fact. Readers following Freud then sometimes follow in this rationalization; put bluntly, the uncanny allows one to believe in ghosts again. Two studies from which I have learned much, yet which I believe exaggerate the prevalence and the power of the uncanny, are Marjorie Garber's *Shakespeare's Ghost Writers* and Ned Lukacher's *Primal Scenes*.

[15] John Maynard Keynes, *The Economic Consequences of the Peace, Collected Writings*, vol. 2, p. 1.

[16] For a suggestive work that constructs its argument along these lines, see José Monléon's *A Specter is Haunting Europe*.

form part of the stock of the late-nineteenth-century imagination. This is not to argue that the preeminent note was not the celebration of those "advantages" in the public sphere's massed appreciation of progress. The apprehension of reenchantment was a small part of the language and, I suppose, the lived experience of the period.[17]

A crucial background for this book is the work of Max Weber. To insist on the actuality of the perception of reenchantment is not to reject Weber's anatomy of the distinctive features of modern culture—bureaucracy, the division of labor, money, representative government, and so on. But reenchantment does point to ways in which the instrumental rationality of the structure of the social world in which we live may by no means correspond to what we like to think of as reason. A stock market panic, to use one of Weber's examples, can happen at the heart of an institution that is highly rationalized from the formal point of view; these "irrational, affectually determined elements" are, writes Weber, deviations "from a conceptually pure type of rational action."[18] The crucial Weberian category of charisma, after all, found its most frightening embodiment in the middle of this century. Charismatic rule with irrational, sometimes even occult, underpinnings is in no way incompatible with highly efficient, formally rationalized administration.[19] (That this disjunction remains shocking helps, I think, to account for the still reverberating reaction to Hannah Arendt's *Eichmann in Jerusalem*.) One way

[17] For studies that open up questions of the supernatural analogous to those I pursue here, see Jonathan Arac's *Commissioned Spirits*, Henri Lefebvre's *Critique of Everyday Life*, and T. J. Jackson Lears's *No Place of Grace*. Also important to me is the work of Geoffrey Hartman, who has been insisting for some time on the supernatural remainders in modern culture. His recent *The Fateful Question of Culture* is an especially powerful antidote to the argument that modernity is fully disenchanted.

[18] Max Weber, *The Theory of Social and Economic Organization*, p. 92. See also p. 110.

[19] Weber himself argues that modernity saw the return of "old gods," which "ascend from their graves," but are "disenchanted" and "take the form of impersonal forces." Max Weber, "Science as Vocation," p.149. It is not clear to me how a god can remain a god and yet be "disenchanted," and the works on which I concentrate here are ones that are less confident than Weber that the modern forms of the irrational are severed from enchantment.

the figures I consider in this book differ is over the question of whether reenchantment is the necessary sequel to rationalization in its capitalist form. Part of the effect of Marx's genealogy of the commodity in the first part of *Capital* is to imply that capitalism is, at least in certain respects, by necessity irrational, with a fetish at its core. Keynes, on the other hand, firmly believed in the possibility of the rational reform of capitalism from within. I do not intend, by pointing out a similarity in these two very different economic and political thinkers, to erase this great gap between them.

The supernatural, then, provides a way to defamiliarize the naturalness, the illusive permanence of the society Keynes describes, a society taken for second nature; "our late advantages," Keynes implies, are *not* "natural." Marx's use of the term "fetishism" is a familiar and telling example of this sort of defamiliarization. As W. J. T. Mitchell puts it: "In calling commodities fetishes, Marx is telling the nineteenth-century reader that the material basis of modern, civilized, rational political economy is structurally equivalent to what is most inimical to modern consciousness."[20] Marx defamiliarizes the commodity by linking it to fetishistic practices "modern consciousness" flatters itself it has long outgrown. It is telling for this project that in closing his crucial chapter on "The Fetishism of Commodities and its Secret," Marx quotes Shakespeare. Discussing the chimerical nature of exchange value and the way in which economists naturalize it, Marx refers to the bumbling night-watchmen of *Much Ado About Nothing*:

> Who would not call to mind at this point the advice given by the good Dogberry to the night-watchman Seacoal?
>
> "To be a well-favoured man is the gift of fortune; but reading and writing come by nature."[21]

[20] W. J. T. Mitchell, *Iconology*, p. 191. For the Russian formalists' concept of "defamiliarization," see especially Victor Shklovsky, "Art as Technique." Tony Bennett's discussion of defamiliarization is especially useful: ". . . the Formalists sought to reveal the devices through which the total structure of given works of literature might be said to defamiliarize, make strange or challenge certain dominant conceptions—ideologies even, although they did not use the word—of the social world." Bennett, *Formalism and Marxism*, p. 21.

[21] Karl Marx, *Capital*, p. 177.

Dogberry is a parodic version of the misrecognition of second nature; his inversions become the image of a society built around the fetishistic reification of exchange value. This quotation from *Much Ado*, however, is not what I call a scare quote. The scare quote requires that struggle of which Harold Bloom has been the most influential phenomenologist. It is not only that the writer appropriates the quotation or allusion; allusion may also appropriate the writer. Allusion can indicate a struggle with a predecessor, and the location of an unresolved aesthetic, intellectual, or psychic dilemma in the later writer.[22] Marx's appropriation of Shakespeare is the subject of a large part of the first section of this book; there I look at moments where Marx's Shakespeare is less manageable than in this passage from *Capital*.

Another passage in political economy, and one that has resonated far more than Marx's invocation of *Much Ado*, provides this study with a paradigmatic example. Adam Smith's "invisible hand" has at once become a powerful scare quote in its own right, and has a possible origin in *Macbeth*. Smith's suggestive figure conjures a supernatural index at the heart of a rationalized economy, pointing the way to, controlling, or grasping the wealth of nations. That the phrase so often appears outside of its context is also germane to this study; as slogan, the scare tactic inherent in "the invisible hand" goes unexamined. The success of the phrase relies on its not being subject to examination; it is not part of a syllogism, but an article of economic faith. Indeed, the phrase discourages examination. It demarcates an area where investigation must necessarily encounter a dead end: the hand promises the faithful that the series of effects called the economy has an organizing force at its core, but at the same time warns that this force will never be seen. In the work of editorialists and speech writers, the "invisible hand" is then the perfect quotation

---

[22] For the most part, I differentiate allusion from quotation by a simple distinction: the allusion comes without attribution, while the quotation includes a tag (for example, blatantly, "as Shakespeare said," or, in the example above, "the advice given by the good Dogberry") that helps the reader identify the source. Clearly these categories are not wholly separable: will everyone remember Dogberry?

of the kind Debord has in mind. The phrase alludes to an authoritative concept, but the phrase figures the concept in such a way that challenging it is impossible. If one illuminates the hand, it is no longer "invisible," no longer the object one hoped to investigate. The phantom heart of the economy is unrepresentable.

Smith raises the "invisible hand" in a discussion of the benefits of free trade and of what came to be called laissez-faire mercantile policy:

> As every individual . . . endeavours as much as he can both to employ his capital in the support of domestick industry, and so to direct that industry that its produce may be of the greatest value; every individual necessarily labours to render the annual revenue of the society as great as he can. He generally, indeed, neither intends to promote the publick interest, nor knows how much he is promoting it. By preferring the support of domestick to that of foreign industry, he intends only his own security; and by directing that industry in such a manner as its produce may be of the greatest value, he intends only his own gain, and he is in this, as in many other cases, led by an invisible hand to promote an end which was no part of his intention.

Smith continues: "By pursuing his own interest he frequently promotes that of the society more effectually than when he really intends to promote it."[23] There is a paradox implicit in Smith's discussion of intentions and the market: society will be better off if all the members of society forget that society exists. Charity begins, but also ends, at home.

The unexamined "invisible hand" has become a talisman of economic faith, and this phrase and its powerful afterlife call for scrutiny. To try to picture the invisible hand is to concentrate on the irrational core that assures the rationalization of the economy, and this effort is in error, just as one would err in trying to substitute real human hands for invisible ones:

> The statesman, who should attempt to direct private people in what manner they ought to employ their capitals, would not only load himself

[23] Adam Smith, *The Wealth of Nations*, vol. 1, p. 456; all quotations from Smith fall on this page. Smith anticipates this discussion of the "invisible hand" in a very similar passage in *The Theory of Moral Sentiments*, p. 184.

with a most unnecessary attention, but assume an authority which could safely be trusted, not only to no single person, but to no council or senate whatever, and which would nowhere be so dangerous as in the hands of a man who had folly and presumption enough to fancy himself fit to exercise it.

Those who presume to have knowledge of society are dangerous. If the "invisible hand" is the unimaginable icon of a society that best reproduces itself in the absence of human intention, these dangerous, fanciful, and presumptuous "hands," invested with authority, form Smith's counter-image.

Smith's discussion suggests that the best intentions are those motivated by a self-interest it would be odd to call enlightened. In fact, enlightenment of a certain kind seems to be fatal to these interests: one should go about one's business and not indulge in too much speculation about society. (Should one write *The Wealth of Nations*?) Or, alternately, one might begin to ask questions about the "invisible hand" and discover that the phrase possesses not only a powerful afterlife but also, possibly, a genealogy that preceded *The Wealth of Nations*. The phrase may be a scare quote; it appears in *Macbeth*:

> *Lady M.*   What's to be done?
> *Macb.*   Be innocent of the knowledge, dearest chuck,
>   Till thou applaud the deed. Come, seeling night,
>   Scarf up the tender eye of pitiful day,
>   And with thy bloody and invisible hand
>   Cancel and tear to pieces that great bond
>   Which keeps me pale!   (III.ii.44–50)[24]

Smith rejects the efficacy of intention and knowledge: it is precisely by going about one's own business that one does the business of society. The Shakespearean precedent offers a weird, and disturbing, parallel; one might say, with the curse of retrospection, that Smith occults much in erasing "bloody" from Shakespeare's phrase. Smith attributes the usefulness of the action of the capitalist for society to the absence of the capitalist's social intention; society should make no part of his calculations. Macbeth's veiled plan for the murder of

[24] Quotations from Shakespeare follow *The Riverside Shakespeare*.

Banquo and Fleance similarly relies on Lady Macbeth's intention not playing a role in his actions. Or, more precisely, the pact represents the planned murder of Banquo and Fleance as belonging to an intention outside both of them, as an act of the "bloody and invisible hand" of night. Behind Smith's capitalist, who efficiently ignores the existence of society, lurks Shakespeare's representation of knowledge that leaves no evidence of itself and ensures the appearance of innocence. The joint refusal to acknowledge responsibility for the plot is, in many ways, the obverse of the sort of failure of acknowledgement Stanley Cavell has observed as part of Shakespeare's grappling with the consequences of skepticism. If, for Cavell, the failure to acknowledge other minds is a tragic consequence of skepticism, Macbeth's urging "innocence" on Lady Macbeth—that is, knowing nothing, ignorance and a lack of responsibility—shows the disowning of knowledge as a political strategy.[25] The political force of this scene from *Macbeth* lies in its representation of a stratagem by which an unspoken agreement assures an action, but also assures that even conspirators will have agreed to nothing that resembles a contract or "bond." Macbeth has assumed the role of sovereign to the extent that he can attribute his power to something outside himself. One of the king's bodies is a force of nature, the night with its "invisible hand." The sovereign has a monopoly on violence, but where such a monopoly makes contracts that go against the law that authorizes the sovereign's power, it can establish franchises and delegate its control of violence to murderers whose actions will have the appearance of those of free agents.

The disowning of intention in Smith and Shakespeare has an equivalent in the field of language and culture I am concerned with here. The repetition of the "invisible hand," one might object, is sheer coincidence, and to make a connection between its appearance in *The Wealth of Nations* and in *Macbeth* is to strain credulity. This

[25] For Stanley Cavell on disowning knowledge and skepticism, see especially "The Avoidance of Love: A Reading of *King Lear*." (Cavell discusses the "invisible hand" passage, along quite different lines, in "Macbeth Appalled (II)," p. 13). For a reading of the passage that directly attends to its political valences, see Christopher Pye, *The Regal Phantasm*, pp. 148–50.

objection points to the unlikelihood of a reference to such an occult moment in *Macbeth* in the pages of Smith's seminal tome. Did Smith intend to refer to *Macbeth*? Perhaps not, but Smith's passage champions the effects of what one does not intend. Skeptical readers may dismiss the notion that Smith refers to *Macbeth* as a *jeu d'esprit*. The allusions on which I focus in the body of this book are less doubtful, and it requires little or no ingenuity to spot them. The question, that is, is not whether these later examples are allusions at all, but why they are there, and why these writers return so insistently to the supernatural. We know Marx alludes to *Hamlet* when he invokes the old mole, but why?

Marx borrows from Hamlet's first encounter with the Ghost of his father. The words are Prince Hamlet's, directed to the Ghost. Hamlet arranges a ritual by which his friends of the nightwatch, Horatio and Marcellus, will swear that they "Never make known" what they "have seen to-night" (I.v.144). "*Ghost cries under the stage,*" punctuating the ritual three times with the word "Swear" (I.v.149, 155, 181) and once with "Swear by his sword" (I.v.161). It is to this last command of the Ghost that Hamlet responds with the line at hand: "Well said, old mole!" One crucial detail completes the synopsis. The second time the Ghost cries, "Swear," Hamlet responds, "*Hic et ubique?* Then we'll shift our ground" (I.v.156). Hamlet, it seems, tries to evade the Ghost while arranging his oath, shifting the position of his more or less impromptu ritual. But this evasive maneuver fails; the Ghost is able to move agilely beneath the stage, and follows Hamlet and his companions. It is after they shift their ground that the Ghost delivers the climactic command, "Swear by his sword," which inspires Hamlet's invocation of the mole. This scene, which I shall discuss at greatest length in my chapter on *Hamlet*, strikes me as the paradigmatic scene of reenchantment within Shakespeare's work. On the one hand, Hamlet's bluntly recognizes that he is a performer on a stage by calling to the Ghost in the "cellarage" and his foolery while performing the oath appears to debunk the authority of the supernatural. On the other hand, that oath is no less in earnest following this debunking. The supernatural remains despite these demystifying maneuvers. Such, in a nutshell, is how I understand reenchantment. Naming it, with whatever ironic force or skeptical charge, does not make it vanish.

Shakespeare's work has resonated in discussions of the psychopathology of social and economic life. The nineteenth century, with its dislocations, its vast changes due to the spread of industrialization and commodification, and its social upheavals and revolutions, had a notable investment in the supernatural in Shakespeare. Rather than trying to write a general history of that investment, I have focused on selected examples, looking at specific forms that it has taken, and suggesting how these forms enable a renewed understanding of *Hamlet* and *Macbeth*. First, however, I introduce Henry Dircks, a phantasmagoria inventor of nineteenth-century Britain, whose encounter with a supernatural element in culture forms a paradigm for the chapters that follow. A man of the Enlightenment who encounters a social world organized by no visible intention, Dircks imagined a mysterious conspiracy. Dircks was shaken by the invisible hand, but it was a shake of dispossession, not of welcome.

PART I

Phantasmagoria

Where was that ad some Birmingham firm the luminous cruci-fix? Our Saviour. Wake up in the dead of night and see him on the wall, hanging. Pepper's ghost idea. Iron nails ran in.

James Joyce, *Ulysses*

1

Henry Dircks, Inventor of
Pepper's Ghost

Why not begin with Carlyle? No figure before Marx, perhaps, responded to the nineteenth century with so vituperative, so intense,
and so engaging a supernatural lexicon. The opening pages of *Past
and Present* are a peculiarly vivid example of Carlyle's tangling with
modern magic. There, Carlyle describes the agricultural and industrial wealth of England, and then conjures a strange logic whereby all
this wealth is inaccessible:

> . . . some baleful fiat as of Enchantment has gone forth, saying, "Touch
> it not, ye workers, ye master-workers, ye master-idlers; none of you can
> touch it, no man of you shall be the better for it; this is enchanted
> fruit!"

Carlyle pictures those in workhouses as "pent up, as in a kind of horrid enchantment; glad to be imprisoned and enchanted, that they
may not perish starved." Writing of parents accused of poisoning
their own children, he asks: "And we here, in modern England, exu-

berant with supply of all kinds, besieged by nothing if it be not invisible Enchantments, are we reaching that?"[1] A word crucial to this
book, "enchantment," is crucial in these opening pages: Why not begin with Carlyle?

Carlyle does not belong with the figures on whom I concentrate in
this book because, for him, *everything* from the eighteenth century
onwards has been the reverse of enlightenment, has been, in a word,
Enchantment:

> The Dryasdust Philosophisms and enlightened Scepticisms of the
> Eighteenth Century, historical and other, will have to survive for a
> while with the Physiologists, as a memorable *Night-Mare-Dream*. All
> this haggard epoch, with its ghastly Doctrines, and death's-head Phi-
> losophies 'teaching by example' or otherwise, will one day have be-
> come, what to our Moslem friends their godless ages are, the 'Period of
> Ignorance.'[2]

There can be no scare quote for Carlyle because there is no zone in
modern culture free of enchantment; the "Phantasm," to use a word
that becomes prominent later in *Past and Present*, is not the exception, but the rule. The expectation of rationalization and disenchantment is, for Carlyle, simply stupidity; only the duped expect
the rational.[3] The prevailing nightmare of Enchantment leaves no

[1] Thomas Carlyle, *Past and Present*, pp. 1; 2; 4–5.

[2] Carlyle, *Past and Present*, p. 278. Compare this wonderful attack on the eighteenth-century in Carlyle's "Count Cagliostro," p.172: "It was the age of imposters,
cut-purses, swindlers, double-goers, enthusiasts, ambiguous persons; quacks simple, quacks compound; crack-brained, or with deceit prepense; quacks and quack-
eries of all colors and kinds. How many Mesmerists, Magicians, Cabalists, Swe-
denborgians, Illuminati, Crucified Nuns and Devils of Lundun! To which the In-
quisition-Biographer adds Vampires, Sylphs, Rosicrucians, Freemasons, and an *Et-
cetera*. . . . As if Bedlam had broken loose; as if, rather, in that 'spiritual Twelfth-
hour of the night,' the everlasting Pit had opened itself, and from *its* still blacker
bosom had issued Madness and all manner of shapeless Misbirths, to masquerade
and chatter there."

[3] I thank Jeff Nunokawa for emphasizing in conversation that Carlyle well
knows that the surprise of reenchantment exists *for others*. To relieve these others
of their stupid expectation of enlightenment is an important motivation for the
composition of *Past and Present*.

possibility for *re*enchantment. There has been no escape from Enchantment; there can therefore be no return to it.

A contrast with Weber will clarify what separates Carlyle from the
figures I consider in this book. In the passage immediately following
his introduction of his resonant notion of the "iron cage" near the
end of *The Protestant Ethic and the Spirit of Capitalism*, Weber
imagines the last vestiges of the Protestant calling as a kind of spirit:

> To-day the spirit of religious asceticism—whether finally, who knows?—
> has escaped from the cage. But victorious capitalism, since it rests on me-
> chanical foundations, needs its support no longer. The rosy blush of its
> laughing heir, the Enlightenment, seems also to be irretrievably fading,
> and the idea of duty in one's calling prowls about in our lives like the
> ghost of dead religious beliefs.[4]

Compare Carlyle, celebrating Transcendentalism and the dethron-
ing of the "Demiurgus Dollar" in "Yankeeland":

> Old godlike Calvinism declares that its old body is now fallen to tat-
> ters, and done; and its mournful ghost, disembodied, seeking new em-
> bodiment, pipes again in the winds;—a ghost and spirit as yet, but her-
> alding new Spirit-worlds, and better Dynasties than the Dollar one.[5]

The happy coincidence of the association of moribund Calvinism
with a "ghost" in these two writers should not disguise the massive
differences between them. For Carlyle the re-embodiment of the
ghost of Calvinism he thinks he has spotted in the stirrings of the
Transcendentalists is desirable: he hopes this re-embodied ghost will
counter the Enchantment he attacks in the rest of his jeremiad. So a
certain kind of reenchantment, in the form of a renewed spirituality,
is what Carlyle wants, whether it takes the form of the critique of the
rule of the dollar in Transcendentalism, or a return to the monastic
life, or the glorified ethic of work he celebrates in *Past and Present*.
Nostalgia motivates Carlyle: the past was better and, with any luck,
we can return to it. For Weber, there can be no such return. The triumph of capitalism does not require the rejuvenation of that "idea of

---

[4] Max Weber, *The Protestant Ethic*, pp. 181–82.
[5] Carlyle, *Past and Present*, p. 341.

duty in one's calling [that] prowls about in our lives like the ghost of dead religious beliefs." The structural solidity of capitalism no longer requires the conviction that one has been called to serve it; capitalism has no need of the "spirit" that, according to Weber, decisively set it in motion. That slightly pathetic, prowling ghost is all that remains of that originating spirit. For Weber, capitalism is a fact of practice, resting on its perpetual "mechanical foundation," not a spell; the material basis of modern culture, and not an ephemeral curse. The same is true for Keynes and Marx, with all their differences.[6] Something may well come after laissez-faire capitalism, but this thing will not be the return of a pre-capitalist past.

So, I do not start with Carlyle, but, instead, with Henry Dircks, a figure whom I offer as an allegorical representative of the "enlightened" encounter with reenchantment. Civil engineer, patent agent, author, inventor, lecturer, life member of the British Association from 1837 onwards, recipient of the LL.D. from the "so-called college of Tusculum in Tennessee, U.S.A.," Dircks (1806–73) invented Pepper's Ghost, perhaps the most successful phantasmagorical device of the nineteenth century.[7] The machine took its name from the impresario who popularized it, "Professor" John Henry Pepper, for a time head of the Polytechnic Institution and himself a jack of many trades. As the vogue of Pepper's Ghost grew in 1863, Dircks became disconsolate. The machine he had designed, in part, to unmask the theatrical techniques and legerdemain of the spiritualist showmen that were so popular in his day, became the source of his own dispossession. His plight helps us picture the encounter with reenchantment. An enlightenment project of a literal-minded kind—the mechanical production of ghosts in order to debunk superstition—ends in an encounter with the stubborn recalcitrance of the supernatural.

[6] For an intriguing account that illuminates the difficulties Carlyle's thought poses for Marx and Engels, see Peter Demetz, *Marx, Engels, and the Poets*, pp. 34–46. Engels, Demetz relates, submitted a piece called "The Situation in England" to a journal Marx co-edited. This piece was an extremely truncated translation of *Past and Present*; it omitted, for example, every passage in praise of England in the Middle Ages (pp. 37–39).

[7] I draw some details and the snobbish quotation about his degree from the entry "Henry Dircks" in the *Dictionary of National Biography*, 1942 ed.

The comparison with Marx and Keynes only goes so far. It is true that Dircks encounters occult disappointments that he thinks enlightened progress should have erased, but he remains the staunch advocate of the position that progress is slowly eradicating superstition and the irrational. He never imagines that the supernatural language he applies to his own predicament might point to more than a few narrow zones of the world beyond him. Dircks, that is, is in a historical predicament he never begins to see. He was not a critic of reenchantment, but, rather, subject to it. Marx and Keynes, on the other hand, acknowledge the difficulty the supernatural poses to the representation of history, and move beyond local instances to more troubling questions about what reenchantment means for our notions of modernity.

SPIRITUALISM AND THE DIRCKSIAN
PHANTASMAGORIA

The British Patent Office registered a patent for "A stage phantom or 'Pepper's ghost,'" on February 5, 1863.[8] Later in that year, this patenting of a ghost became the subject of ridicule, jokes, and even legal hearings. How could one claim exclusive rights to something so capricious and otherworldly as a ghost? John Henry Pepper quotes a contemporary article in a book he wrote many years later:

> Modern researches in Spiritualism have led to one practical result—the discovery of a ghost. Not of an ordinary old-fashioned ghost, appearing in the midnight hour to people with a weak digestion, haunting graveyards and old country mansions, and inspiring romance-writers to the mischief of three-volume novels; but of a well-behaved, steady, regular, and respectable ghost, going through a prescribed round of duties, punctual to the minute—a Patent Ghost, in fact. This admirable ghost is the offspring of two fathers, of a learned member of the Society of Civil Engineers, Henry Dircks, Esq.; and of Professor Pepper, of the Polytechnic. To Mr. Dircks belongs the honour of having invented him, or, as the disciples of Hegel would express it, evolved him out of

---

[8] See patent number 326, in Terence Rees and David Wilmore, *British Theatrical Patents*, pp. 9–10. Descriptions of other relevant patents follow on pp. 10–11.

the depths of his own consciousness; and Professor Pepper has the merit of improving him considerably, fitting him for the intercourse of mundane society, and even educating him for the stage.[9]

This passage captures some of the ghostly contradictions of capitalism, of which the story of Dircks, however idiosyncratic, is representative. This chapter follows the strange path of "Pepper's Ghost" to show how the rhetoric of reenchantment works in a particular case, how arguments about enlightenment formed in the shadow of spiritualism, how arguments about property encounter the problem of owning the Ghost, how a "rational" fabrication of ghosts ended in mystification. Dircks begins, confident that he can manufacture the Ghost while remaining true to his rationalist principles; combinations that struck many as contradictory—ghosts and a patent, ghosts and money, ghosts and enlightenment—seemed to Dircks not only possible, but desirable. But Dircks lost his association with the Ghost, and he experienced this loss as mystifying, even supernatural. The purveyor of "rational entertainment" became the victim of the irrational circulation of the ghostly commodity he had invented.[10]

A crucial context for the case of Dircks is the rage for spiritualism in England in the early 1860s. Many desired conversation with dead family and friends, and spiritualism promised this communication. In a world in which communication was more and more quick, there seemed no reason that progress in what Shawn Rosenheim has called "electrospiritual technologies" might not also bring regular dispatches from the dead.[11] In England, in 1863, the year of London's rage for Dircks's machine, it was possible to see a ghost, and some-

[9] "The Patent Ghost," qtd. in John Henry Pepper, *The True History of the Ghost*, pp. 22–23; Pepper notes that the name of the journal containing this article was "cut off and lost," and I have not found it. For another amusing account of the patent war over the Ghost, see W. Bridges Adams, "Patent Ghosts."

[10] Richard Altick's *The Shows of London* provides an encyclopedic account of the "rational entertainments" of nineteenth-century London.

[11] Shawn James Rosenheim, *The Cryptographic Imagination*, p. 121. Alex Owen has noted, indeed, that spiritualism thought of itself as a challenge to, but also as an extension of, scientific work; "spirit matter" was spiritualism's uneasily "materialistic" solution to the problem of the stuff of ghosts. Owen, *The Darkened Room*, unpaginated introduction.

times several competing ghosts, any day of the year. In *The Ghost!*,
Dircks writes about successes made possible by his perfection of a
superior phantasmagorical apparatus. He strikingly imagines it as in
competition with the theatrical displays of the spiritualists:

> Mesmerism throughout all its harlequinades, down to its present dis-
> guise under spiritualism or spirit-rapping—with all its music, its passes,
> and its mediums—has never had nerve enough or *nous* enough to pro-
> duce such thorough full-length ghosts as are now every day to be seen
> at the Polytechnic, Drury-lane, the Britannia, Canterbury Hall, and
> other popular establishments of every grade in the metropolis.[12]

The function of the phantasmagoria is the same as the desire of the
spiritualist: to produce ghosts. Dircks's technology, however, allows
for the better ghost. That the apparitions produced by Pepper's
Ghost were excellent seems indisputable. Even many of those writers
who disparaged the Ghost's chief theatrical vehicles—quickly written and long forgotten melodramas—mostly praised the powerfully
convincing apparitions it produced. Some writers even echoed
Dircks's declared motives. Dircks always contends that his technological perfection aids the triumph of enlightenment over superstition. Because of the superiority of his apparatus over less sophisticated phantasmagorical shows, it will exorcise the superstitions of
those who have believed in the inferior apparitions produced by the
less advanced mechanisms of mesmerists and other charlatans. Technology in the service of enlightenment will drive out optical delusions in the service of humbug.

It will be useful to understand what Dircks's device achieved. His
invention made possible the projection of the image of a human actor onto a playing stage. Earlier phantasmagorias had relied on min-
ute painted images, inverting them, and projecting their images
through concave mirrors; the degree of detail and realism they could
obtain was minimal. With Dircks's invention, "full-length" ghosts,
ghosts the size and shape of people, were suddenly among available
special effects. The actor occupied something like the "middle stage

---

[12] Henry Dircks, *The Ghost!*, p. 62. Further references to *The Ghost!* will appear
in parentheses in the text.

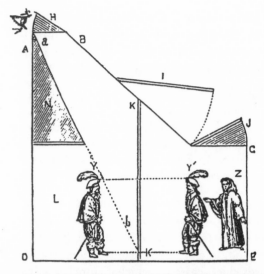

Fig. 1. From Henry Dircks, *The Ghost!*

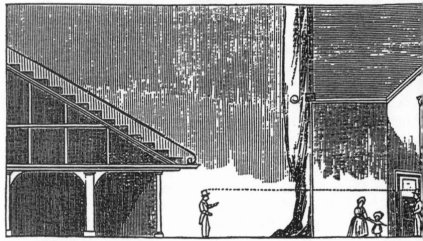

Fig. 2. From Henry Dircks, *The Ghost!*

between presence and absence" that André Bazin describes as the place of the film actor.[13] Dircks adapted the theater to hold what he calls a "second" or "spectre stage" underneath the audience (44, 54). Constructed on this stage is the reverse image of the playing stage visible to the audience. Between the two stages Dircks puts "a good, clear, and even surface of thin patent plate glass" (48). According to the distribution of light, which the "operator" of the apparatus carefully regulates with a system of flaps and doors, this glass serves both as a window onto the playing stage and as a mirror of the second, "spectre stage."[14] As desired by the producers, the audience

[13] Bazin, "Theater and Cinema—Part Two," p. 97, offers a telling analogy: "It is false to say that the screen is incapable of putting us 'in the presence of' the actor. It does so in the same way as a mirror—one must agree that the mirror relays the presence of the person reflected in it—but it is a mirror with a delayed reflection . . ." Pepper's Ghost appears in several accounts of the pre-history of cinema. Erik Barnouw, for instance, stresses how magic and magicians prepared the way for cinema in *The Magician and the Cinema*; Barnouw discusses Dircks (pp. 28–30). There is also a model of Pepper's Ghost in London's Museum of the Moving Image, which charts the pre-history of cinema as well as the development of cinema itself. Dircks himself writes, as if looking ahead: ". . . I am warranted in saying that I am the first inventor in the history of optical science who has ever shewn a phantom or spectre opposed to and throwing its shadow on A WHITE SCREEN" (p. 53).

[14] Figures from *The Ghost!* make Dircks's technique clearer (figs. 1 and 2). In figure 1, the "operator," represented here by the iconic eye whose line of sight follows "the dotted line a,b," can see the entire mirror, K,K, and controls the light. A denotes "the eye of the spectator." "If two figures now be introduced, one Y, the other Z, and the eye of the spectator be fixed at A, he will observe two images, one the real figure Z, the other Y1, the mere reflection of Y. By this arrangement it is evident that the plain, unsilvered glass, thus viewed at an angle of about 45° has all the properties of a mirror, but owing to its transparency two figures are seen, possessing little or no distinguishable difference between them. Of course a person placed at Z, sees only the figure Y, but, as a piece of acting may, under proper arrangements of a suitable stage, approach the situation apparently occupied by Y1, and thus indicate to a spectator placed at A, any pre-arranged dramatic scene, requiring Z to be in correspondence with the visionary figure Y1" (p. 48). This is only a short excerpt from Dircks's extensive description of the operation of his apparatus (pp. 40–54). Figure 2 renders the relationship between the audience and the stage more clearly. The actor to the left occupies the "spectre stage" and appears, as a "visionary figure," in the door on the playing stage to the right.

sees either through the glass and onto the playing area, or sees both
the playing area and the ghostly reflections of actors in the second
stage. The essential point is that Dircks's invention made possible
the projection of an unreduced human image. As figure 2 suggests, it
did not, at least in theory, rely on the freakish, distorted spirits of
former apparatuses. It could project the ghost of a "full-length"
bourgeois gentleman shown in figure 2, gesturing—one can only
guess what scenario the diagram represents—to his grieving and now
frightened family. Pepper's important alteration to Dircks's machine
was to adapt it so that it could fit most normal theaters; Dircks's version had the serious drawback, as George Speaight writes, "that a
special building needed to be constructed to house it, and that only
the spectators in the circle or gallery could see the illusion."[15]

Dircks always insists that enlightened motives led him to invent
the Ghost:

> Among the happy results of modern discoveries we may particularly
> notice the different use made of whatever pertains to the wonderful, as
> compared to the use to which the same would have been subject in su-
> perstitious ages. Our natural magic makes no pretension to occult sci-
> ence, but on the contrary tends to dissipate many vulgar errors, by
> disabusing the public mind, even on matters long considered super-
> natural. (40)

Dircks still calls his work "natural magic"; what he disowns is any
pretension of such magic to the status of an "occult science." What
makes this magic "natural" is precisely the severing of its links to
the supernatural, to occult causes. In the era of the phantasmagoria,
which Dircks implicitly contrasts to earlier, "superstitious ages,"
such technological magic may serve as a tool of the disenchantment
of the world. Optics will replace conjuration. By perfecting the
production of ghosts attempted by conjurors and spiritualists, and
then unabashedly demonstrating the mechanical basis of this production, showing that such a machine must also have lain be-

[15] See George Speaight, "Professor Pepper's Ghost," p. 17. Speaight's article, invaluable in researching the Ghost, includes in its opening pages the clearest available explanation of the various forms of Pepper's Ghost (pp. 16–19).

hind earlier supernatural frauds, science will enlighten and entertain.[16]

The problem, however, is that audiences were just as likely to consider the Ghost's ghosts as somehow equivalent to spiritualism's ghosts as opposed to them. Some accounts did give the phantasmagoria credit for helping to diminish belief in ghosts. In October 1863, *Punch* noted that "there is just now a glut of ghosts everywhere," and the magazine, too, drew a connection between these ghosts proliferating the theaters and music halls, and those summoned by the spiritualists. The skeptical humorist argued that the ghosts raised by the spiritualists should protest against the simulacral ghosts produced in the theaters:

> Now, if, whilst these factitious ghosts are in course of exhibition for public amusement under the well understood denomination of optical illusions, real and genuine departed spirits, in private "circles," are actually showing their hands, and making use of them by patting people's legs, drawing flowers and other objects, ringing handbells, and lifting MR. HOME into space, how is it that these *bonâ fide* ghosts allow themselves to be insulted by mimicry? The ghosts that were invented by PROFESSOR PEPPER are exhibited with the avowed design of demonstrating the unreality of those ghosts which spiritualists believe to be real. If there are any real ghosts, and if they can communicate with the living by raps, why do they suffer their authenticity to be impugned without a sensible protest against a calumnious misrepresentation? Why do they not give PEPPER, and the other professors who produce the sham ghosts, a rap over the head, or at least a rap on the knuckles? Take a theatre containing a crowded audience; the deuce is in it if there is not at least one medium in it out of so many people, mediums being actually as plentiful as they are alleged to be by those who believe in them.[17]

The logic here is impeccable, but it evades both the arguments of spiritualists that those in "circles" needed to provide a sympathetic

[16] In "Phantasmagoria and the Metaphorics of Modern Reverie," Terry Castle has shown that such rhetoric of enlightenment was typical among the early inventors and purveyors of phantasmagoria, such as the famous Etienne Robertson (p. 159).

[17] "Ghosts Without Spirit."

environment for the raising of spirits—a crowded and boisterous theater would never do—and it also assumes that the "denomination of optical illusions" was "well understood."

It is worth looking at this from another angle, sharing the *Punch* author's suspicion of the spiritualists, but absolutely opposed in believing in the reality of spirits themselves. There were anti-spiritualist writers who shared the spiritualists' belief in the actuality of the spirit world, but who also thought any raising of spirits had to be necromancy or the work of the devil. One of this number objected to the debunking of spiritualism—and the writer might well have been thinking of the Ghost—because such an "imitation of spiritualism" would only lead the audience astray, towards the belief that the work of "the *great deceiver*" himself was only show. By hiding the devil, the sham, theatrical debunking of spiritualism itself performs the "devil's work": "Many persons, having examined the tricks of those who profess to act as mediums, and discovering the fallacy, are led to suppose that spiritualism is itself an unreality, and therefore are led to regard it as a harmless amusement at first, until practically they are ensnared into an acceptance of and delight in its diabolical influence."[18] This writer would have a ready answer to the critique of *Punch*: spirits don't rap showmen because the latter are in league with the devil without knowing it.

These examples from *Punch* and E.S. both point, despite their divergence, to a single unanswerable question. To what extent was the Ghost a tool of skepticism? To what extent might it, on the other hand, have fostered belief in the very spirits it simulated and claimed to expose as frauds? Dircks was himself inconsistent in his presentation of the debunking "Dircksian phantasmagoria." Phantasmagoric demystification, Dircks is at pains to stress, brings in profit. Dircks imagines a carnival of ghost consumption. He contrasts the Ghost's success in central London to its first triumphs at the Britannia Theatre, in Hoxton, a suburb of North London:

> "Haunted Hoxton" is nothing as compared to Haunted London, and the occasional itinerating hauntings of ghosts in the provinces. That

[18] E.S., *Spiritualism and Other Signs*, p. 18.

they are real and not evil spirits amounts to the certainty of a mathe-
matical demonstration, for see the congregated crowds around every
door where a ghost is to be exhibited! Hear you not the money dropping into the till—the cries of women and children, who squeeze to
their smallest proportions in the too narrow passages—the large rents
paid, fees received, and profits accumulated—plays, once dead, re-
animated by "The Ghost"—institutions once not-overburdened with
wealth, now enriched—advertisers wondering at the rush of advertising
ghosts—then the many actors, lecturers, lime-light operators, printers,
artists, "The Ghost" gives employment to? Is it not anything but a demon or evil-spirit? (63)[19]

Dircks echoes the dilemma of Hamlet's first act—the question of
whether the Ghost is "a spirit of health, or goblin damn'd"
(I.iv.40)—and concludes that the "Ghost" is "anything but a demon
or evil-spirit." According to Dircks, the spirits are unequivocally
"real"; box office receipts attest to that reality. In Dircks's imagination, the Ghost is like Carlyle's "mournful ghost" of Calvinism: it re-
animates what has been thought dead. A thriving economy with the
phantasmagoria at its center replaces both the mesmerist or charlatan
hawking tawdry spiritualist wares and the cheap amusement at the
largely working-class theater in Hoxton.[20] This economy also, however, eclipses the scene of the champion of reason demonstrating the
mechanical basis behind the reproduction of the supernatural. There
is more than a suggestion that the superiority of the Dircksian phantasmagoria lies not only in the scientific or rationalist motives behind
it, or in its demystifying effects, but also, and perhaps more importantly, in its more efficient, more profitable mobilization of more
people. Does the desire for disenchantment motivate this audience?
Certainly Dircks publishes no testimonial to the vanishing of "vulgar
errors." Instead, the audience is of interest because, without it, there
would be no sound of "money dropping into the till." The ontologi-

[19] In the first phrase of this passage, Dircks may be referring to an amusing article, "Haunted Hoxton," possibly by Dickens, which appeared in Dickens's journal, *All the Year Round*.
[20] For an illuminating sociological account of this venue, see Clive Barker, "The
Audiences of the Britannia Theatre, Hoxton."

cal status of the illusory projections that drive this whole economy built around the profitable phantasmagoria is no longer important. Or, that is, the measure of the "real" has moved from the category of the ghostly to that of the economic. The mechanical supernatural, no longer the province of a narrow, superstitious, mesmerist or spirit-rapping clique, is instead the center of a growing, vibrant economy, promising employment for "actors, lecturers, lime-light operators, printers, artists." Dircks forgets both enlightenment and superstition in his celebration of the production of capital in the representation of ghosts.

Dircks's phantasmagoria was an attraction in a great variety of entertainments, from the Polytechnic's rational amusements to the Britannia's melodramas to the Crystal Palace's ark of attractions, and it would be reckless to generalize about the response of so large and various an audience. Diverse testimony survives in the wake of the Ghost. One anecdote describes young Brechtians before the fact, boys who, in the 1870s, tossed paper at the glass panel, thus destroying the illusion.[21] But many other accounts describe mystification. In many ways George Augustus Sala, evincing amused distance and a knowing rapture at once, might have been typical. First he dismisses the skeleton in a melodrama at the Britannia, *Faith, Hope, and Charity*, saying, "I didn't mind him much, for his anatomical development did not appear to me to be quite accurate . . ."

> But when the Ghost of the widow came up, lurid and menacing, seemingly palpable and tangible, yet wholly unsubstantial—when she pointed at the baronet and reproached him with his sins, and cried, "Ha! Ha!"—and when, like a flash of summer lightning, she disappeared,—I too, knowing always this to be a clever optical delusion, shook more than ever in my shoes, and felt unwonted moisture on my forehead.[22]

Perhaps the Ghost succeeded as "rational amusement," and created skeptics. However, it is hard to measure any check it might have put in the way of spiritualism, which was at the start of its "golden age" in

---

[21] See Catherine Haill, "Spirits and Ghosts That Glide by Night," p. 67.

[22] George Augustus Sala, "On Having Seen A Ghost at Hoxton," p. 512.

Britain "during the 1860s, 1870s, and 1880s . . ."[23] It is even possible
that the Ghost worked quite the reverse of the rationalizing magic its
inventor had in mind, and fostered spiritualism by helping people to
picture the ghosts they desired to see.

THE GHOST ON STAGE AND THE DISAPPEARANCE
OF HENRY DIRCKS

Dircks's forgetting of the interests of enlightenment in the joy of
ghostly income foreshadows another important aspect of his text,
where enlightenment and disenchantment are hardly complete. If
one strain of Dircks's tract celebrates a new spirit of capitalism, another, of at least equal importance to him, mourns the loss of his
claim to his own invention. That thriving economy excluded the inventor. As it became a popular theatrical machine, Dircks's name
slowly vanished from circulation, overwhelmed by that of Pepper;
"every effort," Dircks writes, "has been industriously made to mys-
tify my having any part or lot in my invention . . ." (18). Mystification shifts from the circles of conjurors and spiritualists to the
machinations of those who profit from Dircks's invention while ob-
scuring his name. The supernatural, emptied from the realm of nature and science, returns as an aspect of the social world. Describing,
for instance, the complicated language of a patent obtained for his
invention, Dircks, himself a patent agent, writes: "it is not to be expected that general readers of any class outside of the legal or some
kindred profession should be able to penetrate the deep mysteries
that obtain under a very large seal and still larger sheets of parchment" (58). The sealed document concealing mysteries is a microcosm of the picture of the social world that comes to dominate *The
Ghost!*.

As the conspiracy widens, Pepper's Polytechnic, which Dircks at
first seems sure represents the center of his troubles, begins to shift
responsibility for advertisements that do not mention his name to
editors of newspapers, one of whom then blames a clerk:

[23] Alex Owen, *The Darkened Room*, p. 1

this shifting of the burden from the Polytechnic office to outside offenders in ubiquitous clerks, agents, and reporters, had grown quite
stale with me. There was singular method in this simulated bungling.
But by whom I never learnt, nor can I succeed in interesting others in a
search after the offender or offenders. How, why, or wherefore done, I
have been unable to fathom. (77)

Earlier Dircks celebrates the functionaries who work to popularize
his ghostly apparatus, including the "advertisers wondering at the
rush of advertising ghosts." Now he suspects that same group of in-
volvement in a great conspiracy to strip his name from him. There is
more than a trace of Polonius's finding "method" in Hamlet's "madness" in Dircks's perceiving a "method" in this "simulated bungling"
(II.ii.205–6). Dircks never explicitly pursues the similarity between
his mystification in the face of the workings of the bureaucracy and
that of believers before the conjurations of charlatans, and also never
wonders whether his instrument might lead to increased mystification for its audience rather than to the spread of enlightenment. Instead, he deals with his dilemma evasively, allusively, without naming what troubles him.

Dircks's work quickly becomes a fantasy of dispossession that
borders on paranoia. Writing to a "referee" brought in to mediate
between his claims and those of the Polytechnic, he writes of his fast
fading hope that the "referee" would have conveyed to him "the solution of a great mystery":

My previous acquaintance with you as a publisher induced me to hope
that you were about to enlighten me in regard to a certain ubiquitous
set of pirates, clerks, agents and reporters, leagued together to upset my
claims to my invention, at every theatre and other establishments in
London as well as in the country, and especially in all newspaper para-
graphs. (95)

Dircks's tract swerves from his faith in enlightenment to his disillu-
sionment in the very possibility of being enlightened on this particular point: a simple problem of responsibility has no answer. The
referee is not able to "enlighten" him, of course. In what follows, it
becomes clear that Dircks does not even know who appointed the
referee:

Mr. —— at the same time adds that you were '*our* mutual arbitrator.'
Who (I again ask) proposed you? Was it Mr. ——? or the Polytechnic?
or the solicitors? I never asked for a referee or arbitrator; therefore,
Who was the first mover? and who ratified the appointment? (95)

Dickens meets Aquinas in the age of bureaucracy: What "first mover" appointed "our mutual arbitrator"?

There is evidence that Dircks had some reason to suspect that
there was a campaign to disguise his contribution, if not a conspiracy
against him, and that the Polytechnic might have had something to
do with it. There does indeed seem to have been a remarkable pattern
of mistaken attributions, mistaking the inventor of the Ghost. At the
very least, newspapers had trouble spelling his name correctly.[24] *The
Shoreditch Observer*, the paper that covered Hoxton and the East End
more generally, faithfully reported the various incarnations the
Ghost took at the Britannia, from *Faith, Hope, and Charity*, the first
melodrama that used the "marvellous effect," to the last at the Britannia, a drama with the tantalizing title, *The Jewess of the Temple*.[25] I
have found only one article in the editorial sections of the paper that

[24] Several papers also attributed the invention initially to a "Mr. Rose." See, for
instance, *The Times* (Dec. 27, 1862), p. 4, and "The Theatres," *The Illustrated
London News* (Jan. 3, 1863), p.19. For "Dircks'" as "Dyrch's," see "The Theatres,"
The Illustrated London News (Mar. 14, 1863), p. 270. *The Shoreditch Observer* presents coverage of the Ghost in some ways typical. In this paper, one finds a divergence between advertising matter and editorial content. Quite regularly the paper
ran advertisements for "Britannia, the Great Theatre," to which even the vigilant
Dircks, with his eye open for conspiracies, could have had no real objection:
"Tenth week of the real Ghost at the Britannia. One of the great facts of 1863. The
secret still undiscovered. Still the wonder of the Metropolis! By special arrangement no other Theatre in London can produce this marvellous effect. Every evening, at half-past 6. THE WIDOW AND ORPHANS, FAITH, HOPE, AND
CHARITY. . . . Illustrated by Professor Pepper's adaptation of Mr Dircks's living
spectres, recently patronised by Royalty." *The Shoreditch Observer*, no. 336 (June 6,
1863), p. 4. But it is true that even this scrupulous newspaper ran one advertisement, for *The Wishing Glen*, trumpeting a "New drama, written expressly for illustration of Professor Pepper's adaptation of Mr. Dirck's [sic] astounding Spectral
Illusion!" See no. 338 (June 20, 1863), p. 4.

[25] Of the plays featuring the Ghost at the Britannia, I have been unable to locate two—the first, *Faith, Hope, and Charity*, and the fourth, *The Jewess of the
Temple*—among the Lord Chamberlain's manuscripts at the British Library.

mentions Dircks at all. A review of *Faith, Hope, and Charity*, for instance, comments:

> ... real ghosts make their appearance upon the stage—by arrangement
> with Professor Pepper, of the Polytechnic—and we are glad to find that
> the "real" article, like the imitations which have preceded them, only
> appear for the purpose of punishing evil-doers and promoting the interests
> of the good. The ghosts of Monday night, however, had this advantage
> over their predecessors, that they could not only defy firearms,
> but when a sword was passed clean through a shadow it was none the
> worse for it. The audience showed their appreciation of the efforts
> which had been made for their amusement, by loud applause, and demands
> for the appearance of Mr. Pepper—demands which, however,
> were silenced by the assurance that he could not appear because he was
> not there, having just left to be present at the Polytechnic. The effect
> upon the stage of the Pepper ghosts was very good, and there is this
> also, that by subsequent arrangements the scientific apparatus may possibly
> be so employed that we shall not be able to tell the ghosts which
> walk the stage from those which are supposed to appear on rare occasions
> when we are more solitary, and when there is less gas light; and
> possibly in time the scientific ghost may so improve as to leave nothing
> but contempt for superstitious ones.[26]

In this review from April, Dircks's invention becomes "Pepper
ghosts." By July, in a review of *The Wishing Glen*, which calls the
Ghost "probably the most valuable addition yet made to the appliances
of the stage," the paper uses the name that stuck: "Professor
Pepper's Ghost is again triumphant at this favourite Eastern house
..."[27] In itself, Pepper's eclipsing Dircks may seem quite trivial, but
it was precisely the *name* of the device that concerned Dircks.[28] Especially
intriguing here, however, is the newspaper's endorsement of
the enlightened program Dircks himself championed. The notion
that the increasingly sophisticated "scientific ghost" will leave people

[26] *The Shoreditch Observer*, no. 328 (Apr. 11, 1863), p. 3.

[27] *The Shoreditch Observer*, no. 341 (July 11, 1863), p. 2.

[28] "Dircks possessed independent means," George Speaight points out, "and
had no wish to benefit financially from his invention . . ." Speaight, "Professor
Pepper's Ghost," p. 21. The Ghost, Pepper testifies, made some 12,000 pounds for
the Polytechnic. See Pepper, *The True History of the Ghost*, p. 35.

with contempt for "superstitious ones" is precisely the sort of progress for which Dircks hopes. But as the enlightened program of "rational amusement" survives, Dircks's own contribution as inventor vanishes in the tumultuous applause for the resolutely un-spectral Pepper, who "could not appear because he was not there . . ." So it is precisely in a "newspaper paragraph," to use Dircks's phrase, at once in praise of the enlightening effect of the Ghost and in praise of Pepper, that Dircks might have sensed the nefarious conspiracy to strip the phantasmagoria of its proper name.

PEPPER'S GHOST, AND SHAKESPEARE'S

Dircks dreamed of using his machine to stage Shakespeare; instead, it created its sensations in melodramas and stereotyped tableaux. What concerns me is not the dubious but delectable achievements in playwriting the Ghost inspired, but a fantasy shared by inventor and critics alike. Many imagined that the Ghost's greatest contribution would be to the staging of Shakespeare, and in particular to *Macbeth* and *Hamlet*. I argue in this book that Shakespeare provided the privileged vocabulary for intimations of the supernatural in this period; Shakespeare certainly provided a privileged rhetoric for the history of the Ghost.

An anonymous writer in the *New-York Daily Tribune* recognized the strange intertwining of strands in the reception of Pepper's Ghost. Calling the Ghost the "great dramatic sensation in London and Paris for some weeks past," and remarking that it is "said to have been summoned from the vasty deeps of science by one H. Dircks, Esq., and to have been first applied to scenic uses by Professor Pepper, of the London Polytechnic Institute," the article notes that the many articles "exposing the mystery of the said ghost" have only worked to "to increase its celebrity and multiply its followers":

> The credulous portion of the people are disposed to believe in the positive reality of the thing, and it would not surprise us any day to see a letter from Mr. Hume or Mr. Howitt attempting to prove that it is nothing more than the disembodied spirit of Shakespeare, revisiting the

glimpses of the moon and seeking an engagement in his favorite role in "Hamlet!"[29]

The writer alludes to the exchange between Owen Glendower and Hotspur in the first part of *Henry IV*:

> *Glend.*   I can call spirits from the vasty deep.
> *Hot.*   Why, so can I, or so can any man,
>   But will they come when you do call for them?
>   (III.i.52–54)

Shakespeare invented both the paradigmatic English apparition in the Ghost of Hamlet, and the paradigmatic figure of skepticism about the supernatural in Hotspur's retort to Glendower. The skepticism of the journalist applies both to the assertion of the supernatural itself, and to Dircks's claim to invention. (The rest of the article is bent on proving that a machine like that invented by Dircks had existed long before; Poe, the writer asserts, "makes an allusion to this fact" in his "Marginalia."[30]) Especially intriguing here is the writer's assertion that the "credulous portion of the public are disposed to believe in the positive reality of the thing . . ." How does the writer know this? It is as if the arena of special effects were a pure instance of Adorno and Horkheimer's dialectic of enlightenment: the technological advance in producing the more "realistic" special effect, pursued as a technical problem with a "scientific" solution, becomes the new source of the old belief in ghosts. Hume or Howitt will write a

[29] "Amusements," *The New-York Daily Tribune* 23, no. 6967 (Aug. 3, 1863), p. 7. On the same page is an advertisement for Wallack's Theater, where the Ghost appeared, calling it the "LAST EUROPEAN SENSATION/A WALKING, TALKING PHANTOM,/pronounced by all the Professors and Savans of London and Paris/THE GREATEST SCIENTIFIC WONDER THE WORLD EVER BEHELD . . ." The names here refer to two famous spiritualists, William Howitt and "the most successful and controversial spiritualist of the nineteenth century, Daniel Dunglas Home, pronounced and often misspelled *Hume*." See Russell M. and Clare R. Goldfarb, *Spiritualism and Nineteenth-Century Letters*, p. 77.

[30] What is important to me is Dircks's sense of his dispossession, not the actual merit of his claim to invention. Speaight shows that no English claim to priority may be valid; a French invention anticipated Dircks's. Speaight, "Professor Pepper's Ghost," p. 22.

letter testifying that Shakespeare is announcing a return engagement in "his favorite role," the Ghost. In this joke the motives of the inventors have simply vanished, and the critic imagines that spiritualists and showmen have a common interest in promoting the Ghost. The authoritative spiritualist will vouch that the Ghost is a medium for the Ghost of Shakespeare, seeking to play the Ghost of Hamlet. The "disembodied spirit" will return to play the stage Ghost.

What seems playful in this passage from the *Tribune*, however, returns more or less in earnest in the *New-York Times*: "How vastly will SHAKESPEARE'S plays of 'Macbeth' and 'Hamlet' gain in impressiveness by this singularly appalling invention of Prof. PEPPER!"[31] Dircks himself shared this goal, seeing his invention as the culmination of a literary tradition. With an epigraph from *Macbeth* on the title page, *The Ghost!* declares its investment in Shakespeare from the outset. Yet Shakespeare is not some transcendent authority Dircks invokes to sanctify his project; Shakespeare is, instead, among those authors whose "frenzied fancies" Dircks has designed his mechanism to realize. Stage representations of the supernatural, inadequate for so long, will finally be made wholly convincing. Behind Dircks's invocations of Shakespeare lies a sense that Shakespeare lacks something crucial, and that Dircks works to remedy this lack. Dircks writes:

> In my youth I had been awed by the stately and statue-like ghost in "Hamlet;" but [despite] all the vigorous imagination of youth, united to the natural overlooking of many discrepancies arising from inexperience, I well remember I was more struck with the language and unearthly eloquence of the spectre than I was with the mailed and plumed spectre itself. The very playbills gave me his name; and to my young mind it was, with all its majesty of mien, but the "Boo! boo!" of the nursery. There was no mistaking it for other than a very well got up, real blood and life ghost. And although its bedtime was regulated by the crowing of the chanticleer, I did not for a moment suppose it had retired to any neighbouring churchyard. Dramas introducing apparitional appearances have hitherto always obtained their success for other

---

[31] "Wallack's Theatre," *The New-York Times* (Aug. 7, 1863), p. 5.

merits than any attributed to the lusty sprites brought on to the stage.
(64)

Dircks appears as a twisted late incarnation of the Romantic tradition of readers and theater-goers, exemplified by Lamb and Hazlitt,
for whom the supernatural element in Shakespeare had been essentially unrepresentable. As David Marshall writes,

> . . . Lamb and Hazlitt could be accused of reading Shakespeare from
> the standpoint of English Romanticism—of trying to turn public plays
> into private poems. Both are also reacting to the conventions of the
> nineteenth-century stage: what Lamb calls "contemptible machinery"
> and "the elaborate and anxious provision of scenery."[32]

Lamb and Hazlitt correct the inadequate excesses of the stage by delivering the plays to the privacy of the reader's imagination. Dircks,
by contrast, improves the "contemptible machinery." When he
writes that dramas "have hitherto always obtained their success for
other merits than any attributed to the lusty sprites brought on to the
stage," the confident tone underlying that "hitherto" trusts that the
supernatural on stage will, from now on, have its proper power. In
Hamlet, "the mailed and plumed spectre itself" will, at last, have a
powerful effect.[33]

The extent of the ambition behind Dircks's project becomes particularly clear in considering this rehabilitation of the Ghost of
Hamlet in 1863, on the eve of the much anticipated Shakespeare Tercentenary of 1864. On at least a few occasions, the phantasmagoria
did indeed project the Ghost of Hamlet. Among the ghosts exhibited
at the Polytechnic, Pepper lists

> . . . Scrooge and Marley's Ghost, by Charles Dickens; the Ghost of the
> diving bell; the knight watching his armour; the poor author tested; the
> Ghost of Napoleon I. at St. Helena; and the Ghost in *Hamlet*, pro-
> nounced by a leading R.A. as being nearly perfect, only wanting a little

[32] David Marshall, "Exchanging Visions," p. 544.

[33] It is worth wondering whether fig. 1 does not represent the Ghost of Hamlet.
Certainly figure Y is a "plumed spectre."

different colour in the walls of the ramparts, which I adopted with his ultimate satisfaction and approval.[34]

These ghosts were tableaux, little scenes on familiar subjects to show off the device. Especially intriguing here is Pepper's suggestion that to make the Ghost of Hamlet "perfect" is merely a matter of decoration; the spirit has become a special effect, isolated from the play in which it appears, grander but in other ways not very different from the other types Pepper lists.

One response to the Ghost deserves more extended examination here. Tom Taylor's burlesque play, *The Ghost! The Ghost!! The Ghost!!! Or The Late Lawful Rise in Spirits*, satirizes Dircks and Pepper and their efforts to patent ghosts.[35] First Professor Kepper and then Professor Quircks enter a "Churchyard in the City" on a dark night, hunting for ghosts they might capture and patent, both unaware that the other is also among the graves. The men do manage to raise ghosts, but these ghosts are all past theatrical and literary phantoms, including the Bleeding Nun, Mrs. Veal, the Corsican Brothers—and the Ghost of Hamlet, who intones:

> I am the Ghost of Ghosts—List, list, oh list,
> Murdered by most slow stages—Royal Dane,
> Who walked for centuries in Drury Lane,
> And Covent-garden, till the minors got
> License to show me, then I went to pot;
> By third-rate strollers my prestige was floored,
> And, an old mole, I did mole's work—I *bored*. (4)

Taylor's joke superimposes the theatrical history in which the minor theaters gained the right to produce Shakespeare onto the supernatural burrowing of the Ghost. (This is the first of many rewritings of the mole I discuss in this book.) Taylor is looking back to *Hamlet*, of

[34] Pepper, *True History of the Ghost*, p. 30.

[35] Tom Taylor, *The Ghost! The Ghost!! The Ghost!!!* (Lord Chamberlain's plays ms. 53024 W, British Library, London). This copy is a printed version of the play with significant corrections and additions in handwriting, among the most interesting being the alteration of the printed names of Dircks and Pepper to Quircks and Kepper.

course, but he is also underlining his own earlier use of the cellarage
scene. Kepper and Quircks, after rancorous exchanges, have agreed
to settle their "ghostly rights and wrongs":

> QUIRCKS—(*Tenderly*)   Kepper! Shake hands once more:
>   We'll work our small still spirits as before.
> GHOSTS (*Without, above, and below*)
>   Beware!
> QUIRCKS—(*in alarm*)   What's that?
> KEPPER—   From earth was it?
> QUIRCKS—   Or from air?
> 1ˢᵗ GHOST—(*Without, above*)   Beware!
> 2ⁿᵈ GHOST—(*female voice below*)   Beware!!
> 3ʳᵈ GHOST—(*male voice, right*)   Beware!!!
> 4ᵗʰ GHOST—(*female voice, left*)   Beware!!!!!
> QUIRCKS—Should they be true Ghosts and resent our thievin 'em?
> KEPPER—True Ghosts! oh lord! tell 'em we don't believe in 'em.
> QUIRCKS—(*with forced composure*).
>   Go along with your nonsense, no intrusions!
>   We're up to you!
> KEPPER—   We know you're mere illusions. (3)

Taylor rewrites the crucial Shakespearean scene of reenchantment,
the cellarage scene. Kepper and Quircks, who together patented the
Ghost, discover that there are in fact ghosts. These "real" ghosts are,
however, the inventions of the theater. Quircks and Kepper are, for
the moment, a comic version of the audience of the Ghost. They
know that there are no ghosts, but theatrical ghosts convince them
that there are ghosts. And they have precisely that mixture of fear and
disbelief of which Sala is representative, at once able to keep the "eye
to business" (3) open, and terrified. Taylor has, in his burlesque,
caught the logic of the problem that shapes the whole history of the
Ghost. The convincing theatrical Ghost does not undo the power of
the ghostly: even the inventors of mechanical ghosts are frightened
by ghosts, on and off the stage.

Shakespeare, it would seem, is himself the subject of satire in
Taylor's play: "Well said, old Ham," says a Mrs. Veal, burlesquing
the line—"Well said, old mole"—that reverberates throughout this

book. The Ghost of Hamlet, the "Ghost of Ghosts," does not seem any more authoritative than any of the other ghosts, and he sees himself in league with these somewhat less grand theatrical creations, for whom he holds Shakespeare responsible:

> And *we*, the offspring of a Shakespeare's brain,
> Shall we hold up a Quircks and Kepper's train?
> Come old original Ghosts, gaunt, ghastly, grim,
> And tear these vile Ghost-forgers limb from limb.
> From earth and air, moorland and mountain mist,
> 'Tis Hamlet senior calls—List! list! oh list! (5)

The Ghost of Hamlet speaks for the whole parade of ghosts, and one prepares for a comic sparagmos where the ghosts will dismember the inventors. Instead, a comic song or two follows, along with a burlesque of *Romeo and Juliet*. Taylor's original intention was apparently to end the short play with a speech by Wilkie Collins's Woman in White, but he scratched that out, replacing it with—what else?—a speech by the true ghost of ghosts, the "ruler of the spirits," the Ghost of "Shakspere."

The tone of the burlesque changes somewhat as Shakespeare's Ghost laments the condition of the British stage, fallen "To mere sensation and base arts or thrall" and adaptations of French drama. He berates the old ghosts:

> *You* were sensations once, and ruled the roast
> As Kepper *now* rules with his patent Ghost.
> And 'twixt the two if I *must* make a choice
> For Quirks and Kepper here I give my voice!
> *Their* phantom has with *science some* relation,
> *You* but with second rate imagination!
> (*General burst of indignation.*)
> Silence! outworn abortions of the Stage,
> Cheats for grave children of an earlier age—!
> Hence, *stale* sensations! mouthing mockeries, hence!
> Sensation yields, but not to *you*—to *sense*!
> *Kepper*   Return, great King, to the Theatric sphere!
> *Ghost of Shakspere*   When the age needs—my motto's '*I am here*'!

> I live in my creations—they can wait
> Till show, sensation, slang are out of date . . .

The play ends with a chorus of ghosts, followed by a dance:

> At mighty Shakspere's chiding voice
> Let Kepper smile and Quirks rejoice
> But grimly, grimly, walk we still
> To the echoes *of* the graveyard chill.

"Professor Pepper's machine was plainly the hero and chief attraction of the entertainment," writes Taylor's biographer of *An Awful Rise in Spirits*, and so it might seem, as the older spirits slink away, announcing Shakespeare's approval of Kepper and Quircks.[36] But the biographer repeats the ghosts' misunderstanding. The Ghost of Shakespeare quite reluctantly endorses Quircks and Kepper as the lesser of sensational evils, and precisely on grounds dear to Dircks: Pepper's Ghost has at least *some* relation to science. But this Ghost would be happy to see the rage for "sensation" vanish completely.

An Awful Rise in Spirits enacts in its giddy way a problem that marks the intersection of Shakespeare and the supernatural. On the one hand, Taylor distances Shakespeare from the world of sensational drama; on the other, Hamlet's Ghost is the "Ghost of Ghosts," monarch of this world. The effort to reserve Shakespeare for the purposes of enlightenment quickly looks suspect, especially when it is the *Ghost* of Shakespeare who speaks for Quircks, Kepper, and the advancement of "science."

The same anti-spiritualist writer who attacked those who tried to debunk the raising of spirits also criticized the cult of Shakespeare as at least similar to, if not complicit with, spiritualism. Spiritualism, argues E.S., paves the way for hell: "This awful future must be of necessity the full development of what is now indulged in as an amusement by those who are asleep in the arms of witches, necromancers, magicians, and demons."[37] Shakespeare, implies E.S., is the opiate of the elite:

---

[36] Winton Tolles, *Tom Taylor and the Victorian Drama*, p. 58.
[37] E.S., *Spiritualism and Other Signs*, p. 14.

We would here digress, just to remark on another subject, but bearing out the same principle—the Shakespeare tercentenary. "The stuff that has forced its way into the public press has been most humiliating to the common sense of the country generally. No one has taken the trouble to wade through the nonsense that has been written on the subject, without perceiving that it has been confined to a few professionals and their dupes. The idolatry of Shakespeare has never yet extended to the masses; and no attempt to make his work popular *with them* will ever succeed."[38]

For E.S., idolatry of Shakespeare is of a piece with spiritualism, Romanism, necromancy, and other targets. My point is not that E.S. is somehow "right" about the nature of Bardolatry, but that this extreme critique is oddly consonant with what Taylor dramatizes. Both suggest the difficulty of disentangling Shakespeare from the supernatural. There will be no "scientific" Ghost of Hamlet.

In *The Ghost!*, Dircks, too, momentarily makes Shakespeare the spokesman for the forces that have stolen his invention from him. Dircks wistfully considers the status of his struggle to have his name returned to his invention with a series of rhetorical questions:

And after all what was my claim? What to make a fuss about? What to go to law about? or, What even to send floating on the ocean stream of daily press publication? It was like a squabble for a mere ribbon which tied up the rolls of bank notes rolled into the Polytechnic. So old as Shakespeare has been the enquiry—"What's in a name." (80)

Juliet's question becomes a flat statement. It is a mark of Dircks's confusion, even despair. Shakespeare, whose work the phantasmagoria was to bring to completion, has given a motto to uncaring attempts to strip Dircks's name from his invention. Ghostly effects, among which one can class this strange "quotation" from Shakespeare, continue to surface away from the phantasmagoria itself. Dircks is peculiarly relevant to my project as a whole in that, at one

---

[38] E.S., *Spiritualism and Other Signs*, p. 15. The source of the quotation is unclear; E.S. stresses that one purpose of the book is to bring together "quotations from pamphlets and papers which have been too little regarded, although containing facts of stern and solemn importance . . ." (p. 1).

moment, his sense of mystery, of an ordering or disordering force
elsewhere, takes the form of a quotation from Shakespeare. He does
not ask, but instead states, "What's in a name," as if Juliet's question,
as question, had lost its point. The scare quote would seem to indicate that there is nothing in a name, only what he calls "the mere ribbon which tied up the rolls of bank notes rolled into the Polytechnic," an incidental ornament to a process of capitalist accumulation
with its own laws and no need of his name or any other. (One can recall the blank that subsumes the name of his adversary, "Mr. ——.")
But Dircks quotes a text that proceeds to make a fetish of the proper
name. Juliet may ask, "What's in a name?" (II.ii.43), but she calls
Romeo later in the scene:

> Hist, Romeo, hist! O for a falc'ner's voice
> To lure this tassel-gentle back again!
> Bondage is hoarse, and may not speak aloud,
> Else would I tear the cave where Echo lies,
> And make her airy tongue more hoarse than mine,
> With repetition of my Romeo's name. Romeo!
>   (II.ii.158–64)

And so it goes: "Romeo" is the play's last word (V.iii.310). Dircks's
quotation belongs to a text that pretends to discount the importance
of the proper name, only to make that name an obsessive refrain of
the scene and play. The moment of Dircks's quotation from Shakespeare is a plaintive hiatus that does not return. Dircks wants his own
name to echo, and repetition of it to make clamorous London
crowds hoarse. The rest of *The Ghost!* concerns his obsessive attempts
to have his name returned to his invention and to attain recognition
in the public sphere. So Dircks's dispirited quotation from Shakespeare, with its suggestion of resignation, is instead a refusal of resignation, an insistence on his right to his name.

   I have insisted on Dircks's despair over his having been dispos-
sessed of even his own name. But the case is more specific than that.
Dircks's dilemma is not a matter of mourning for the loss of an
ahistorical aura attached to "the" name. The violation was a com-
mercial one; Pepper had usurped Dircks's right to a trademark, to
having his name become the brand name for his invention, the mark

by which the public knows the product and keeps it distinct from other products. What's in a name is both the sign of a particular brand and, for Dircks, the assurance that he will not be alienated from his product, that the Dircksian Phantasmagoria will be identified with him and not Pepper. (It is probable that Pepper's name disappears in the blank of Mr. ——; Dircks enacts his "typographical" revenge.)[39] Walter Benjamin had particular insight into the new order of language associated with the trademark: "Today's fantasies nest deep within the names of companies, whereas in former times these fantasies were believed to be hoarded in the vocabulary of 'poetic' words."[40] Dircks's fantasies, it seems, nest in the notion of "Dircks" becoming the brand name for the finest phantasmagoria, and using this machine to perfect Shakespeare's Ghost.

Amid advertising matter for Dircks's books at the end of his *Scientific Studies*, this blurb for *The Ghost!* appears:

> "A few months ago all London was rushing off to see Professor Pepper's Ghost, as it was called, but which now it appears was the property of Mr. Dircks, and from which his good name was filched in a very unhandsome manner. Here then he tells us about it, how the spectre was raised, and how we may ourselves at pleasure call spirits from the vasty deep."—The Bookseller, February 29.[41]

This sympathetic account harmonizes with Dircks's tract to the extent that its two allusions to Shakespeare are ones that Dircks might have used. The filching of the "good name" alludes to Iago's speech in Othello—". . . he that filches from me my good name/ Robs me of that which not enriches him,/And makes me poor

---

[39] "Typographical" is a term Dircks himself uses. He wanted his name both spoken as inventor in lectures using the Phantasmagoria and printed on posters and in advertisements: " . . . I therefore required equal justice typographically and verbally" (p. 11). Evidently those he spoke with at the Polytechnic believed he would be satisfied simply with spoken attribution: "In short it was no doubt hoped at first that *verbal* truths were of vital importance to me, while *typographical* misrepresentations were certain to benefit those whom they most concerned" (p. 17).

[40] Qtd. in Winfried Menninghaus, "Walter Benjamin's Theory of Myth," p. 311.

[41] Dircks, *Scientific Studies*. This blurb appears on the fourth numbered advertising page.

indeed" (III.iii.159–61)—while the second sentence alludes to the exchange between Hotspur and Glendower discussed above. The allusions in the blurb almost summarize Dircks's contradictory concerns. On the one hand there is the debunking spirit of Hotspur, granting slender recognition to the techniques of spirit-raising and questioning their efficacy. Dircks is happy to perfect the optical apparatus for raising ghosts, only unwilling to have its apparitions taken for supernatural occurrences. On the other hand, there is the migration of fetishization, of giving a positive value to the unreal, from belief in ghosts to the conferring of value on what Iago calls the "immediate jewel" of the soul (III.iii.156)—the "good name"—and the consequent demonization of those "agencies" bent on its theft or destruction. Indeed, one can see Dircks, claiming not to care about money but wanting his name to be the brand name for a machine to project ghosts, as a typical, if exaggerated, commodity fetishist in the phantasmagorical age, longing to sink his identity into the machine.

But the blurb has another value, which lies in its description of the fleeting vogue of the phantasmagoria: "A few months ago all London was rushing off to see Professor Pepper's Ghost. . ." This blurb, probably from February 1864, marks the Ghost, whatever its name, as a passing trend, a vanished entertainment. By the time of the publication of *The Ghost!*, frenzied scenes of ghost consumption had moved on to other spots in the metropolis. The Ghost did not simply vanish in later years, but the sensation was past.[42] Dircks's battle had at its center a machine no one cared about, one of a raft of more or less transient entertainments of the mid-nineteenth century.

Dircks, dedicated to the eradication of belief in bogus spirits and mysterious agencies, debunks some of the sources of that belief in one area, apparitions, only to encounter mystery in the new form of a fantastic conspiracy against him. This new mystery arises in a social world that one would expect to encounter, following Weber, as thoroughly disenchanted, emptied of supernatural content. Weber's

[42] Altick's discussion of Dircks comes in the epilogue of his monumental study of the nineteenth century's "shows of London," as a sort of last gasp. See Altick, *The Shows of London*, pp. 504–5. For the afterlife of the Ghost on stage—but especially in touring fairs—see Speaight, "Professor Pepper's Ghost."

The Protestant Ethic and the Spirit of Capitalism pictures religion as a rationalizing, disenchanting force; Dircks's *The Ghost!* represents a machine meant to rationalize a world of spectral effects as itself the center, even genesis, of a world of mystery, as an irrational, enchanting instrument of dispossession.

2

Homo Alludens: Marx's
Eighteenth Brumaire

Marx's concepts of the fetishism of commodities and of reification have proven almost endlessly useful interpretative tools. The notion of the saturation of consciousness by reified thought, especially after Lukács and the reverberations of his chapter "Reification and the Consciousness of the Proletariat" in the work of the Frankfurt School, has provided a subtle tool for tracing the intersection of the economic and the aesthetic. It sometimes seems as though Marx's decisive linkage of the fetish and the commodity form had decoded the determining kernel of modern culture, charting the resonant core of almost every object in it, back to which we might, with some ingenuity, trace its origin.[1]

It also seems at times, however, that Marx was anticipated in his insight not only by the high literary works such as *Timon of Athens,*

---

[1] A group of literary studies focusing on commodity culture has been especially suggestive for me. See Jonathan Freedman's *Professions of Taste*, Regenia Gagnier's *Idylls of the Marketplace*, Jeff Nunokawa's *Afterlife of Property*, and Jennifer Wicke's *Advertising Fictions*.

which he used to discuss the corrosive power of the money form, but also by the freaky profusion of popular magical shows and optical tricks that marked nineteenth-century culture. If "phantasmagoria" has, as I will discuss later, become an important term in the Marxist vocabulary, it also strikes me that linking magic to the money form was a commonplace of magical performance, as it remains today, where nothing is so likely to be a magician's prop as a coin or piece of paper money. One instance is especially striking to me. Among the popular magicians of early-nineteenth-century England, one M. Henry left behind a particularly vivid archive. His shows included the usual mixture of puns, hot-air balloons, laughing gas, and Shakespeareana. At the Adelphi Theater, on Friday evening, February 18, 1825, and, no doubt, on many other nights as well, M. Henry performed a show called "Table Talk" with the Shakespearean subtitle "Shreds and Patches." The program included a long shaggy dog story interspersed with illusions, including one called, startlingly, "The Quick Circulation of Capital."[2] A contemporary pamphlet records M. Henry's show and describes this sleight of hand: "Mr. Henry borrows a purse, which he envelopes in paper, holds it between his finger[s], and discharges a pistol, which affixes the purse to a board at the back of the scene."[3] This is a joke among many jokes. M. Henry literalizes the metaphor of the "circulation" of capital with a sort of visual pun: he takes a purse from a (planted?) member of the audience, and transforms this purse into a projectile. But this trick also supplies a condensed image of the violence with which capital circulates. There is, the gag implies, a randomness to capital's movement that only a more or less arbitrary magic trick can capture. The sleight of hand lets us "see" the movement of the invisible hand, and yet it remains mysterious.

Later in 1825, in Liverpool, M. Henry anticipated Marx's making commodities talk in *Capital*, and performed a mysterious trick billed as the "SILVER VASES OF METAMORPHOSES; or the IN-

[2] For a poster, see the British Library's collection, "Henry's Conjuring Entertainments, 1817–29," poster no. 49.
[3] *Table Talk, Or, 'Shreds and Patches.'*

VISIBLE EXCHANGE!—/ *The Speaking Money!!!/* Which will answer any Question, and correctly accompany music in a dance . . ."[4] The titles of these tricks are as deeply suggestive as the tricks themselves are amusing to imagine. (The spectacle of money's not only speaking, but also dancing to music, whether correctly or not, was surely worth the price of admission.) The movement from the invisibility of exchange to talkative cash enacts something like the movement in Marx from the overlooked enigma of the commodity to the speaking commodity. My larger concern here, however, is to explain why I move from the case of Henry Dircks to Karl Marx's *The Eighteenth Brumaire*, from the magical stages of the mid-nineteenth century to one of its most influential works of political theory.

Moving from Henry Dircks to Marx's *The Eighteenth Brumaire of Louis Bonaparte* takes one from an individual encounter with reenchantment to a study that focuses on the reenchantment of a whole nation. The moment of *The Eighteenth Brumaire*, first published in 1852, or roughly a decade before Dircks's machine had its spectacular year, is that of the dissolution of the revolutions of 1848 and its subject is the political history of the successful coup d'etat of Louis Bonaparte, nephew of Napoleon I, in 1851. Marx continually suggests that supernatural forces are responsible for Louis Bonaparte's rise to power. Indeed, it is no exaggeration to consider the events in France as emblematic, for Marx, of the reenchantment of a whole continent following the failures and disappointments of the revolutions of 1848. Like the representative Dircks, Marx imagines his project as a disenchanting one; in particular, Marx stresses the necessity of forging a disenchanted revolutionary language. Yet *The Eighteenth Brumaire* is notable for its allusions and its scare quotes. 1848 promised a break with the past and hope for new,

---

[4] "Henry's Conjuring Entertainments, 1817–29," unnumbered poster for performance at the Liverpool Theatre of Variety, June 27, 1825. In the same collection (no. 53), a poster for Monday, April 18, at the end of an 1825 run at the Adelphi ("POSITIVELY THE LAST NIGHT"), similarly announces: "ANIMATED SPECIE!/THE SILVER VASES OF METAMORPHOSES,/ *Or, THE INVISIBLE EXCHANGE.*"

democratic, revolutionary alternatives: Marx reads the failure of 1848 as the result of reenchantment.

Marx announces himself as a critic of enchantment. His engagement with the supernatural, however, at times also seems to be an inextricable entanglement with it. Marx is, in this way if no other, like Dircks, with whom, I like to imagine, he may once or twice have exchanged grumbles beneath the dome of the Reading Room in the old British Library. Marx's self-conscious effort to find a language for historical change, and his hope that to find such a language might also help to achieve change, is, however, a project that marks the far greater ambition of his work. Dircks, as I have suggested, never sees his situation as typical of a historical moment, and his own misfortune never leads him to question the general progress of enlightenment in which he believes. It is important to stress the strangeness of Marx. The conditions of mid-nineteenth-century Europe suggested to Marx a world of antitheses.[5] Hegel had defined the progress of Reason; Marx, probably more vividly than any other critic working in the Hegelian tradition, described the antithetical movement by which that progress brought with it a horrifying growth of the irrational. At moments, however, it seems as if Marx can imagine a positive counterforce to reenchantment only in enchanted or magical terms. The words he uses to describe what he detests, the reactionary coup, for instance, are not wholly opposed to those he uses to picture what he desires, revolution.

SMELLS LIKE WORLD SPIRIT: ALLUSION, REVISION, FARCE

In his 1869 preface to the second edition of *The Eighteenth Brumaire*, Marx discusses the troubling issue of "allusions" in his text: "A revision of the present work would have robbed it of its particular colouring. Accordingly I have confined myself to mere correction of printer's errors and to striking out allusions now no

---

[5] David McLellan points out Marx's love for antitheses in a discussion of Marx's favorite tropes in *Marx Before Marxism*, p. 73.

longer intelligible [nicht mehr verständlicher Anspielungen]."[6] Marx's preface in many ways recapitulates the concerns of the text it introduces. In *The Eighteenth Brumaire*, Marx already declares that the coup d'etat of Louis Bonaparte has formed "the second edition [die zweite Auflage] of the Eighteenth Brumaire"; that is, it has been a repetition of the coup of Napoleon I (15, 96).[7] This 1869 publication is, then, the second edition of a study of a second edition. Marx's emphasis on revision is important: The preface introduces the notion of a certain confinement in revision that is crucial to *The Eighteenth Brumaire*; Marx investigates material, linguistic, and historical barriers to thorough revision. He assures us that he is the source of his own confinement: "I have confined myself . . ." There is a trace of a certain regret here, as though Marx would like to free himself, but knows he cannot. He will not allow himself to be the thief of his own work's "colouring." Revision, whatever pleasures it might liberate, would be stylistic theft. In fact, Marx insists that he has not revised *The Eighteenth Brumaire* at all. Correction and striking out allusions must, then, be something else.

The question of how striking out no longer intelligible allusions is not revision points to some of the ambiguities that surround Marx's use of allusion in *The Eighteenth Brumaire*. One can sketch a program at once historical, critical, and linguistic. On the one hand, allusion should be an intelligible kind of repetition. Allusion in *The Eighteenth Brumaire* forces an awareness of the repetitive structure of a phrase; this awareness of repetition can itself become a crucial historical tool. Awareness of the provenance of the phrase can provoke critical awareness of genealogy and other potentially devious forms of historical transmission. Allusion is also, however, part of the nightmare of repetitive history. The revolutionary project of *The Eighteenth Brumaire* involves imagining a history that

[6] Karl Marx, "Author's Preface to the Second Edition," in *The Eighteenth Brumaire*, p. 8; "Vorwort [zur zweiten Ausgabe]," p. 304.

[7] Page numbers in parentheses follow *The Eighteenth Brumaire of Louis Bonaparte* and *Der achtzehnte Brumaire des Louis Bonaparte*; I cite the English edition first. In places I refer to the matching volume of commentary and notes to this volume of the *MEGA*, which I refer to as *Apparat*.

seizes the future, and this project includes escaping allusion and its repetitive confines, confines that recall Marx's own refusal to revise himself, to escape his own language. Allusion is part of that famous "tradition of all the dead generations" that "weighs like a nightmare on the brain of the living" (15, 97). Joyce echoes Marx: "History, Steven said, is a nightmare from which I am hoping to awake."[8] In Marx, it seems, waking up from this nightmare would put an end to allusion. There is, then, a certain historical responsibility not to erase allusions prematurely, since only such a historical awakening can truly rid the world of them.

However much it is the aim of *The Eighteenth Brumaire* to raise the prospect of a revolutionary awakening from nightmarish, allusive language, allusion nevertheless marks this contradictory work from the outset. Even its title works by installing the historical events the text analyzes into the space of allusive repetition. From the start, repetition figures the disappointment of hopes at the very least, if not nightmare itself. The promise Marx and others sensed in the revolutions of 1848 dissolves in the disillusioning repetition that is Louis Bonaparte's coup. The date of Marx's title is not the date of that coup, which culminated on December 2, 1851, but that of the coup d'etat of his uncle, Napoleon I, on the eighteenth Brumaire in the year VIII of the French revolutionary calendar (November 9, 1799, according to the Gregorian calendar).[9] This superimposition of the revolutionary calendar over the reactionary coup d'etat of Louis Bonaparte serves many functions. Marx is able to represent Louis Bonaparte's seizure of power as archaic, belated

---

[8] James Joyce, *Ulysses*, p. 35. Margaret Cohen has discussed the language of awakening in Walter Benjamin as part of his "Freudian-Copernican revolution" in Marxist thought, and her comments are relevant here: "The use of dream rhetoric in Marxism is thoroughly Enlightenment, underwritten by precisely the conceptual project that Benjamin invokes dream language to dislodge." See Cohen, *Profane Illumination*, p. 53. It is true that Marx never abandons his conviction that to awaken from nightmare is the goal. He does, however, acknowledge the great effort such awakening would entail, even if a large part of this acknowledgment is allusive.

[9] For a compelling account of some of the events Marx discusses, see Priscilla Robertson's *Revolutions of 1848*, pp. 11–103.

by half a century, belonging to a time the calendar of which, even, is defunct. It also ironically and unflatteringly compares Louis Bonaparte, whom Marx will characterize in disparaging terms, with his uncle. The disparity between the events of Napoleon I's Eighteenth Brumaire and the coup d'etat of his nephew makes the title's allusion a strong form of parody.

Yet the title also anticipates some of the more complicated, less resolved concerns of *The Eighteenth Brumaire* as a whole. By inscribing Louis Bonaparte in a calendar that set itself off as revolutionary, Marx suggests that Bonaparte has himself seized a revolutionary past, even if only belatedly or in parodic form. Marx will analyze this seizure of the past as reactionary, as farcical historical revision, but Bonaparte's appropriation of the past raises questions deeply connected to those surrounding Marx's discussions of revolutionary practice. In *The Eighteenth Brumaire*, Marx faces the difficulty of an odd homology between revolutions, which often attempt to seize history in parodic form, and Bonaparte's regressive coup d'etat, which does the same. The fear that such allusive seizure of history may always lead to regressive delusions is part of the reason Marx insists that the "social revolution of the eighteenth century cannot draw its poetry from the past, but only from the future" (18, 101).

The title itself is typical of a work both teeming with allusions and deeply concerned with allusive structures. To ask whether this tissue of allusion implicates *The Eighteenth Brumaire* itself in farcical revision is to ask a question suggested by the text's famous opening itself: "Hegel remarks somewhere [irgendwo] that all facts and personages of great importance in world history occur, as it were, twice. He forgot to add: the first time as tragedy, the second as farce" (15, 96). This invocation of Hegel suggests some of the critical work allusion performs in *The Eighteenth Brumaire*. Attribution here takes the form of a fractured quotation, of a scare quote. The word "somewhere" dislocates the heavy authority of Hegel's name; its gesture to some more or less unimportant place in Hegel's corpus undermines the weight of the attribution. In Hegel, history repeats; in Marx, repeating Hegel, history repeats, but historical repetition takes the form of generic difference. Marx, too, is engaging in a sort of repetitive action, the repetition of Hegel's dictum. The difference there, it would seem, is one of correction, or completion. Where Hegel "forgot" to mention that repetition has its tragic and farcical extremes, Marx repeats Hegel with the difference that he remembers to mention this generic distinction in the repetitions of history.

Bruce Mazlish has convincingly shown that Marx alludes in his offhand way to a passage from Hegel's *The Philosophy of History*. This passage is a reflection on Caesar's putting an end to the Roman Republic:

> But it became immediately manifest that only a *single* will could guide the Roman State, and now the Romans were compelled to adopt that opinion; since in all periods of the world a political revolution is sanctioned in men's opinions, when it repeats itself. Thus Napoleon was twice defeated, and the Bourbons twice expelled. By repetition that which at first appears merely a matter of chance and contingency becomes a real and ratified existence.[10]

In *The Eighteenth Brumaire*, what repeats does not attain a "real and ratified existence"; "we are," as Mazlish notes, "in the presence of another of Marx's famous inversions."[11] The mention of Hegel, it would seem, is among Marx's intelligible allusions, one of those which survived the non-revision that produced the second edition; the attribution to Hegel, in fact, simply reverses Hegel. Where Hegel invokes the sanction of repetition to justify one dictatorship, Marx turns this sanction topsy-turvy to attack another. Where repetition in Hegel produces a "real and ratified existence," in Marx it produces an unreal, questionable, and theatrical one.

The 1869 preface to *The Eighteenth Brumaire* also anticipates the body of the work in suggesting a relationship between theater and allusion. When Marx writes of those discarded "allusions now no longer intelligible," the German word is "Anspielungen." (The sense of play latent in the Latinate English term, allusion—whose

---

[10] Georg Wilhelm Friedrich Hegel, *The Philosophy of History*, p. 313.
[11] Bruce Mazlish, "Tragic Farce," p. 336.

root is the Latin, "ludere," or to play—is more immediately apparent in German, where "Spiel" is the general term for play, and "Anspielung" is clearly a variety of play.) Marx links this notion of allusion as play to theater by using another form of "Spiel" in the preceding sentence, where Marx distinguishes his efforts in *The Eighteenth Brumaire* from those of Hugo in *Napoleon le Petit* and Proudhon in *Coup d'Etat*: "I . . . demonstrate how the *class struggle* in France created circumstances and relationships that made it possible for a grotesque mediocrity to play a hero's part [einer mittelmässigen und grotesken Personage das Spiel der Heldenrolle ermöglichten]."[12] In distinguishing his work from that of Hugo and Proudhon, Marx emphasizes that an accurate depiction of historical forces reveals what made possible "Spiel" of a particular kind, theatrical representation. And Marx's interest is not "theatrical representation" as such, but theater that sounds like farce, where a fool impersonates a hero. Mazlish notes that Marx was hardly alone in sensing farce in the events following the revolutions of 1848.[13] Engels, he shows, likely provided a catalyst for the opening of *The Eighteenth Brumaire* in a letter to Marx dated December 3, 1851: "it really seems as if old Hegel in his grave were acting as World Spirit and directing history, ordaining most conscientiously that it should be unrolled twice over, once as a great tragedy and once as a wretched farce."[14]

Part of the supposed intelligibility of Marx's reversal of Hegel lies in the assumption that Marx retains, despite his overturning

[12] Marx, "Author's Preface," p. 8; "Vorwort," p. 304.

[13] Mazlish provides a similar theatrical description of events of 1848, which, however, does not directly mention farce, from de Tocqueville's *Recollections*. Mazlish, "Tragic Farce," 336. Proudhon, whose published account of the coup Marx criticizes in his 1869 preface, strikes a similar note when he writes in a letter dated February 25, 1848: "Drunk on historical novels, we have given a repeat performance of the 10th of August and the 29th of July. Without noticing it, we have all become characters from some farce." Pierre-Joseph Proudhon, *Selected Writings*, p. 154. Alexander Herzen writes of a crowd gathered before a massive demonstration in 1849: "Had those people found real leaders the day would not have ended in farce." Herzen, *My Past and Thoughts*, p. 354.

[14] Karl Marx and Frederick Engels, *Selected Correspondence* (Moscow, n.d.) 75, qtd. in Mazlish, "Tragic Farce," 336.

mood, a traditional generic hierarchy, where debased farce is the unequal partner to grand tragedy. This assumption is questionable. Part of the work of *The Eighteenth Brumaire* is the disruption of forms of play. Farce and the play of allusion become strategies of historical analysis. Marx not only revises Hegel in his opening, but he also simultaneously borrows from and alters Engels's suggestive passage. Engels qualifies genres in ways Marx does not: "great tragedy" and "wretched farce" are not necessarily Marx's categories. Or, that is, they are, and they are not. In the first edition of *The Eighteenth Brumaire*, Marx uses terms that repeat those in Engels's letter. There, Marx writes that history repeats itself, the first time as great tragedy, "grosse Tragödie," the second time as wretched or shabby—"lumpige"—farce.[15] (This "lumpige" farce looks forward to that famously unstable group, the lumpenproletariat.) In the 1869 revision, apparently, Marx decides those adjectives are no longer intelligible. In any case, they disappear, leaving, simply, tragedy and farce. If, in the first edition, Marx retains tragedy as the supreme theatrical genre, he has turned Hegel the political theorist upside down only to repeat without difference Hegel the aesthetician's valorization of tragedy.

Certainly there are reasons for ascribing to Marx the prejudice that denigrates farce and exalts tragedy, among them Marx's campaign to ridicule Louis Bonaparte, to cast him as the lead player in a farce, to reveal the "mediocre and grotesque personage" beneath the heroic, but empty, Napoleonic facade. Yet the very possibility of the generic reconfiguration of history suggests the power of farce as a tool not only of denigration but also of critique. The worth of farce as genre does not assume the worth of figures in farce; the critical value of farce in the *Brumaire* may be precisely that its force as a representational tactic is independent of the "value" of the characters it represents. Marx's farce is distinguishable from tragedy, which, classically, assumes tragic consciousness on the part of figures in it. Farcical consciousness, instead, belongs outside farce, is the product of a critical distance from the action of farce itself.[16]

[15] See the *Apparat*, p. 706.
[16] Stephen Tifft's article on *The Rules of the Game*, "*Drôle de Guerre*," includes a

Marx had critical support for a less dismissive characterization of farce. Franz Horn wrote in 1823 of a (specifically German) taste for mixed genres: "Love of so-called pure tragedy was never common, but the inherent romantic impulse demanded rich sustenance, as did the delight in farce, which is usually most alive in thoughtful dispositions."[17] Horn's formulation is distinctly at odds with Hegel. (Hegel, indeed, was in fact almost always forgetting to mention farce.[18]) Hegel's thought on comedy, however, illuminates the theatrical rhetoric of *The Eighteenth Brumaire*. For Marx, the first occurrence of the facts and persons of history is tragedy, and the second farce. Hegel's conception of comedy forms an intriguing counterpart: comedy begins where tragedy ends. Comedy "possesses . . . for its basis and point of departure that with which it is possible for tragedy to terminate . . ." Reconciliation, which is for Hegel the final result of the collisions of tragedy, is present at the onset of comedy. "The true course of dramatic development consists in the annulment of *contradictions* viewed as such, in the reconciliation of the forces of human action, which alternately strive to negate each other in their conflict," writes Hegel. For Hegel, the "true course" of dramatic development is an allegory for that of historical development: "in a work of art the matter of exclusive importance should be the display of that which is conformable with reason and the truth of Spirit . . ."[19] The value of genres such as tragedy and comedy lies, for Hegel, in their accurate "display" of the substantial content of history. Tragedy and comedy are the masks of *Geist*. For Hegel, then, the collisions of tragedy are the crises of history.

The Hegelian equivalence between the content of theatrical representation and the content of Spirit-directed history is not totally

---

compelling reading of *The Eighteenth Brumaire* (pp. 147–53). Especially relevant here is Tifft's reevaluation of farce as "a matter of ill-tuned ideology" (p. 151) and his emphasis on its critical potential and force.

[17] Horn, qtd. in Walter Benjamin, *The Origin of German Tragic Drama*, p. 123.

[18] Hermann Glockner's *Hegel-Lexikon* lists only a single use of the word in the *Jubiläums-Ausgabe* of Hegel's work; the *Lexikon* comprises the twenty-third and twenty-fourth volumes of this edition.

[19] Hegel, *On Tragedy*, pp. 76, 71, 50.

alien to the use of theater in *The Eighteenth Brumaire*. Yet Marx's work makes a crucial break. Just as, for Marx, Hegel's reconciliation would harmonize too easily with resignation, co-optation, or submission, so the notion that theatrical and historical content coincide would signal a suspension of critique. In *The Eighteenth Brumaire* farce is equivalent to an evasion of history and Bonaparte's farce is the mask of what stalls history. The crisis of political representation in the *Brumaire* finds its apogee when Marx discusses Bonaparte's ruling despite his lack of class affiliation. As David Fernbach writes, Marx "confronts the paradox of a state power that appears not to express the rule of a social class at all, but to dominate civil society completely and to arbitrate class struggles from above."[20] Marx explains this contradiction by demonstrating, among other things, Bonaparte's problematic representation of a class that is not a class, the lumpenproletariat, "the only class upon which he can base himself unconditionally" (75, 142). The notorious catalogue Marx offers to describe this class—"vagabonds, discharged soldiers, discharged jailbirds, escaped galley slaves," etc. (75, 141)—has drawn more attention than what follows; the discussion following the catalogue of bohemians is important in following through the implications of theatrical discourse in Marx's work.[21]

Theater in *The Eighteenth Brumaire* often figures political self-consciousness, and awareness of dramatic genre looks oddly like discernment of the political. This is nowhere clearer than in the passages following Marx's description of the lumpenproletariat:

> An old crafty *roué*, he [Bonaparte] conceives the historical life of the nation and their performances of state [Haupt- und Staatsaktionen] as comedy [Komödie] in the most vulgar sense, as a masquerade where the grand costumes, words and postures merely serve to mask the pettiest knavery [Lumperei]. (75–76, 142)

[20] David Fernbach, introduction, *Surveys from Exile*, p. 9. See Terry Eagleton, *Walter Benjamin*, pp. 162–70, for an especially rigorous discussion of this problem of class representation in *The Eighteenth Brumaire*.

[21] For an important discussion of that list and other issues surrounding Marx's representation of the lumpenproletariat, see Peter Stallybrass, "Marx and Heterogeneity."

Marx's admiration for Bonaparte's political acumen here is clear; he appreciates Bonaparte's manipulation of a theatrical masquerade. Bonaparte's savvy takes the form of an ability to discriminate between genres; he sees the "Haupt- und Staatsaktionen" of politics as comedy. The "Haupt- und Staatsaktionen" is itself a genre of German drama; the translation's vague "performances of state" misses Marx's use of a specific form. Horn's comment on farce, quoted above, is an aside in a discussion of this genre in which he describes its most notable features:

> The kings and princes appear with their crowns of gilt paper, very melancholy and mournful, and they assure the sympathetic public that nothing is more difficult than to rule, and that a wood-cutter sleeps more soundly at night; the generals and officers hold fine speeches, and recount their great deeds . . . The ministers are correspondingly less popular with these authors, and are usually portrayed as evil-intentioned and with a black, or at least a grey, character . . . The clown and fool is often a nuisance to the *dramatis personae*; but they simply cannot get rid of this incarnation of parody who, as such, is of course immortal.[22]

One might do worse than to describe Marx's Louis Bonaparte as such an "incarnation of parody." His ghostly repetition of Napoleon even constitutes a kind of ghoulish claim to immortality. Marx's analysis collapses the prominent roles of the "Haupt- und Staatsaktionen"; Bonaparte is at once sovereign, "evil-intentioned" courtier, and clown. More important, like Marx, Bonaparte, remembering tragedy but witnessing farce, has the perspicacity to analyze "the historical life of the nation" as a form of theater. In discussing Bonaparte, who is able to conceive of the "historical life of the nation and their performances of state" as something like farce—"comedy in the most vulgar sense"—Marx seems to repeat his own opening to *The Eighteenth Brumaire*, where he conceives of events and persons in history as farce. *The Eighteenth Brumaire* presents the dilemma of a homology between the historical critic, Marx, and his putative subject, Bonaparte. Bonaparte, it seems, has

---

[22] Horn, qtd. in Benjamin, *Origin*, pp. 123–24.

already mastered and put into practice the generic criticism of history which Marx uses against him.[23]

The "Lumperei" masked by masquerade clearly links Bonaparte's theatrical escapades to the lumpenproletariat Marx has just discussed. Bonaparte's success lies in his lack of self-delusion:

> The Society of December 10 belonged to him, it was *his* work, his very own idea. Whatever else he appropriates is put into his hands by the force of circumstances; whatever else he does, the circumstances do for him or he is content to copy from the deeds of others. But Bonaparte with official phrases about order, religion, family and property in public, before the citizens [öffentlich vor den Bürgern], and with the secret society of the Schufterles and Spiegelbergs, the society of disorder, prostitution and theft, behind him—that is Bonaparte himself as original author, and the history of the Society of December 10 is his own history. (76–77, 143)

For the moment, Bonaparte, to paraphrase *The Eighteenth Brumaire*'s second paragraph, makes his own history, and just as he pleases, under circumstances chosen by himself. And he accomplishes this by manipulating the difference between what is open and public, "öffentlich," and what is "behind him," the "secret society" of December 10. Political and theatrical representation

---

[23] Jeffrey Mehlman's reading in *Revolution and Repetition* suggests that Marx is not only a theorist of farce but also a victim of farce. For Mehlman, farce, aligned with the lumpenproletariat, is a de-stabilizing third term in Marx's text that disrupts the classical opposition of comedy and tragedy; the "specular—or reversible—relation" of tragedy and comedy "is exceeded by a heterogeneous, negatively charged instance whose situation is one of deviation or displacement in relation to one of the poles of the initial opposition" (p. 14): the relation is exceeded, that is, by farce. Farce, for Mehlman, is typical of the "'third terms' active in the text" in uncannily breaking "with the *philosopheme of representation*" upon which Marx's text relies (p. 20). Farce is an uncanny blockage in Marx's system, according to Mehlman, and Bonapartism is the farcical, uncanny crisis that undoes Marx's dialectic. Mehlman's classically deconstructive reading has generated much debate. See especially Eagleton, *Walter Benjamin*, for a concentrated critique of Mehlman's argument (pp. 162–70). In addition to those already cited, other valuable readings of the *Eighteenth Brumaire* include Edward W. Said, "On Repetition"; Paul Bové, "The Metaphysics of Textuality"; and Sandy Petry, "The Reality of Representation."

work by inversion here; "the secret society of the Schufterles and
Spiegelbergs" expresses itself as the open society of "order, religion,
family and property." Yet this inversion is by no means simple. The
"Schufterles and Spiegelbergs" are characters from Schiller's *The
Robbers*. Bonaparte's inversion works by putting the theatrical backstage; his robbers stand "behind him," offstage, while "phrases" do
the work of drama.

Bonaparte is author simultaneously of what is backstage and
what is onstage, of what is open to the public and what is hidden
from view. In Bonaparte's

> society of December 10, he assembles ten thousand rascally fellows
> [Lumpenkerls], who are to play the part of the people, as Nick Bottom
> that of the lion [wie Klaus Zettel den Löwen]. At a moment when the
> bourgeoisie itself played the most complete comedy [Komödie], but in
> the most serious manner in the world, without infringing any of the
> pedantic conditions of French dramatic etiquette, and was itself half
> deceived, half convinced of the solemnity of its own performances of
> state [ihrer eignen Haupt- und Staatsaktionen], the adventurer, who
> took the comedy as plain comedy [der die Komödie platt als Komödie
> nahm], was bound to win. (76, 142)

French comedy, played "in the most serious manner in the world,"
becomes a German dramatic genre, the "Haupt- und Staatsaktionen." Marx's mention of Bottom, chief among the "rude
mechanicals" in *A Midsummer Night's Dream*, is the first of the significant Shakespearean moments in *The Eighteenth Brumaire*. Bottom never plays the lion, though at one point he asks for the role
and has much to say about how it should be played. The mechanicals' comic dilemma is how to play their drama without having it
mistaken for reality, and thus frightening their elegant Athenian
audience. Bottom's solution for the lion is for Snug, who has been
cast in the role, to give a speech in which he allays the fears he
imagines the audience might have: "'If you think I come hither as a
lion, it were pity on my life. No! I am no such thing; I am a man as
other men are . . .'" (III.i.42–44).

Bottom's strategy of distancing oneself from the role one plays,
Marx thinks, is precisely what the savvy Bonaparte finally forgets.

Bonaparte's political and theatrical acumen, his generic cunning, is not infinite:

> Only when he has eliminated his solemn opponent, when he himself now takes his imperial role seriously and under the Napoleonic mask imagines he is the real Napoleon, does he become the victim of his own conception of the world, the serious buffoon [der ernsthafte Hanswurst] who no longer takes world history for a comedy but his comedy for world history. (76, 142)

The *Hanswurst* is a stock character of the "Haupt- und Staatsaktionen"; for analogous characters in English plays, one can think of Iago, or Edmund in *King Lear*. A particular type of court intriguer in a genre intrigued by the court, the *Hanswurst*, according to a certain Weiss, "armed with the weapons and irony and scorn, usually got the better of his fellows . . . and did not even have any inhibitions about taking over the task of directing the intrigue of the play . . ."[24] It is in the figure of the *Hanswurst* that the "ill-intentioned minister" and the clown meet. Walter Benjamin comments: "The comic figure is a *raisonneur*; in reflection he appears to himself as a marionette."[25] It is a similar process of reasoning and reflection that makes Marx's Bonaparte superior to his bourgeois rivals; he is aware of himself as an actor and is aware of the value of the convictions about drama held by others. It is precisely when he becomes aware of himself as "marionette," as subject to conflicting generic and political constraints, that he attains a position from which he can manipulate the theatrical arrangements of society, become "original author." As "ernsthafte Hanswurst," however, he becomes an unaware stock figure in the sort of historical drama for which the bourgeoisie has mistaken its comedy.

If, as W. J. T. Mitchell has shown, in *The German Ideology* a key figure for ideology is the *camera obscura*, in *The Eighteenth Bru-*

---

[24] Weiss, qtd. in Benjamin, *Origin*, p. 126.

[25] Benjamin, *Origin*, p. 127. It would be worth contemplating Shakespeare's second tetralogy as an extended *Haupt- und Staatsaktion*, as it includes Hal's speech on the difficulties of rule and the heaviness of the crown, and Falstaff, the immortal, corpulent "incarnation of parody" whom no imperious refusal to acknowledge can dismiss.

maire not only theater but, in particular, the distinctions between foreground and background, onstage and offstage figure ideology.[26] Bonaparte becomes subject to an ideology he has earlier recognized as false, and has manipulated as the public representation of an entirely different "secret society." It is when Bonaparte, wearing the Napoleonic mask, "imagines he is the real Napoleon" that "he becomes the victim of his own conception of the world," farcical repetition rather than original author, victim rather than producer of false consciousness. One of Brecht's theses in "A Short Organum for the Theatre" has particular resonance here. Brecht writes of the actor: "At no moment must he go so far as to be wholly transformed into the character played. The verdict: 'he didn't act Lear, he was Lear' would be an annihilating blow to him."[27] For Marx, the verdict on Bonaparte—he didn't act Napoleon, he was Napoleon—should be an annihilating blow. Partial transformation is a necessity of ideological manipulation; Bonaparte must seem to believe his "official phrases about order, religion, family and property." But the ideologue who remains partly outside the theatrical constructs of ideology knows that belief in such phrases is error. Fooled by his own belief, the "raisonneur" becomes marionette. The theatrical discourse of *The Eighteenth Brumaire* in the end privileges a position outside of theater; it has as its project a knowledge that is not theatrical. Bonaparte has such knowledge, but then, according to Marx, loses it.

Engels's characterization of the coup d'etat of 1851—"it really was as if old Hegel were in his grave acting as World Spirit and directing history"—contains a similar theatrical dialectic. Acting and directing, performing and controlling, Hegel, like Bonaparte, seems to manipulate history into a desired shape. Yet Hegel's historical manipulation is from a position not so much onstage or offstage, but underneath the stage. As ghost in his grave playing

---

[26] W. J. T. Mitchell, "The Rhetoric of Iconoclasm: Marxism, Ideology, and Fetishism," pp. 151–208.

[27] Brecht, "A Short Organum for the Theatre," in *Brecht on Theatre*, p. 109. For a similar reading of this passage, see Michel Chaouli, "Masking and Unmasking," pp. 62–63.

"World Spirit," as *Geist* playing *Weltgeist*, this Hegel recalls nothing so much as another Shakespearean figure recalled in *The Eighteenth Brumaire*: the Ghost of Hamlet, beneath the stage, who acts the revenge ghost and directs the history of Hamlet.

GHOSTS IN 'THE GERMAN IDEOLOGY' AND 'THE EIGHTEENTH BRUMAIRE'

Like the Ghost of Hamlet, the ghostly Hegel haunts the letter by Engels. Before turning to this spirit, I will examine the larger background of supernatural discourse behind *The Eighteenth Brumaire*. Ghosts, spooks, and specters abound. Evidently these supernatural fauna are not among those "allusions now no longer intelligible" that Marx struck from his first edition. To remember Engels's letter, however, is to remember that Marx's attribution to Hegel may also be an allusion to Engels, however obscured. Marx's opening sentence is both fractured quotation and hidden allusion. The association of ghosts and allusion is not accidental; the allusion, like the ghost, is a revenant partly unloosed from its historical moorings. Nor is the prominence of this constellation of allusion and ghosts in *The Eighteenth Brumaire* an accident. Allusion and ghosts are aspects of a concern central to the work: the problem of the tenacity of an oppressive political and historical inheritance.

1848 suddenly made necessary the recognition of ghosts. A striking peculiarity of Marx's prominent supernatural rhetoric is that it seems inconsistent with the thorough materialism one expects from the Marx of this period. Comparison with *The German Ideology*, for example, written only a few years before, in 1845–46, is telling. In *The German Ideology*, Marx and Engels write:

> It is self-evident . . . that "spectres," "bonds," "the higher being," "concept," "scruple," are merely the idealistic, spiritual expression, the conception apparently of the isolated individual, the image of very empirical fetters and limitations, within which the mode of production of life and the form of intercourse coupled with it move.[28]

---

[28] Karl Marx and Friedrich Engels, *The German Ideology*, p. 52.

According to this program, such terms as "spectre," it seems, require translation from the expressive, imagistic, individual register
to one that reveals what those obfuscating terms tend to conceal:
the material circumstances that have generated them. One impetus
behind this campaign against mystification and the vocabulary that
underwrites it is certainly Marx's political and philosophical campaign to reverse Hegel and his master trope, *Geist*. The critique of
"idealistic, spiritual expression" will call for a critical praxis, and a
critical vocabulary, which better represents the material circumstances of the social world. Yet it is worth noting that even in *The
German Ideology*, Marx and Engels concede that those terms in
scare quotes remain "the image of very empirical fetters and limitations." Supernatural language may be inadequate, a poor translation of these "fetters and limitations," but it still bears a relationship, as "image," to the underlying material conditions.

Later in *The German Ideology* Marx and Engels discuss their
conception of history:

> It has not, like the idealistic view of history, in every period to look for
> a category, but remains constantly on the real *ground* of history; it does
> not explain practice from the idea but explains the formation of ideas
> from material practice; and accordingly it comes to the conclusion that
> all forms and products of consciousness cannot be dissolved by mental
> criticism, by resolution into "self-consciousness" or transformation into
> "apparitions," "spectres," "fancies," etc., but only by the practical
> overthrow of the actual social relations which gave rise to this idealistic
> humbug; that not criticism but revolution is the driving force of his-
> tory, also of religion, of philosophy and all other types of theory.[29]

Marx and Engels put the supernatural terms here among the errors
of "mental criticism." But a gap remains between the new practice
of history Marx and Engels claim to introduce and the dismissal of
the mystifying terms of moribund idealist analysis. If these mystifying terms are images of "actual social relations," then there is the
problem of lag time. Is there a disenchanted language for "the real
ground of history"? How can the materialism of Marx and Engels

[29] Marx and Engels, *German Ideology*, pp. 58–59.

attain a language free of ghosts and spooks, especially in the absence of "the practical overthrow of the actual social relations"?
The danger is that, before the revolution, critique of ideology will
become a form of ideology, an overthrowing in thought of what is
not a product of thought but of "material practice." The facts of
"material practice" will survive. Scare quotes may be an admirable
sign of critical self-consciousness, but in themselves they make no
revolution. The passage above goes further: the "forms and products of consciousness," as well as "material practice," will be transformed only with revolution. The point may be that "'apparitions,'
'specters,' 'fancies,' etc." are the inadequate transformations of a
mental criticism that believes world history is "a mere abstract act"
performed by a "metaphysical spectre."[30] But in *The Eighteenth
Brumaire* a further implicit caveat follows: at this point inadequate
transformations are what any criticism, "mental" or materialist,
must resort to as a provisional working vocabulary. "Geist" is
bunk. Even if Geist, however, is only as an evasive translation of
"actual social relations" it bears witness to these relations.

Is there no alternative to a division that would suggest that critical language is either completely enchanted by or completely liberated from the fantasies of ideology? Progressive disenchantment
may be a satisfactory alternative model. One could say that the new
critical vocabulary of Marx and Engels provides a progressive step
toward the exorcism of supernatural practice from the arena of
critical thought, even if not a complete break from it. The insistence on a severe break between fully liberated revolutionary language and enchanted discourse is, however, partially Marx's. Nevertheless it is also Marx who, in *The Eighteenth Brumaire*, uses a
supernatural discourse similar in kind, if not in effect, to that he
and Engels excoriate in *The German Ideology*.

In *Specters of Marx*, Jacques Derrida has suggested that it is impossible to be sure of any strict break in Marx's work. He argues
convincingly that Marx wants to distinguish the bad "specter" from
the good "spirit," and goes on to argue that this effort shows that

---

[30] Marx and Engels, *German Ideology*, p. 58.

Marx always remains haunted. In a passage of almost lyrical ven-
triloquism, Derrida shifts from the third to the first person:

> Marx tried all the exorcisms, and with what eloquence, what jubilation,
> what bliss! He so loved the words of the exorcism! For these words al-
> ways cause to come back, they convoke the *revenant* that they conjure
> away. Come so that I may chase you! You hear! I chase you. I pursue
> you. I run after you to chase you away from here. I will not leave you
> alone. And the ghost does not leave its prey, namely, its hunter.[31]

This passage captures one of the central points of Derrida's reading
of Marx. To exorcise is always to bring back the ghost. (Derrida's
answer to Hotspur's question for Glendower—". . . But will they
come when you do call for them?"—would be, Why, yes, they do.
They must.) One of the uncharacteristic oddities of Derrida's
reading of Marx, however, is that he is sometimes deaf to the allusive echoes in Marx's work. It is as if, in reducing Marx to "spirit,"
he forgets his usual attention to intertextuality. This matters, I
think, because Derrida presents a straw Marx who is unconscious
of the way ghosts double back, unaware of the vicious circle that
determines that every chase after ghosts is also a proclamation of
the existence of ghosts. While I do not think that Marx is wholly in
control of the ghostly allusions he summons, I also argue that allusion constitutes Marx's partial recognition of his own place, caught
in resilient repetition and supernatural structures.[32]

---

[31] Jacques Derrida, *Specters of Marx*, p. 140. For another compelling deconstructive reading of the role of the supernatural in Marx, see Thomas Keenan,
"The Point Is to (Ex)Change It."

[32] It seems to me that in a few places Derrida is careless in his own *esprit* catalogue, and names ghosts that a "new enlightenment" should not only chase, but
exorcise for good. Derrida describes "the unleashing of racisms and xenophobias,
ethnic conflicts, conflicts of war and religion": "Entire regiments of ghosts have
returned, armies from every age . . ." (p. 80). And below: "Inter-ethnic wars . . .
are proliferating driven by an *archaic* phantom and concept, by a *primitive conceptual phantasm* of community, the nation-State, sovereignty, borders, native soil
and blood" (p. 82). Furthermore, he describes "the mafia and drug cartels on every
continent" as "capitalist phantom-States" (p. 83). One wonders how this works according to the deconstructive contamination of spirit by specter that Derrida describes. Surely these are not what Derrida calls "*spirits* in the plural and in the

Not to be aware that ghosts still walk the earth is indeed, for Marx, the sign of the most thorough enchantment. The world's most enchanted nation, according to *The Eighteenth Brumaire*, is the United States. Marx analyzes the lessons of the defeat of the Paris proletariat in the June days of 1848:

> It had revealed that here *bourgeois republic* signifies the unlimited despotism of one class over other classes. It had proved that in countries with an old civilization, with a developed formation of classes, with modern conditions of production and with an intellectual consciousness in which all traditional ideas have been dissolved by the work of centuries, *the republic* signifies *in general only the political form of revolution of bourgeois society*, and not its *conservative form of life*, as, for example, in the United States of North America, where, though classes already exist, they have not yet become fixed, but continually change and interchange their elements in constant flux, where the modern means of production, instead of coinciding with a stagnant surplus population, rather compensate for the relative deficiency of heads and hands, and where, finally, the feverish, youthful movement of material production, which has to make a new world its own, has left neither time nor opportunity for abolishing the old spirit world [Geisterwelt]. (24–25, 105–6)

The United States, here, is the place where "traditional ideas" have not yet been "dissolved by the work of centuries"; an antiquated "intellectual consciousness," Marx implies, rules its "conservative form of life." With unfixed classes and "modern means of production," means that are a substitute for scarce human labor, there is no time in the United States for the dissolution of "traditional ideas," a process for which French history provides such a fine example. So there is no discrepancy between "the feverish, youthful movement of material production" in the United States and the overpowering world of ghosts that rules it and keeps it locked in

---

sense of specters, of untimely specters that one must not chase away but sort out, critique, *keep close by, and allow to come back*" (p. 87, my emphasis). Can Derrida separate his "spirit" from these "ghosts" or his "new International" from these "phantom-States"? The most valuable response to *Specters of Marx* so far is Fredric Jameson's "Marx's Purloined Letter."

tradition. Rather, it is precisely the absolute rule of production, in a nation with no "surplus population," to use Marx's disturbing phrase, which will determine the tenacity of "the old spirit world." The United States here is part of the world that has not yet experienced the contradictions of capital and is, therefore, pre-political.[33]

France, on the other hand, political nation of the first order, has had some "opportunity for abolishing the old spirit world." Such abolition, however, does not happen all at once. Marx criticizes certain "Democrats" who, in anticipation of "the second Sunday in May 1852," the day appointed for Bonaparte to step down as President of France, performed mental revolutions not unlike those of the Hegelians who are a target of *The German Ideology.* "As ever," writes Marx, "weakness had taken refuge in a belief in miracles, fancied the enemy overcome when he was only conjured away in imagination [in der Phantasie weghexte], and it lost all understanding of the present in a passive glorification of the future that was in store for it . . ." (20, 102). The French may have more time than their hyper-productive American counterparts for demolition of "the old spirit world," but in France that demolition happens only in fantasy.

The Democrats in this passage form a group that mistakenly imagines itself to have a sorcerer's power. As with the Hegelians, their apotropaic overturnings in the world of spirit have no equivalent in the social world. Magic, in fact, returns where they least expect it. Enter Louis Bonaparte, "Hexenmeister": "all has vanished like a phantasmagoria before the spell of a man whom even his enemies do not make out to be a sorcerer [Hexenmeister]" (20, 102–3). Marx contrasts the ineffective hexing of the Democrats with the strong "spell" of Bonaparte. The Democrats, who conjured away ("weghexte") Bonaparte in imagination, encounter their antagonist as the unacknowledged master—"Hexenmeister"—of the tricks they would themselves use. All the trappings of bourgeois Democratic resistance, under Bonaparte's counter-magic, vanish

[33] A small irony attending *The Eighteenth Brumaire* is that it was first printed in New York. For a somewhat bathetic account of the circumstances of this publication, see Franz Mehring, *Karl Marx,* pp. 240–44.

"like a phantasmagoria." If the United States in *The Eighteenth Brumaire* is the place where industrialization and "the old spirit world" co-exist, the Democrats are like those "industrialists of philosophy" Marx and Engels describe in *The German Ideology*, who experiment with a whole range of "new substances" and "new combinations."[34] The phantasmagoria, both a mechanical ghost machine and the illusions produced by it, is Marx's figure for the material basis of the ideological production of the Democrats; Bonaparte is able to spirit it away, it seems, in part because he recognizes the phantasmagoria for what it is: an ideological factory. The Democrats have no defense against Bonaparte's "spell"; they cannot disenchant the political arena when they have no notion of where the magic comes from.

The Eighteenth Brumaire constitutes an important text in what Margaret Cohen has resonantly dubbed "Gothic Marxism." She describes a Marxist genealogy "fascinated with the irrational aspects of social processes, a genealogy that both investigates how the irrational pervades existing society and dreams of using it to effect social change."[35] Derrida's "spirit" of Marx, herald of the New International, is perhaps the most remarkable recent addition to this tradition. It is certainly true that one of the fascinations of *The Eighteenth Brumaire* is Marx's engagement with the irrational. Marx, however, would never have endorsed the notion that the irrational might become the engine of social change, and this is not only because he "lacked the terms" Freud provided to imagine how this movement from the irrational to social change might work, as Cohen argues. (Cohen contends, via Benjamin and Althusser, that Freudian dreamwork supplies a model for decoding the relations between base and superstructure.)[36] Marx and some of his recent critics, such as Cohen and Derrida, agree in insisting on the perseverance of irrational forces at the heart of modernity. As I have suggested in my introduction, Marx anticipates a critique of the Weberian model of rationalization in his own representations of a

---

[34] Marx and Engels, *German Ideology*, p. 39.
[35] Margaret Cohen, *Profane Illumination*, pp. 1–2.
[36] Cohen, *Profane Illumination*, p. 53.

more haunted modernity. Where Marx and some of his recent critics part company, however, is over the question of the potential uses to which the irrational may be put. Marx may have dreamt of putting the irrational to use "to effect social change," but in his waking hours he had less faith in such a use.

Marx's American example clarifies the question of the role of the supernatural. The paradox of the United States, as presented by Marx, lies in the lack of correspondence between modern productive forces and "the old spirit world." In those most rational of Marxist terms for figuring the relationship between production and ideology, one could say that the case of the United States offers an example of a lag between base and superstructure: the workers on the ground floor have not yet caught up with the ghosts in the attic. So overwhelming are the imperatives of the base, so irresistible the mandate of production, that there is "neither time nor opportunity for abolishing the old spirit world." The defunct superstructural apparatus is already doomed; Americans simply have had no time to do the demolition. So the use of supernatural discourse here names an archaic phantom, residue of an outdated ideological formation that is still dominant because those subject to it have no basic imperative to revise it. The "Geisterwelt" is just that: a world of ghosts that co-exists with the world of the living without getting in its way, a dead but not yet dismissed ideological inheritance. The supernatural in Marx's discussion of the United States encodes a superfluous superstructure.

The promise of the example of the United States seems to be that one will be able to enact similar translations of other of Marx's supernatural terms, decoding ghosts as remnants of outdated ideologies. But it may be that Marx's supernatural discourse also figures the recalcitrance of such ideologies. There is a certain resistance to such translation even in the American example. The term "Geisterwelt" revises Hegel's "Weltgeist," and the simplest aspect of this revision is perhaps also its most crucial. "Geister" is plural, "Geist" singular. The world of plural ghosts confronts the world of unified Spirit. The United States in *The Eighteenth Brumaire* is a unitary example to put beside the variegated political world of

France. But the dissolution of ideological totality in the American example, where "Geisterwelt" revises "Weltgeist," suggests that even in the United States the ideological terrain is more varied than unified, more contested and fluid than single and solid. In many ways *The Eighteenth Brumaire* anticipates later discussions of the complexity of hegemony. Raymond Williams, for instance, stresses that the process of hegemony "isn't just the past, the dry husks of ideology which we can more easily discard."[37] There is certainly an aspect of *The Eighteenth Brumaire* that suggests that Marx imagines the cultural critic as "Hexenmeister," able to cast counter-spells which quickly and thoroughly scare off ideological ghosts. The supernatural rhetoric of *The Eighteenth Brumaire*, however, marks a recognition that the reenchantment of the world is deep, and that "the real *ground* of history" is harder to survey than the authors of *The German Ideology* imagined. What this rhetoric does not suggest is that the best tools to counter this enduring and oppressive supernatural inheritance will themselves come from the box of the supernatural.

TRANSLATIONS OF THE MOLE

The two previous sections help situate the place of Shakespeare in *The Eighteenth Brumaire*. The theatrical and supernatural come together in the third section of this chapter in what is at once the best known and the most mysterious allusion to Shakespeare in Marx's work, that moment in the *Brumaire* where he alludes to the Ghost of Hamlet's movements under the stage. If the "real ground" of history concerns Marx, so too does the underground of history. He sounds this underground through allusion to *Hamlet*. It is the task of this section to unravel some of the complexities of this resonant allusion.

In the seventh and last section of *The Eighteenth Brumaire*, Marx describes the progress of the revolution in a paragraph that begins: "But the revolution is thoroughgoing [gründlich]. It is still jour-

---

[37] Raymond Williams, "Base and Superstructure in Marxist Cultural Theory," p. 39.

neying through purgatory" (121, 178). With the solidification of
Bonaparte's executive power, and the steady dissolution of any opposition, there is little outward sign of revolution and it must un-
dergo an invisible underground rite of purification. Marx's description of the revolution continues:

> It does its work methodically. By December 2, 1851, it had completed
> one half of its preparatory work; it is now completing the other half.
> First it perfected the parliamentary power, in order to be able to over-
> throw it. Now that it has attained this, it perfects the *executive power*,
> reduces it to its purest expression, isolates it, sets it up against itself as
> the sole target, in order to concentrate all its forces of destruction
> against it. And when it has done this second half of its preliminary
> work, Europe will leap from its seat and exultantly exclaim: Well
> grubbed, old mole! (121, 178)

Purification and destruction are a pair. With the reduction of executive power to its purest form in the perfection of the power of
Louis Bonaparte the revolution will find an easy target. On the one
hand, Marx suggests that the revolution is undergoing a purifying
journey through purgatory; on the other, revolution itself is the unseen, underground agent that purifies executive power in order to
destroy it. Revolution itself should embody a dialectic of purification and destruction.

Marx alludes to a phrase from Schlegel's translation of *Hamlet*:
"Brav, alter Maulwurf! Wühlst so hurtig fort?"[38] Schlegel translates
Shakespeare: "Well said, old mole! Canst work i' th'earth so fast?"
(I.v.162). Europe, Marx writes, will greet the outcome of the revolution with the victorious cry, "Well grubbed, old mole! [Brav
gewühlt, alter Maulwurf!]." That Marx has called the revolution
"gründlich" ("thoroughgoing") now appears as a pun. It is not only
thorough, as one translation of the word suggests, but thoroughly
of the earth, of the ground. "Brav gewühlt, alter Maulwurf!" Well
subverted, old mole! Well undermined, old mole! The phrase is
difficult to translate with a single equivalent: "wühlen" can mean to

[38] *Hamlet, Prinz von Danemark*, trans. A. W. von Schlegel, p. 40.

burrow, to dig, to undermine, or to grub; a "Wühler" is an agitator or subversive.[39]

Marx was generally reluctant to picture post-revolutionary society, so his imagining the revolutionary moment at all is of particular interest. That the climax of this description of revolution should take the form of an allusion is all the more striking. Allusion, always doubled, counters the "pure expression" of executive power. The suggestion of a linguistic aspect to the purification of executive power—the suggestion that the revolution's underground task is to reduce executive power to its purest "expression [Ausdruck]"—is consistent with other moments in this text. Revolution, opposed to executive power, never finds pure expression; its forms are parodic or allusive. Marx describes a paradoxical revolution that has no visible features yet nevertheless does its invisible, subterranean work. He analyzes a historical formation—Bonaparte's coup d'etat—which seems, on the surface, to spell the revolution's doom; the historian's analysis discovers what that formation represses and finds that the symptoms of the surface, properly considered, reveal a depth, a burrowing, and a mole. The linguistic tactic of allusion, then, may figure the disjunction between surface appearance and the facts of the underground that is the true historian's subject. The moment in *Hamlet* to which Marx alludes offers an exemplary instance of such a disruption in the field of theatrical action. That moment draws attention to an unsuspected representational space beneath the stage. Marx, similarly, draws attention to an unsuspected field of historical activity. Allusion figures not only the farce that is Bonaparte's recapitulation of Napoleonic history, but the materialist analysis of history that reads contradictions not simply as conflict on the surface but as allusions to or symptoms of what that conflict represses.

[39] Grimm's dictionary counts a passage from an 1848 letter of Engels to Marx among its examples for "wühlerei," or subversive political activity. See the *Deutsches Wörterbuch von Jacob Grimm und Wilhelm Grimm*: "für den (*vater*) ist schon die Kölner zeitung ein ausbund von wühlerei [for him (*father*) the Cologne newspaper is already the height of subversion]." (My translation.)

In alluding to *Hamlet* Marx engages a play whose concerns are in many ways those of the *Brumaire*: legitimacy, usurpation, ghostly intervention, theatrical and historical repetition. In Shakespeare's scenario, the son must avenge his father's death by murdering his uncle and claiming his father's place. In Marx's, the nephew has displaced his father by claiming a false one. Louis Bonaparte claims to be the nephew of and rightful successor to Napoleon the First. A convenient law—"*la recherche de la paternité est interdite* [Enquiry into paternity is forbidden]" (124, 180)—assures that no one can question that claim; no one can legally give evidence to the contrary.[40] One needs to conjure the ghost of the father in order to reveal the illegitimacy of the nephew. Accurate genealogy becomes a revolutionary act. In *Hamlet*, the critical genealogist is also the wronged party; the murdered father brings the story of his own murder to light. Marx, then, is like the ghost in uncovering the genealogical lie. Both Marx and the Ghost offer competing narratives of the genealogy of their antagonists' coming to power, narratives which threaten that power's legitimacy.

I suggested earlier that Engels's letter, with its phantasmatic scene of Hegel "in his grave acting as World Spirit and directing history," may have echoed with *Hamlet* for Marx. Indeed, in alluding to the mole in *Hamlet*, Marx again slyly reworks Hegel, who had himself alluded to the mole in his *Lectures on the Philosophy of History*. Hegel writes:

[40] I retain the English edition's version of the French text. The German is slightly different, beginning "*Toute recherche* . . ." Petry explains the genealogical problem in this way: "Marx's reference above to the Napoleonic Code alludes to the widespread rumor that Napoleon III was not in fact the son of Napoleon's brother but was the offspring of his mother's adultery. The jibe is petty, but its dissociation of the name of Napoleon from *any* connection with the reality of Napoleon emphasizes that the social function of a name in no way depends on material reality. Like the referent, paternity is not a physical fact but a social performance." Petry, "Reality of Representation," p. 464. A British observer of the turmoil of 1848, Walter Bagehot, whose account is for the most part a defense of the coup as Bonaparte's making France safe for capitalism, had heard these rumors. In a parenthetical aside, he notes, "if you believe the people in the *salons*, the President is not the son of his father, and everybody else is the son of his mother . . ." Bagehot, *Letters on the French Coup d'État of 1851*, p. 42.

It goes ever on and on, because spirit is progress alone. Spirit often seems to have forgotten and lost itself, but inwardly opposed to itself, it is inwardly working ever forward as Hamlet says of the ghost of his father, "Well done, old mole" [Brav gearbeitet, wackerer Maulwurf]—until grown strong in itself it bursts asunder the crust of earth which divided it from its sun, its Notion, so that the earth crumbles away.[41]

Hegel, Ned Lukacher writes, uses "the 'old mole' as a figure for philosophy's attainment of absolute knowledge"; indeed, according to Lukacher, "Shakespeare's enigmatic 'old mole' is Hegel's figure for the overcoming of figure itself, for the end of deferrals, for the end of representation."[42] Lukacher's argument about the mole seems to me doubtful. The passage does not warrant associating the mole with breaking through the earth; rather than being a figure for the "attainment of absolute knowledge," it is more the case that the "old mole" is the emblem of that subterranean, self-contradictory stage before Spirit's attainment of any "absolute knowledge." The Ghost is, pointedly, underground when Hamlet calls to it. Doubtless, the "progress" of Spirit as "old mole" is a necessary preliminary stage in the attainment of any "end" to this progress, but the mole does not figure this end.

Lukacher's reading of the "old mole," by the very hastiness with which it assigns to the mole a value Hegel withholds from it, helps one understand the way in which Marx rewrote Hegel. Marx criticizes the too rapid assumption of attainment in Hegel's thought; it is a forerunner of that pretended dissolution of the "products of consciousness . . . by mental criticism" among the Young Hegelians which Marx and Engels criticize in *The German Ideology*.[43] Put beside Hegel's passage, one of Marx's discussions of proletarian revolutions earlier in *The Eighteenth Brumaire* shows both clear

[41] G. W. F. Hegel, *Lectures on the Philosophy of History*, trans. E. S. Haldane and Frances H. Simpson, 3 vols. (New York: Humanities Press, 1974), 3: 546–47, qtd. in Ned Lukacher, *Primal Scenes*, p. 198. Lukacher has modified the translation.

[42] Lukacher, *Primal Scenes*, pp. 202, 198. For a more playful though equally instructive tracing of the tracks of the mole in German thought, see David Farrell Krell, "Der Maulwurf."

[43] Marx and Engels, *German Ideology*, p. 58.

signs of its Hegelian underpinnings and indications of Marx's divergence from Hegel:

> . . . proletarian revolutions, like those of the nineteenth century, criticize themselves constantly, interrupt themselves continually in their own course, come back to the apparently accomplished in order to begin it afresh, deride with unmerciful thoroughness the inadequacies, weaknesses and paltrinesses of their first attempts, seem to throw down their adversary only in order that he may draw new strength from the earth and rise again, more gigantic, before them, recoil ever and anon from the indefinite prodigiousness of their own aims, until a situation has been created which makes all turning back impossible, and the conditions themselves cry out:

> > *Hic rhodus, hic salta!*
> > *Here is the rose, here dance!*   (19, 101–2)

Again, a passage in which Marx describes the process of revolution ends in an allusion, this time to Aesop's fable of the Swaggerer, and, again, this allusion is at the same time an allusion to Hegel. Hegel, explaining in the Preface to the *Philosophy of Right* that the "endeavour" of his work is "to apprehend and portray the state as something inherently rational," himself translates the imperative from Aesop (Here is Rhodes, jump here!): "Here is the rose, dance thou here."[44] Hegel criticizes those who substitute utopias for political analysis: "To comprehend what is, this is the task of philosophy, because what is, is reason."[45]

Clearly Marx found a model for his stuttering, self-interrupting revolution in Hegel's self-contradictory Spirit, which "seems to have forgotten and lost itself." Yet, it is just as clear that Marx has no interest in borrowing Hegelian notions wholesale. The task Marx set for his philosophy was anything but "To comprehend

[44] Hegel, *Philosophy of Right*, p. 11. Knox explains that the Greek word for Rhodes also means "a rose. *Saltus* means a jump, but *salta* is the imperative of the verb 'to dance'. The rose is the symbol of joy, and the philosopher's task is to find joy in the present by discovering reason within it. In other words, philosophy may 'dance' for joy in this world; it need not postpone its dancing until it builds an ideal world elsewhere" (p. 303, n33).

[45] Hegel, *Philosophy of Right*, p. 11.

what is"; the Marxist task, according to the last and best known of
the theses on Feuerbach, is to change it. Why then does Marx borrow Hegel's borrowings? Why does Marx repeat Hegel's allusions?
Marx's revision of Hegel is clearly far too huge a topic for me to do
it justice here. I will therefore focus on that element of it that is
most germane to my project and concentrate on the intersection in
The Eighteenth Brumaire between translation and allusion.

In the English edition of Marx I am using, "Brav gewühlt, alter
Maulwurf!" becomes "Well grubbed, old mole!" This translation of
the phrase—perhaps any translation—would have been of interest
to Marx, who is in *The Eighteenth Brumaire* nothing if not a theorist of translation. In a passage early in the text, Marx compares the
parodies that litter revolutions to an extreme model of language ac-
quisition:

> In like manner a beginner who has learnt a new language always trans-
> lates it back into his mother tongue, but he has assimilated the spirit
> [Geist] of the new language and can freely express himself in it only
> when he finds his way in it without recalling the old and forgets his
> native tongue in the use of the new. (15–16, 97)

By allusion, Marx offers an example for the art of translation and
forgetting. "Brav gewühlt, alter Maulwurf!" does not suggest, exactly, "Well said, old mole!" Has Marx's revision of Shakespeare
acted in the revolutionary manner Marx describes? Has some old
language been forgotten? Allusion's intersection with translation further vexes this question. Allusion invites one to consider precisely
those instances where discourse refutes its own pretensions toward
closure, towards a pure state untainted by historical difference. If
amnesia, forgetting one's "native tongue," is, strangely, the model for
the revolutionary language that Marx imagines, allusion offers a
contrary language that one can never fully sever from the past.

Marx's gesture to Hegel here, his allusion to Hegel's allusion, is
at once citation, translation, and revision. It may be useful to have
the four crucial passages here side by side:

> Well said, old mole! Canst work i' th'earth so fast? (Shakespeare)
> Brav, alter Maulwurf! Wühlst so hurtig fort? (Schlegel)

Brav gearbeitet, wackerer Maulwurf! (Hegel)
Brav gewühlt, alter Maulwurf! (Marx)

There is no way to reproduce Shakespeare's English from the German. Nor does Marx simply use Schlegel's translation; his slight alteration makes a past participle ("gewühlt") of Schlegel's present tense verb ("Wühlst"), and moves it from the beginning of the second phrase of Schlegel's line to the second position in the first phrase. There is a strange restoration here. A parallel to Shakespeare not found in Schlegel appears in Marx: Marx "translates" Shakespeare's "said" with "gewühlt," it is true, but there is at least some word that takes the place of "said." Schlegel, in his translation, has no room for speech. Shakespeare's "said" disappears, to resurface in the varieties of action imagined by Hegel and Marx. For Hegel, the "valiant" mole ("wackerer Maulwurf") works bravely; Marx restores Schlegel's "alter Maulwurf" while upending Hegel's sense of work. "Arbeiten" becomes "wühlen"; work, subversion. The mole's emergence, only potential in Hegel, is fulfilled in Marx. Marx's alteration of the present tense in Schlegel's translation into his own past participle is then, in miniature, a way of rehearsing his conception of his own subversive work, his "Wühlerei," as at once the completion and the overturning of Hegel's work.

Marx's revision of Hegel here suggests that the work of allusion serves as an allegory for Marx's revolutionary reversal of Hegel. This reversal, in turn, serves the text as an allegory for the work of revolution itself. Yet the allusions that jostle the margins of *The Eighteenth Brumaire* make it clear that Marx did not conceive of the seizing of such a post-revolutionary language as something easily achieved. Marx, like the parodists of historical actions he describes, appropriates ghosts, foremost among them the Ghost of Hamlet. The model of production without recollection that characterizes Marx's discussion of revolutionary translation belongs to an impossible world or to the future. In another important passage near the opening of *The Eighteenth Brumaire*, Marx uses another linguistic model for the revolution:

The social revolution of the nineteenth century cannot draw its poetry from the past, but only from the future. It cannot begin with itself before it has stripped off all superstition in regard to the past. Earlier revolutions required recollections of past world history in order to drug themselves concerning their own content. In order to arrive at its content, the revolution of the nineteenth century must let the dead bury the dead. There the phrase went beyond the content; here the content goes beyond the phrase. (18, 101)

The last phrase would seem to imply that "here," where content surpasses phrase, there will be no need for the poetry of the past. The future will be the subject and the subject will take its substance, its phrase, from the future. This would be the antithesis of allusion, which takes its substance from the past. Revolutionary action must be disenchanting in its most immediate sense: it must strip "off all superstition." Yet in a passage where Marx posits the radical dumping of "recollections of past world history," he borrows a key phrase from one of the most influential "world-historical" myths of the West. In stressing the absolute fissure with the past and the "superstitions" attached to it, Marx locates his work squarely in the New Testament. It is at the moment that Marx stresses the need for the revolution to come to its own content that he borrows from the New Testament: may one say that "here the content goes beyond the phrase"? It seems that it is not so much that content goes beyond the phrase but that the phrase recalls the difficulty of even imagining any place stripped of superstition and the poetry of the past.[46]

The passage to which Marx alludes presents a detail in Christ's gathering of disciples:

And another of his disciples said unto him, Lord, suffer me first to go and bury my father.

But Jesus said unto him, Follow me; and let the dead bury their dead. (Matt. 8: 21–22)

---

[46] Chaouli has also described this strange reliance on the Bible here; see Chaouli, "Masking and Unmasking," pp. 67–68. Derrida's discussion of this passage provides an example of the inattention to intertextuality that vitiates some of his readings of Marx. See *Specters*, pp. 113–16.

Another inadequately buried father emerges in the text. The Ghost of Hamlet, figure of the emergence of the revolution, closes his colloquy with his son with the commandment, "Remember me" (I.v.90). This father in Matthew is the figure for forgetfulness, even for the commandment to forget. It should not come as a surprise that what survives of the dialogue as usually remembered is the commandment that Jesus delivers to his disciple. The phrase goes beyond content, erases it. One could say that Marx finds in this Christian slogan a model for his own condemnation of old super-stitions and attachment to dead poetry. One remembers the phrase about the dead burying the dead as a powerful phrase of some ob-scure but powerful religious import, forgetting or never knowing that there was ever a question of a corpse that one of the disciples wanted to bury. But to use the phrase invites the kind of genealogi-cal research Marx practices in *The Eighteenth Brumaire*. Allusion in *The Eighteenth Brumaire* is a technique opposite to that of Louis Bonaparte's strategy of eradicating the maintenance of accurate ties to the past. Marx installs a commandment to forget the past at a point where the borrowed language of that commandment pro-vides an indirect inducement to excavate a historical source for that language. The scare quote forces one to recognize the uses a dis-course finds in the past, even the genealogy of a phrase.

One could argue that Marx uses these phrases casually and means for them to be read so, as cliches without history. One does not need to know the origin of the phrase about the dead's burial of the dead for it to have some power any more than one needs to know the etymology of "Maulwurf" to think of a mole when one hears it. But then one could forward this suspect model of casual, "everyday" speech as a version of that revolutionary language that abolishes its origins, busts its ghosts, and lets the dead bury their dead. *The Eighteenth Brumaire* does not suggest or champion such a notion of language, nor does it offer a sanguine prospect for the achievement of revolution in the material world that the linguistic figures. It does not exhibit much confidence in the ease with which one may jerry-build a revolutionary language or find one ready-made in everyday conversation. One must conclude that Marx never claims to have discovered the revolutionary language of the nineteenth century: "It cannot begin with itself before it has stripped off all superstition in regard to the past" (18, 101). If Marx describes his own practice in the text, it is here, as stripping off superstition, preliminary preparation for a revolution in progress that he can predict but never anticipate in a language similar to that the revolution will use. *The Eighteenth Brumaire* can only allude to the future.

GHOSTS AND CONTRADICTION

Why, if *The Eighteenth Brumaire* is at work stripping off superstition, is it so marked by the constellation of ghosts and politics? This constellation, which is never far from the text's surface, resurfaces again around the question of Bonaparte's coup d'etat. It is at the point of the purification of "executive power" that the familiar spirits of haunted pre-revolutionary times come out in force: "The shadow of the *coup d'état* had become so familiar to the Parisians as a spectre that they were not willing to believe in it when it finally appeared in the flesh [Der Schatten des Staatsstreiches war den Parisern als Gespenst so familiär geworden, dass sie nicht an ihn glauben konnten, als er endlich in Fleisch und Blut erschein]" (112, 170). The familiar ghost becomes the unbelievable "real" appearance. The National Assembly falls victim to this shadow: "It had nothing better to do than to recapitulate in a short, succinct form [in einem kurzen bündigen Repetitorium] the course it had gone through and to prove that it was buried only after it had died" (112, 170). In the paragraph where Marx alludes to the mole he writes that the revolution reduces executive power "to its purest expression" (121, 178). Part of this reduction will entail the shedding of the obsolete National Assembly. Marx here suggests that the Assembly itself will provide an "Ausdruck," an expression of its own demise. The Assembly repeats its death in the form of a summary in a "Repetitorium," or exercise book, like a penitent student. Marx describes the Assembly's demise as a kind of writing, of a rote, and perhaps childish, kind. The Ghost of Hamlet famously reports the death of King Hamlet; the assembly, unable to cope with the incarnation of the spirit of the coup d'etat, performs a dialectical reversal and makes itself a ghost, delivering its own obituary notice not as an inspiration to revenge but as a careful school assignment written to please the master.

In what comes closest to a theoretical description of the role of ghosts in *The Eighteenth Brumaire*, Marx writes:

> One sees: *all* "idées napoléoniennes" *are ideas of the undeveloped small holding in the freshness of its youth*; for the small holding that has outlived its day they are an absurdity. They are only the hallucinations of its death struggle, words that are transformed into phrases, spirits transformed into ghosts. But the parody of the empire . . . was necessary to free the mass of the French nation from the weight of tradition and to work out in pure form the opposition between the state power and society. (130–31, 185)

In perhaps the best-known formulation from *The Eighteenth Brumaire*, Marx writes: "The tradition of all the dead generations weighs like a nightmare on the brain of the living" (15, 97). There, Marx argues that it is this nightmare that inspires people to create something that has never been. This creative effort, however, often takes its forms from history; this seizure of the past degenerates into parody or farce. In Marx's discussion of "idées napoléoniennes," the parody of imperialism that follows the coup d'etat of Louis Napoleon becomes a liberating force. Having recognized the incompatibility of Napoleonic ideas with the contemporary state of society the mass of French society will begin to understand the contradiction between the power of state and society. Indeed they will be able to see this contradiction in its pure form.

Once more, purity is a preparation for a revolutionary dismantling of oppressive conditions. It is clear, however, that there is nothing singular about this purity. Purity here is a state of contradiction that suddenly becomes easily recognizable. In the passage about the journey of the revolution through purgatory that culminates in the praise of the mole, Marx writes that the revolution brings executive power to an end, "reduces it to its purest expression, isolates it, sets it up against itself as the sole target, in order to concentrate all its forces of destruction against it" (121, 178). Reduction to purity prepares for destruction. Attendant upon such violent preparations will be the crowds of ghosts that accompany historical parody. Similarly, in discussing the "parody of the empire," he analyzes Napoleonic ideas and "words [Worte] that are transformed into phrases [Phrasen], spirits [Geister] transformed into ghosts [Gespenster]." Words and spirits, phrases and ghosts; the second terms are among the "hallucinations of [the] death struggle" of Napoleonic ideas. Marx here reserves the term "Geist" to characterize ideas that belong to their time. It is as remnants of an archaic system, as surviving expressions of a defunct stage of development, that "Geister" become "Gespenster." One may usefully consider these phrases and ghosts aspects of what Raymond Williams calls "residual" culture:

> By 'residual' I mean that some experiences, meanings and values, which cannot be verified or cannot be expressed in terms of the dominant culture, are nevertheless lived and practised on the basis of the residue—cultural as well as social—of some previous social formation.[47]

Bonaparte's peculiar politics may have its power and its appeal in achieving present domination in the name of the residual. Bonaparte's phrases conjure ghosts of an outmoded agrarian "social formation" and establish rule in their name, only to usher in the triumphant capitalism of the Second Empire. Where the "Geist," or spirit, at least has the virtue of being an expression of its culture, the "Gespenst," or ghost, camouflages the operations of the dominant group.

The ghost, then, is a sign of a contradiction between a society's archaic conception of itself and the actual dominant forces within it. Marx's demonology, his supernatural lexicon, is, however, not susceptible to easy translation. To name a ghost is not to exorcise it. The central example of the Ghost of Hamlet is again suggestive. That Ghost would seem to contradict Marx's purposes; Marx summons the archaic Ghost of the revenging father as a figure of future revolution. The ghost, spirit of social contradiction, would seem also to represent a contradiction in Marx's thought. This notion,

---

[47] Williams, "Base and Superstructure," p. 40.

however, rests on an embedded notion of the Ghost as archaic
visitor from the feudal past. It is the aim of the next chapter to
show that this received notion of the Ghost is not wholly sound.
The contradiction in Marx, the coexistence of the archaic and the
future, the residual and the emergent, already characterizes Shakespeare's Ghost.

3

The Ghost of Hamlet in the Mine

[*Aside*] This mole does undermine me—heard you not
A noise even now?

John Webster, *The Duchess of Malfi*

Marx's allusions to *Hamlet* may have a root in this dialogue between
Hamlet and one of the gravediggers:

Ham. How long hast thou been grave-maker?

1. Clo. Of [all] the days i'th'year, I came to't that day that our last
king Hamlet overcame Fortinbras.

Ham. How long is that since?

1. Clo. Cannot you tell that? Every fool can tell that. It was that
very day that young Hamlet was born—he that is mad, and sent into
England. (V.i.142–48)

According to a sort of mythical causality, the fates of the gravedigger
and Hamlet are related before they meet: The gravedigger comes to a
job; King Hamlet overcomes Fortinbras; Prince Hamlet comes into
the world. In one way, this seems immediately appropriate: the death
of Fortinbras is the kind of event that provides work for gravediggers.
This conjunction reinforces the possibility that the scene belongs to
the *memento mori* tradition, a point here stressed by the iconic skulls

the Clown lobs out of the grave he is digging. But such humanist pathos does not explain why Marx, at work inventing the hidden historical mission of the proletariat, appeals to *Hamlet*. There are other ways to read this odd convergence. In short, one can say that in the character of Hamlet Marx finds a model for his central historical narrative: born of the decay and decline of feudalism, Hamlet comes into the world as capitalism does, mysteriously engendering his own gravediggers.[1]

Hamlet provides a vivid image of the "hidden ground of history" Marx and Engels describe in the *German Ideology*. The story of the gravediggers belongs to an underground world in *Hamlet* that Marx's scare quote appropriates and illuminates. One can compare a pathetic story Marx offers as an allegory of the predicament of France in *The Eighteenth Brumaire*, which also combines digging, madness, and England:

> The nation feels like that old mad Englishman in Bedlam who fancies that he lives in the times of the ancient Pharaohs and daily bemoans the hard labour that he must perform in the Ethiopian mines as a gold digger, immured in this subterranean prison, a dimly burning light fastened to his head, the overseer of the slaves behind him with a long whip, and at the exits a confused welter of barbarian mercenaries, who understand neither the forced labourers in the mines nor one another, since they speak no common language. "And all this is expected of me," sighs the old mad Englishman, "of me, a free-born Briton, in order to make gold for the old Pharaohs." (17–18, 98)

The melancholy consciousness of the "free-born Briton" in Bedlam here stems from the certainty of being compelled to perform an archaic task. Marx's anarchic narrative combines suggestions of Genesis and Exodus with a contemporary tale of madness in the London insane asylum: the confusion of tongues at Babel and the Egyptian

---

[1] The inaugural formulation of this trope of burial comes at the end of the first section of Marx and Engels's *Manifesto of the Communist Party*: "The development of Modern Industry, therefore, cuts from under its feet the very foundation on which the bourgeoisie produces and appropriates products. What the bourgeoisie, therefore, produces, above all, is its own grave-diggers. Its fall and the victory of the proletariat are equally inevitable" (p. 483).

exile are the setting for the meek protest of the bourgeois lamely asserting his rights in the prison of the mine. Part of the oddity of
Marx's story lies in the fact that the man in Bedlam knows who he is,
"a free-born Briton"; his madness is only partial. Marx's point is that
such madness, the sense of knowing one lives under impossibly
anachronistic conditions, is a real condition of existence: "An entire
people . . . ," writes Marx of the French, "suddenly finds itself set
back into a defunct epoch . . ." (17, 98).

This story is not only a fine example of Marx's tragicomic imagination of reenchantment, but it also forms an important link between *The Eighteenth Brumaire* and *Hamlet*. A peculiar irony surrounding Marx's text is that it ushers in as a "defunct epoch" an era
that has come to seem prophetic: the hallucinating Briton figures the
entire French nation, which is suddenly subject to the antiquated
Bonaparte. Yet Bonaparte's Second Empire, with its profusion of
commodities and its concentration of state power, has seemed a clear
forerunner of subsequent historical formations. In a way, Marx was
right to imagine the perfection of Napoleon III's executive power as
a revolutionary moment—but it was a moment that introduced not
a workers' revolution but a revolution in the workings of capitalism.[2]
The Eighteenth Brumaire illuminates a similar contradiction between
the archaic and the emergent in *Hamlet*.

Critics often read the Ghost as a standard-bearer for feudalism;
Prince Hamlet, in contrast, is anxious to shed his feudal heritage.
William Empson calls this typical of the "Victorian view of Hamlet":
Hamlet "was morally too advanced to accept feudal ideas about re-
venge, and felt, but could not say, that his father had given him an

---

[2] This is the thrust, for instance, of Rosalind Williams's *Dream Worlds*. According to Susan Buck-Morss, the Second Empire became "increasingly 'legible' in the
1930s" for Benjamin. It became possible to read Napoleon III as "the first bourgeois
dictator; Hitler was his present-day incarnation." Buck-Morss, *The Dialectics of
Seeing*, p. 308. Buck-Morss notes Benjamin's increasing engagement with *The Eighteenth Brumaire* during this period. The historical tangle here is formidable. The
legibility of the pairing of Louis Bonaparte and Hitler has, I would think, faded. To
align Hitler with Marx's farcical Bonaparte must appear a kind of historical misrecognition. (There are good reasons why much of Chaplin's *The Great Dictator*
now falls flat.)

out-of-date duty . . ."³ Indeed, a sturdy tradition casts Hamlet as the quintessential representative of modernity itself. According to this argument, the contradiction between the Ghost's calling of Hamlet into an archaic scheme of revenge and Hamlet's precocious modernity grounds the play's conflicts. The political dilemma—the dead king contracts with his living son for the death of the reigning monarch, brother of the Ghost—may then be taken as a perfect illustration of Marx's dictum from *The Eighteenth Brumaire*: "The tradition of all the dead generations weighs like a nightmare on the brain of the living." Much supports reading the Ghost as feudal revenant. Indeed, it is crucial to my argument that one recognize these feudal aspects in the Ghost. The project of this chapter, however, is to show that this association of the Ghost with a nightmarish, powerful past needs expansion.

A central point of *The Eighteenth Brumaire* is that the anachronism is a real condition of a particular historical moment, the moment Adorno associates with the phantasmagoria:

> . . . phantasmagoria comes into being when, under the constraints of its own limitations, modernity's latest products come close to the archaic. Every step forwards is at the same time a step into the remote past. As bourgeois society advances it finds that it needs its own camouflage of illusions simply in order to subsist. For only when so disguised does it venture to look the new in the face.⁴

For Adorno phantasmagoria answers a need: social subsistence requires a "camouflage of illusions." A specific manifestation of the new, one of "modernity's latest products," the phantasmagoria, becomes a synecdoche for a whole problematic ensemble. So powerful has this synecdoche been that it has required the recent work of Terry Castle and Margaret Cohen to restore the phantasmagoria's material past, to remind us that behind the term lay an apparatus and a technological history.⁵ Marx's phantasmagoric miner in Bedlam has spe-

---

³ William Empson, *"Hamlet," Essays on Shakespeare*, p. 104. For a more recent discussion of related issues which, however, focuses on *King Lear* and *Macbeth*, see John Turner's "The Tragic Romances of Feudalism."

⁴ Theodor W. Adorno, *In Search of Wagner*, p. 95.

⁵ That there was a need for this corrective may be seen, for instance, by locating a

cial relevance to *Hamlet*. A neglected story of the mine lies beneath *Hamlet*, and examining it reveals a peculiarly phantasmagorical play.

Critics have been attentive to the way the cellarage scene complicates the theatricality of *Hamlet*: Hamlet's loudly admitting that the play is a play at a moment that should authorize his subsequent actions is startling. Critics have been less attentive to the way Hamlet's terms insist that the Ghost belongs to a group that haunted the imagination of early modern Europe: the Ghost of Hamlet is a ghost in a mine. The project of this chapter is to suggest that the theatricality of the Ghost and the Ghost's place in the mine are inextricable. "England's literate citizens steeped their response to the placeless market in mythological and magical allusions," writes Jean-Christophe Agnew.[6] The Ghost, which becomes so central a scare quote in the work of Marx, is, in *Hamlet*, already among these "allusions" Agnew describes. The Ghost opens a door onto one of the enchanted spaces of early modern Europe but, as I argue in the last section of this chapter, these spaces are phantasmagorical in Adorno's sense. They are the site of modernity's reenchantment.

The Ghost is an archaic face for a nascent world of economic exchange. This chapter, then, interrogates the "shape" or "figure"—to use two words applied to the Ghost in the first scene—of the new in *Hamlet*. The allusion in Marx that initiates this reading is itself an instance of phantasmagoria of a kind, a moment where what is, in theory, emergent—the rupture caused by the "revolution"—takes the form of the old, in the allusion to *Hamlet*. Marx's appropriation of "Well said, old mole" offers an example in forcefully suggesting that the Ghost belongs to a crucial moment at once part of the scope of his work and outside of its range of figuration; Marx cannot invent the "poetry" of the future, but, instead,

---

blind spot in the otherwise very useful discussion of the question of the phantasmagoric by Gillian Rose: "'Phantasmagoria' means a crowd or succession of dim or doubtfully real persons." Surely the term came to mean this, but it is just as sure that it originally referred to a machine. Indeed, the case of Dircks, phantasmagoria inventor, charts a movement much like that of the word "phantasmagoria" itself: from Dircks's solid apparatus for the production of ghosts to Dircks's becoming a "doubtfully real" person to himself. Rose, *The Melancholy Science*, p. 31.

[6] Jean-Christophe Agnew, *Worlds Apart*, p. 57.

suggests that Shakespeare already has. In *Hamlet*, the Ghost already registers the emergent future. The Ghost in the mine is a spirit of capitalism.

MINING TERMS IN 'HAMLET'

The passage crucial to this investigation, the dialogue in the cellarage scene involving Hamlet and the Ghost under the stage, contains words no one has taken seriously. To take them seriously places the Ghost in the mine. Critics have tended to emphasize Hamlet's supposed stratagem or sheer incoherence at this point—"Hamlet's jocularity" cleverly disguises the seriousness of what has transpired, Hamlet's encounter with the Ghost has so disturbed him that he cannot think straight—rather than asking what sense these particular terms make.[7] Why these words and not others?

> *Ghost. [Beneath.]*   Swear by his sword.
> *Ham.*   Well said, old mole, canst work i'th'earth so fast?
>   A worthy pioner! Once more remove, good friends.
>   (I.v.161–63)

Hamlet's term, "pioner," seems to have had two more or less common and not necessarily exclusive meanings. "A *pioneer*," writes Harold Jenkins, "was originally a foot-soldier who preceded the

---

[7] The phrase in quotation marks is Harold Jenkins's in his long note to the cellarage scene among the Arden edition's appendixes: " . . . Hamlet's jocularity, after the solemnity of the actual encounter, gives more than a touch of burlesque; and this 'comic relief' (for in the strictest sense it is that) has, in a manner characteristically Shakespearean, serious and even sinister overtones." Jenkins, ed., *Hamlet*, pp. 457–58. This long note includes many useful clues that I have followed in this chapter. Stephen Booth also speaks of Hamlet's "jocular behavior" in his discussion of the cellarage scene in "On the Value of *Hamlet*," p. 160. John Dover Wilson, in *What Happens in Hamlet*, writes: "We marvel at Hamlet's levity with his father's spirit, and do our best to explain the strange epithets 'boy,' 'truepenny' and 'old mole' as the hysterical utterances of a mind on the borderland of insanity, an explanation which is in part the truth" (p. 78). The most serious overtone, for Jenkins, is that of the possible diabolism of the Ghost; Eleanor Prosser makes a strong case for this in *Hamlet and Revenge*, pp. 118–43.

main army with a pickaxe . . ."⁸ This first possibility, then, is at
variance with every other indication about the Ghost in the first
act. The Ghost, the play has been at pains to establish, makes en-
trances costumed in full battle regalia: "Such was the very armor he
had on/When he the ambitious Norway combated," says Horatio
(I.i.60–61). With the word "pioner" alone, then, Hamlet lowers the
rank of the Ghost, relegating him to the humblest military caste.
To call the Ghost this sort of "pioner" is to mock the armor he
wore while facing and defeating the elder Fortinbras in single com-
bat. In Jenkins's definition—"pioner" as soldier—the Ghost is already associated with a vanguard, with those in advance of the
main body of troops. The scene presents a military phantasmagoria, where those in the vanguard are also those whose weapons or
tools are most primitive. While this demotion by the force of a single word is intriguing, it is another valence of "pioner" that in-
trigues me most: a "pioner" might also be a miner.

Hamlet's speaking of the speed with which the "old mole" works
in the ground surely suggests a peculiarly efficient miner, not a sol-
dier.⁹ His association of the Ghost with mining is not limited to the
strange epithet, "pioner," or to the speedy mole, however. In Hamlet's first exchange with the subterranean Ghost, quoted above,
Hamlet calls the Ghost "truepenny." Furness records the comment
of (the aptly named) Collier on this term:

> This word is (as I learn from some Sheffield authorities) a mining term,
> and signifies a particular indication in the soil of the direction in which

---

⁸ I quote Jenkins's note to I.v.171. Othello, for instance, uses the word with this
meaning in mind: "I had been happy, if the general camp,/Pioners and all, had
tasted her sweet body,/So I had nothing known" (III.iii.345–47). For "pioner" in
Hamlet, the Riverside edition gives the gloss, "digger, miner (variant of pioneer)"; for
"Pioners" in Othello, on the other hand, the same volume suggests the gloss, "the
lowest rank of soldier, primarily used for manual labor, not fighting." As will be
clear, though I am more interested in the first suggestion, I find both possible and
intriguing.

⁹ There were also, however, soldiers who did a miner's tunneling work, in order
to lay mines underneath enemy positions. See Henry V, III.ii.

ore is to be found. Hence Hamlet may with propriety address the Ghost under ground by that name.[10]

This derivation, it is true, is exceptional; more commonly one finds a gloss for "truepenny" such as the "trusty fellow" in the Riverside edition. As with "pioner," the two glosses for "truepenny" do not cancel each other. Does the "propriety" Collier finds simply lie in the similarity between the "particular indication in the soil" and the Ghost, in their both being underground? Or is the "propriety" in the similarity between the soil, which leads the way to ore, and the Ghost, who leads the way to accurate knowledge of the circumstances concerning the death of King Hamlet? Or is it that among mining terms "truepenny" is a mark of distinction and therefore properly applied to the Ghost?

The association of ghosts and ore is not unique to Collier. Indeed, evidence of such a belief in ghosts as sign of plentiful ore spans the early modern period in Europe. As late as 1747, William Hooson, an English miner, wrote in his *Miners Dictionary*, of the "Knockers," or spirits in the mines:

> This is something which I have heard Miners talk much of, but I think the old ones have more than now a Days they do; and how to give a right Account of it I know not, but by hear say, and these Knockers have been thought to be a Sign of much Ore.

Hooson's suggestion that "old ones" had more knockers than contemporary mines should not be taken as a sign of skepticism, and its evidence of his awareness of a long tradition of such belief is worth note: ". . . for my Part I cannot affirm, or deny anything about them, as having no experience thereof at all, but that there are some kind of living Creatures in the Earth, and that they are heard by Miners sometimes, after one way or other I think is very sure . . ."[11] The si-

---

[10] Collier, qtd. in Furness, ed., *Hamlet*, I.i.150n.

[11] "Knocker," in William Hooson, *The Miners Dictionary*. (There is, sadly, no entry for "Truepenny" in Hooson's manual.) Hooson is the first example in the *OED* for "knocker," sense b: "A spirit or goblin imagined to dwell in mines, and to indicate the presence of ore by knocking." See "knocker," *OED*, new ed., 1991. For accounts of the beliefs of miners after Hooson, see the entry for "Mineurs" in Collin

multaneous vagueness and certainty of Hooson's definition recalls the unsettled state of inquiry into the status of the Ghost at the end of the first scene of *Hamlet*: "after one way or other" the Ghost is a ghost, but what makes a "ghost" is open to debate.[12] In *Hamlet*, part of what makes a ghost is its phantasmagoric aspect, its place as a hinge between the archaic and the new. Popular ghost beliefs, among which one must count the belief in ghosts as a sign of ore, form part of the play's representation of a Ghost. To take another small but telling example, one can remember the Ghost's skulking away at the crow of the cock. (Dircks mocks this detail when he writes that the Ghost's "bedtime was regulated by the crowing of the chanticleer.") Horatio delivers this commentary:

> I have heard
> The cock, that is trumpet to the morn,
> Doth with his lofty and shrill-sounding throat
> Awake the god of day, and at his warning,
> Whether in sea or fire, in earth or air,
> Th'extravagant and erring spirit hies
> To his confine . . .   (I.i.149–55)

Marcellus follows with a more distinctly Christian interpretation of the crowing of the cock (I.i.157–64). Dover Wilson notes this as among the "superstitions" of which there is evidence in *Hamlet*.[13]

---

de Plancy, *Dictionnaire Infernale,* and Paul Sébillot's *Les Travaux Publics et les Mines dans les Traditions et les Superstitions de tout les Pays.* Zola's *Germinal* may mark one of the terminal points of such miners' beliefs in Europe: "They harboured a secret fear of ghosts down in the mine, but scoffed at the empty heavens." Émile Zola, *Germinal,* p. 168. The particularity of miners' beliefs has become, it seems, by the time of Zola's work, a shell, itself "secret." The survival becomes an embarrassment. Note, however, that the OED entry contains this example from *Chamber's Journal* from as late as 1885: "In the Cardigan mines, the knockers are still heard, indicating where a rich lode may be expected."

[12] In addition to works cited elsewhere, valuable studies of the Ghost include Madeleine Doran's "That Undiscovered Country" and Roland Mushat Frye, *The Renaissance Hamlet,* pp. 14–29. I have also found provocative Peter Hughes's discussion of ghostliness, Wittgenstein, Shakespeare, and representation in "Painting the Ghost."

[13] Dover Wilson, *What Happens,* p. 74. In his study, *The Night Battles,* Carlo Ginzburg provides evidence that this belief in the importance of the crowing of the

While there is no question that such beliefs are part of the construction of the Ghost, they are only a part.

Horatio's speech, in passing, also testifies to the existence of "extravagant and erring" spirits "*in* earth," again testifying to beliefs in the ground as inhabited by supernatural beings.[14] Such testimony is in fact consistent with both popular and elite conceptions of the underground in the early modern period. A conception of the mineral earth and its contents as not inert but, instead, organic and capable of reproduction held sway. In addition, many believed that to violate the earth was dangerous because the earth harbored ghosts and spirits. Belief in underground spirits who sometimes aided and sometimes pestered miners was widespread.[15] As Hooson suggests,

---

cock was integral to popular practices among the witches and *benandanti* of Friuli. The *benandanti* engaged in battles for the harvest, their souls leaving their bodies for nocturnal engagements: "if the spirit 'did not return before dawn at cock's crow,'" testified Margherita san Rocco, "'we would not change back into human form, and the body would stay dead and the spirit remain a cat.'" Ginzburg explains this reference to the cat: "The soul which left the body to go to the witches' conventicles or to the jousts of the benandanti was considered in both cases as something very real and tangible, usually an animal." An example involving the soul as a mouse follows immediately. It is worth wondering whether *Hamlet*, which notes a belief similar to the peasants' in the role of the crowing cock, does not also recall this belief in the soul travelling as a small animal: "Well said, old mole . . ."? See Ginzburg, *The Night Battles*, p. 19. I should note that I am not asserting that Shakespeare necessarily took such details from popular practices; I am, however, suggesting that it is also not necessarily the case that scholarly sources alone inform such passages, as notes and commentary often imply. For a development of Ginzburg's controversial thesis that widespread belief in such travelling of souls in the form of small animals is part of a larger structure of shamanistic Eurasian beliefs, see especially his chapter, "Disguised as Animals," in *Ecstasies*, pp. 182–204. For an appreciative and engaging critique of Ginzburg's work, which focuses on *Ecstasies*, see Perry Anderson, "Nocturnal Enquiry."

[14] Dover Wilson, *What Happens*, p. 66, notes the relevance of these lines from Milton's "Il Penseroso": "And of those Daemons that are found / In fire, air, flood, or underground, / Whose power hath a true consent / With Planet or with Element . . ." While the similarity may simply be owing to a commonplace listing of the four elements, it seems worth considering whether Milton's may not be a direct echo of Horatio's line. As Dover Wilson points out, "we may . . . perceive a glance at *Hamlet* and *Macbeth*" in the lines on the "Buskined stage" which follow in Milton.

[15] The last four sentences rely on Carolyn Merchant's *The Death of Nature*, pp. 20–41.

miners held many strong convictions about the underground places where they labored. The notion that the Ghost is a sign of a plentiful vein or ore—Collier's "truepenny"—is also found in a 1572 translation of Ludwig Lavater's *Of Ghostes and Spirites Walking by Nyght*, which has long been considered a possible source for *Hamlet*. In Lavater's description of some of the beliefs of miners the term "pioner" notably resurfaces: "Pioners and diggers for metal, do affirm, that in many mines, there appear strange shapes and spirits, who are apparelled like unto other laborers in the pit."[16] From this suggestive quotation alone, one can imagine the need for a system by which one could distinguish those devils who looked like miners from those miners who looked liked devils. Somehow the miner had to distinguish the "strange shapes" from their apparel.[17] This problem is not unlike that facing Hamlet, who must, in effect, test the Ghost. The Ghost appears to be the spirit of his father—the Ghost introduces himself as such and is "apparelled like unto" his father—but may be a devil, since, among other things, devils have a habit of wearing other people's clothes and urge them to commit crimes in order to damn themselves. It is not clear that Hamlet instantly believes the Ghost, and it occurs to him—as, Dover Wilson suggests, it would to most who speculated about ghosts around 1600 in England—that the Ghost could be a devil in disguise. Lavater's description continues:

> These [strange shapes and spirites] wander up and down in caves and underminings, and seem to bestir themselves in all kind of labor, as to

[16] Ludwig Lavater, *Of Ghostes and Spirites Walking by Nyght*, p. 73. I have modernized the spelling in quotations from Lavater. Jenkins points to this passage, as a gloss for "pioner," in his long note, and Dover Wilson, too, cites it as evidence that the Ghost might be taken for a devil. Dover Wilson, *What Happens*, p. 81.

[17] Peter Burke discusses a "fifteenth-century painting [that] suggests that the outside world did not distinguish between the dwarfs or gnomes who lived in the mines and the miners themselves, small and hooded as they were." Burke, *Popular Culture in Early Modern Europe*, p. 36. Burke has an illuminating discussion of the peculiar culture of miners, including their "legends, dealing in particular with the spirits of the mines . . . who guarded the treasure and needed to be appeased by offerings. Legends of this kind, dealing with the discovery of treasure by supernatural help, were current . . . all over Europe, from Cornwall to the Urals" (p. 35).

dig after the vein, to carry together ore, to put it into baskets, and to
turn the winding wheel to draw it up, when in very deed they do
nothing less. They very seldom hurt the laborers (as they say) except
they provoke them by laughing and railing at them: for then they
throw gravel stones at them, or hurt them by some other means. These
are especially haunting in pits, where metal most aboundeth.[18]

Spirits, Lavater strangely insists, not only appear to do work, but
they *do* do work; the spirits, who "seem to bestir themselves . . . in
very deed do nothing less." Ghosts deceptively seem to be doing
work which in fact they do do. What is one to make of this seeming
to do, which is actually doing? To repeat the last sentence of the
quotation from Lavater: "These are especially haunting in pits, where
metal most aboundeth." The more "metal," the more ghosts. One
can speculate that the reverse of this formula is also true: the more
ghosts, the more metal. The ghosts are "truepennies."[19]

One can recall that the scholarly Horatio wonders whether the
Ghost has come back to haunt some "Extorted treasure in the womb
of earth" (I.ii.137); this and Horatio's other questions to the Ghost
are consistent with beliefs that ghosts might bring valuable messages

[18] Lavater, *Of Ghostes*, p. 73–74. Compare here Paul Sébillot's similar discussion
of miners' beliefs in underground spirits, in *Les Travaux Publics*, pp. 390–91: "The
appearances [manifestations] of these underground spirits are not always the same:
sometimes they content themselves, like goblins [lutins] of the world above ground,
in performing farces for the miners that seldom surpass the rather coarse foolery of
peasants and sailors." (My translation.)

[19] Michael T. Taussig has studied beliefs that in many ways echo those of which
there are traces in *Hamlet*. Twentieth-century Bolivian coal miners, as inhabitants of
early modern Europe, considered the mine a living organism inhabited by spirits. It
is especially startling, with the cellarage scene in mind, to encounter the last item in
Taussig's list of living traits attributed to the mineral ores in Bolivia: "They may be
said to be . . . screaming below the ground." In addition, the devil aided in detection
of "rich ore-bearing veins." Taussig, *The Devil and Commodity Fetishism in South
America*, pp. 147, 14. Again, there is a remarkable coincidence: the devil appears as a
"truepenny," as an aid to the discovery of rich veins of ore. But the coincidences of
detail are less compelling than the similarity of the whole structure of systems of belief. Taussig demonstrates that the Bolivian miners' myths helped them adjust to the
violent shocks of a capitalist incursion; *Hamlet*, too, having no name for capitalism,
identifies its increasing effects in the form of a "figure" at once undeniably authoritative and potentially demonic: the Ghost.

to survivors, be omens of political events, or return to hidden treas-ures.[20] Horatio's expectation that the Ghost will conform to earlier patterns of belief anticipates a tradition of scholarship, most vividly exemplified by Dover Wilson's *What Happens in Hamlet*, which suggests that Elizabethan or early modern ghost beliefs and practices should find themselves transcribed on stage in *Hamlet*. Dover Wil-son's conclusion remains both intriguing and unsatisfactory. After a discussion of the tension in English culture between Catholics, who retained belief in ghosts; Protestants, who accepted ghosts only as demonic; and frank skeptics like Reginald Scot, Dover Wilson con-cludes of Shakespeare: "His patron, the Earl of Southampton, was a declared Catholic at heart, while Protestants, of course, would form a large proportion. It paid him dramatically to let all three schools of thought have their views considered."[21] The ambiguity of the Ghost is, for Dover Wilson, a matter of political and theological compro-mise, a carefully crafted amalgam of doctrinally contradictory posi-tions that concedes something to all while fully conforming to none. The phantasmagoric Ghost, however, is not only Dover Wilson's uneasy transcription of early modern beliefs, not only a symptom of the religious stresses of Elizabethan culture, but also, as Hamlet's "pioner" suggests, an idol of the marketplace.[22]

---

[20] For a thorough account of ghost beliefs in early modern England, see Keith Thomas's *Religion and the Decline of Magic*, pp. 587–614.

[21] Dover Wilson, *What Happens*, p. 84.

[22] Etymologists may take some amusement in considering that it is possible to read "phantasmagoria" as a translation of Bacon's phrase. Cohen discusses the possi-ble etymologies for the word, "coined by Robertson in 1797." One of two, from *Le Robert*, suggests that the word comes "from the Greek *phantasma* 'ghost,' and *agoreuein* 'to speak in public . . .'" Margaret Cohen, *Profane Illumination*, p. 235. Translate "ghost" as "idol," and recall that *agoreuin* is related to *agora*, or market, and one encounters Bacon as an early theorist of the phantasmagoria. There are, etymological shenanigans aside, some similarities between the misrecognition that is Adorno's subject and Bacon's target in *The New Organon*. For "Idols of the Market Place," see Francis Bacon, *The New Organon*, pp. 56–57.

REPLICATION

> ... what replication should be made by the son of a king?
>
> *Hamlet* (IV.ii.12–13)

> Like will to like, quoth the Devil to the collier.
>
> Elizabethan proverb

The cellarage scene links the hollowed-out ground of mines and the hollow space under the stage: the Ghost moves underground, like a miner, if with unworkmanlike speed. The image of the Ghost as miner stalking the cellarage scene is not an isolated moment in the play, but opens up the matter of the relationship between the economic and authority in *Hamlet* as a whole. I argue in this section that the phantasmagorical nexus of the cellarage scene—the mine and the Ghost—provides a way to understand the central problem the Ghost poses: the question of authority. One can summarize much debate about the play in a question: Is Hamlet right to obey this undermining spirit that may be a devil in disguise? [23]

The Ghost authorizes the pact between Hamlet and the other witnesses; Hamlet unsettles the Ghost's authority by pointing out that the moment is a theatrical one. By naming the hollow, raftered area beneath the stage the "cellarage," Hamlet clearly emphasizes that the action in the scene takes place on stage; the effects of this emphasis are, however, less clear. William Empson observes: "It seems the area under the stage was *technically* called the cellarage, but the point

---

[23] The unsettling suggestion that the "ground" beneath the stage is in fact riddled with tunnels and crawl-spaces is part of *Hamlet*'s extended complication of the surface of the stage: the trapdoor in the last scene of the first act becomes the open grave in the first scene of the last. My description of a single trap is, however, perhaps too simple; for the possibilities of staging the Ghost on an Elizabethan stage with a variety of traps, see Diana Macintyre DeLuca's "The Movements of the Ghost in *Hamlet*." DeLuca does, however, conclude that productions probably used the main trap for staging the entrance of the Ghost, and it seems likely that the same would have been used for the grave of Ophelia. Trapdoors were, as well, a feature of mines. Hooson's *Miners Dictionary* contains an entry for "Trapdoor": ". . . this is of very good Use, either against Thieves, or prying Knaves, who may come at unseasonable times to see any Man's Work, and thereby take occasion to do him Damage . . ."

is clear without this extra sharpening; it is a recklessly comic throwaway of illusion . . ."[24] So the calls to the Ghost are a sort of debunking both of the Ghost's authority and of the authority of the illusion of the stage: Hamlet claims a place at least partly outside these authorities. By calling the Ghost "old mole" and so on, Hamlet distances himself from the solemn thralldom of the earlier scene, where he finally talks with the Ghost and pledges allegiance to its antiquated call to revenge. Indeed, Hamlet tries to arrange his impromptu ritual away from the Ghost; Hamlet and the others move about the stage, trying, as Hamlet says, to "shift" their ground (I.v.156). But this moment of debunking passes quickly. In this scene as in the play as a whole, every step away from the Ghost, to paraphrase Adorno, is at the same time a step towards it, "into the remote past." And the Ghost always gets there first. Hamlet appears more pleased than perturbed that the Ghost is able to "shift" as quickly as he and his comrades. Hamlet gestures towards debunking the Ghost by announcing its theatricality and linking it to the mine; that undermining, theatrical power is, however, a source of the authority of the Ghost and, indeed, the source of Hamlet's authority later in the play. Hamlet becomes not only the Ghost's representative but himself a second, surrogate ghost.

Empson elaborates his argument about the discarding of illusion: "the effect is still meant to be frightening . . ."[25] The throwing away of illusion, for Empson, paradoxically heightens the power of the scene. He argues that the audience, having come to the Globe prepared to mock a tawdry, unfashionable revenge tragedy (the so-called *Ur-Hamlet* most likely, Empson believes, written by Kyd), would have been startled, even frightened, by the play's willingness to mock itself in moments like the cellarage scene. What is so audacious in Empson's analysis is that he claims to rediscover the experience of the audience of "*Hamlet* When New."[26] This fear Empson identifies is important to my understanding of the Ghost. As a familiar revenge ghost, it is the object of the knowing contempt of the audience

[24] Empson, "*Hamlet*," p. 85.
[25] Empson, "*Hamlet*," pp. 85–86.
[26] Empson's piece was first published under this title in the *Sewanee Review*.

Empson describes. The cellarage scene, however, links the Ghost and its haunting to one of the crucial phantasmagorical places of early modern culture: the mine. The mine was at once source for raw materials crucial to the growing capitalist culture and, so to speak, a super-nature preserve, a place where the spirits of popular belief had a continuing life. Ashley H. Thorndike observed some time ago that among the convincing contemporary allusions to *Hamlet*—he counts thirteen that "supply us with evidence of the character of the contemporary estimate of the play" in two late-nineteenth-century collections—six "allude to the ghost, four in particular to the business in the cellar": "In these allusions," writes Thorndike, "*Hamlet* was looked upon as a popular ghost play, in which the dodging about of the ghost was especially noticeable."[27] What I want to rescue is the way the cellarage scene aroused fears related to the rising hegemony of capitalist forms of value.

The central scenes for analysis of the continuing authority of the Ghost in *Hamlet* are those surrounding the staging of the play-within-the-play, *The Murder of Gonzago*. "The Mousetrap" is, indeed, a test of that authority in a way that reworks the cellarage scene: in the earlier scene the Ghost below the stage ratifies the contract between Hamlet and the other witnesses of the Ghost, demanding that the witnesses swear to silence. "The Mousetrap," on the other hand, should ratify the Ghost's account. More generally, the scenes with the players very clearly link performance with competition in the theatrical market: The performance of *The Murder of Gonzago* occurs partly because of a disturbance in notions of theatrical value in the city. The players appear in Denmark not on account of any royal invitation but because they have been driven to travel by competition and their dwindling share of the audience in the city. According to the play's logic that links money to sovereignty as related forms of value, this disturbance in the theatrical market leads Hamlet to reflect on similar curiosities in the market in images of kings:

[27] Ashley H. Thorndike, "The Relation of *Hamlet* to Contemporary Revenge Plays," pp. 202–3n. See especially citations from Marston, Fletcher, and E. S. (B. of D.) in the volumes that combine and expand those Thorndike used, John Munro's *The Shakspere Allusion-Book*, pp. 129, 200, 326.

It is not very strange, for my uncle is King of Denmark, and those that would make mouths at him while my father liv'd, give twenty, forty, fifty, a hundred ducats a-piece for his picture in little. 'Sblood, there is something in this more than natural, if philosophy could find it out. (II.ii.363–68)[28]

The link here between strangeness and the inadequacies of philosophy echoes the dialogue between Horatio and Hamlet immediately after the cellarage scene:

> *Hor.* O day and night, but this is wondrous strange!
> *Ham.* And therefore as a stranger give it welcome.
>   There are more things in heaven and earth, Horatio,
>   Than are dreamt of in your philosophy . . . (I.v.164–67)

Both passages represent something mysteriously in excess of the reach of "philosophy." The inflation in the value of images is testimony to the existence of "something more than natural" and the Ghost is evidence that there "are more things in heaven and earth" than philosophy can account for. This pairing of Ghost and inflated values as beyond philosophy's reach locates the phantasmagorical axis of the play. It is as if the phantasmal, second body of the king is more powerful when autonomous, separated from the king's "body natural."[29] Philosophy cannot picture the relationship between "nature" and the Ghost, or that between "nature" and the inflation in the value of images. The archaic Ghost and the wild variation in the cash value of the images of kings both figure an authority unmoored by philosophy, yet paradoxically powerful. Hamlet's speech about the fluctuations in the market for miniature portraits of kings antici-

---

[28] If Empson is right, *Hamlet* challenges an audience who come expecting to be able to laugh easily at an old play of Kyd's. Hamlet's bitter remark about the enhanced value of an old representation might then be taken as a sort of inside joke in the text of *Hamlet* about the value of *Hamlet* itself: the audience now pays to view what it used to laugh at, and the refurbished theatrical commodity—*Hamlet*, when renewed—suddenly has value again. (This also resonates with the renewed usefulness of another old play, "The Mousetrap" itself.) This reflection on the value of the portraits of Claudius foreshadows Hamlet's testing of Gertrude with the pair of miniatures in the bedroom scene (III.iv.53ff).

[29] See Ernst H. Kantorowicz, *The King's Two Bodies.*

pates a theme especially insistent in scenes surrounding the play-within-the-play, that of fortune. The question of fortune first arises in Hamlet's praise of Horatio's temperateness in the face both of success and adversity before "The Mousetrap" begins: ". . . blest are those/Whose blood and judgment are so well co-meddled,/That they are not a pipe for Fortune's finger/To sound what stop she please" (III.ii.68–71). The Player King's longest speech echoes this discussion of fortune:

> This world is not for aye, nor 'tis not strange
> That even our loves should with our fortunes change:
> For 'tis a question left us yet to prove,
> Whether love lead fortune, or else fortune love.
> The great man down, you mark his favorite flies,
> The poor advanc'd makes friends of enemies.
>
> (III.ii.200–205)

The Player King's speech revises Hamlet's praise of Horatio by materializing its key term.[30] In Hamlet's praise of Horatio, "Fortune," for the moment, is the capitalized figure of mythological thought. While such mythological resonance is not absent from the Player King's speech, his translation of Fortune as fortune, as economic worth, is notable: he opposes the "great man" to the "poor." The Player King suggests that the variations in fortune are "not strange," echoing Hamlet's earlier discussion of the miniatures: "It is not very strange . . ." But both Player King and Hamlet, despite their denial of the strange, open up unanswered questions. What Hamlet describes as unfathomable, beyond the reach of "philosophy," sounds a lot like money: objects of disturbing, shifting value that bear the images of kings. To trade coins for miniatures is to trade like for like: it is, in some mystical way, the image of the king that verifies the value of a

---

[30] On *Hamlet* and the materialization of the word, see Margaret Ferguson, "*Hamlet*: Letters and Spirits," pp. 292–309. It is remarkable that in *The New Organon* Bacon classes "Fortune" among those Idols of the Market Place that are "names of things which do not exist" and "which result from fantastic suppositions and to which nothing in reality corresponds." Bacon is a theorist of the materialization of the word here: "For men believe that their reason governs words; but it is also true that words react on the understanding . . ." Bacon, *New Organon*, pp. 57, 56.

coin in the first place. Hamlet challenges "philosophy" to investigate the inflation of the value of Claudius's portrait; the Player King, in turn, prepares a scholastic debate and asserts that "'tis a question yet to prove" whether Love anticipates or merely follows fortune. The weirdness here is like the weirdness of the association of the Ghost with the mine. The Player King, an allegorical version of King Hamlet in Hamlet's manipulation of *The Murder of Gonzago*, is himself a phantasmagorical figure. Like all the characters in Hamlet's "Mousetrap"—and like the Ghost, for that matter—the Player King speaks in the antiquated diction and cadences of the revenge tragedies the audience Empson describes was prepared to laugh at. But the Player King naturalizes that problem of inflated values Hamlet considers beyond philosophy's reach: "'tis not strange . . ." This is perfectly phantasmagorical: The figure from a theatrical past naturalizes the forms of the future.

"Elizabethan and Jacobean theater . . . ," argues Agnew,

> did not just hold the mirror up to nature; it brought forth 'another nature'—a new world of 'artificial persons'— . . . The theater bestowed an intelligible albeit Protean human shape on the very *form*lessness that money values were introducing into exchange . . .[31]

In *Hamlet*, these "artificial persons" appear under the aegis of the phantasmagoria: the "Protean shape" is archaic. The spirit in the mine is a Ghost from the past. To inhabitants of industrialized nations today, the supernaturalization of the earth and of the mine may seem a misrecognition of nature. To the early modern audience described by Agnew, on the other hand, the naturalization of exchange relations would seem no less bizarre. Commodity exchange had not acquired its uneasy status as "another nature"; there was, in Hamlet's words, "something in this more than natural." There was, indeed, to translate Hamlet's words, something supernatural. If the first part of *Hamlet*—before the play-within-the play—supernaturalizes authority, however, the second part authorizes the supernatural. Margaret Ferguson has noted Hamlet's "pervasive concern with debased cur-

[31] Agnew, *Worlds Apart*, p. xi.

rency"[32]; this is matched by his pervasive concerns with inflated values, as with the portraits, and, finally, with the restoration of proper value. If the first act is a supernatural disturbance in the settled values of the state, the rest of the play, especially after the success of "The Mousetrap," marks a naturalization of that disturbance. The rest of the play recuperates those gestures by which, in the cellarage scene, Hamlet seems to lampoon and distance himself from the authority of the Ghost.

The question of the value of the Ghost's testimony, of the "truepenny" or "damned ghost," is never far from the surface after the arrival of the players. Horatio, promising to look for signs of Claudius's guilt, vows: "If 'a steal aught the whilst this play is playing,/And scape [detecting], I will pay the theft" (III.ii.88–89). Horatio offers a sort of bail: if Claudius makes a sign of his guilt that Horatio does not notice, Horatio "will pay the theft." In any case, Horatio's promise suggests that "The Mousetrap" is a financial arrangement, even a wager. The economic terms that have surrounded the Ghost since the cellarage scene return after the staging vindicates the Ghost's testimony. After the play's end, Hamlet cashes in:

> Would not this, sir, and a forest of feathers—if the rest of my fortunes turn Turk with me—with [two] Provincial roses on my raz'd shoes, get me a fellowship in a cry of players?
> *Hor.* Half a share.
> *Ham.* A whole one, I.
>   . . .
> *Ham.* O good Horatio, I'll take the ghost's word for a thousand pound. Didst perceive? (III.ii.275–87)

The nexus of theatricality, money, authority, and the supernatural surfaces in a concentrated dialogue. Hamlet feels that his skills in staging the play-within-the-play confirm his theatrical talent and his thoughts turn to a "fellowship," that is, part ownership in a company.[33] The Ghost wins Horatio's wager. Hamlet, critic of inflation

---

[32] Ferguson, "Letters and Spirits," p. 297.

[33] Jenkins's note is useful here: "A sharer in a company of players, as distinct from a hired man, was joint owner of its property and participated in its profits . . ." Jenkins, ed., *Hamlet*, III.ii.273n.

in his critique of the shifting value of the images of kings, now himself celebrates the multiplication of the value of the "truepenny" to a
"thousand pound." That monetarization of the word of the Ghost by
which Hamlet seemed to distance himself from the Ghost in the cellarage scene reappears here, but as confirmation.

This recuperation of the ghostly economic nexus is particularly
clear in the scene where Hamlet accosts Gertrude in her bedchamber.
Gertrude finds an explanation for Hamlet's seeming madness and
senseless dialogue with the Ghost:

> This is the very coinage of your brain,
> This bodiless creation ecstasy
> Is very cunning in. (III.iv.137–39)

Hamlet, at the end of the play-within-the-play, takes the verification
of the Ghost's testimony as a sort of "coinage," but what Hamlet
celebrates, Gertrude takes as a sign of inauthenticity and fraud:
"bodiless creation," which one might gloss as making ghosts, becomes "coinage." According to Gertrude, the Ghost is a forgery of
Hamlet's brain, and a hallucination, the "bodiless creation" of
Hamlet's "ecstasy" or madness. Hamlet responds by asserting that he
is not mad, and then, typically, offers a wager:

> Bring me to the test,
> And [I] the matter will reword, which madness
> Would gambol from. Mother, for love of grace,
> Lay not that flattering unction to your soul,
> That not your trespass but my madness speaks;
> It will but skin and film the ulcerous place,
> Whiles rank corruption, mining all within,
> Infects unseen. (III.iv.142–49)

Hamlet reads Gertrude's body as a microcosm of the haunted state,
diagnosing a general infection with a local symptom, an "ulcerous
place"; suddenly, Hamlet associates mining with corruption.[34] Ham-

---

[34] This association has a precedent in the first act, where Hamlet discusses the
"vicious mole of nature," the one peculiar fault that causes a general "corruption" of
character (I.iv.24, 35), and then calls the Ghost "old mole."

let also, however, associates the Ghost with mining again; the bedroom scene treats the unseen, the problem that Gertrude does not see
the Ghost. Hamlet aligns the Ghost and mining as forces invisible to
Gertrude that nevertheless are doing work. It is indeed odd that
Hamlet associates mining with corruption, but this may be how he
measures Gertrude's failings. Her failure to recognize the claims of
the Ghost measures her own corruption.

Hamlet recuperates the figure of mining as the scene ends, describing his own future counter-moves against the schemes of Rosen-
crantz and Guildenstern:

> Let it work,
> For 'tis the sport to have the enginer
> Hoist with his own petar, an't shall go hard
> But I will delve one yard below their mines,
> And blow them at the moon. (III.iv.205–9)

The explosive mine meets the underground site of ore. Hamlet takes
on the Ghost's mining work; others may work in dangerous mines,
but Hamlet, father and son, mine better. If Hamlet sees himself as a
miner, in the following scene Gertrude sees Hamlet's madness as the
pure product of a mine. Claudius blames himself for the murder of
Polonius:

> It will be laid to us, whose providence
> Should have kept short, restrain'd, and out of haunt
> This young mad man; but so much was our love,
> We would not understand what was most fit,
> But like the owner of a foul disease,
> To keep it from divulging, let if feed
> Even on the pith of life. Where is he gone?
> *Queen.* To draw apart the body he has kill'd,
> O'er whom his very madness, like some ore
> Among a mineral of metals base,
> Shows itself pure; 'a weeps for what is done. (IV.i.17–27)

Gertrude has associated Hamlet's hallucinatory "coinage" with his
madness; here, suddenly and surprisingly, his "madness" is itself

authentic, the pure "ore/Among a mineral of metals base."[35]
Claudius, however unknowingly, wants to prevent Hamlet from becoming too much like the Ghost—he wants to keep him "out of
haunt"—while Gertrude, rapidly revising the false "coinage" with
the pure "ore," reproduces in the space of two scenes the movement
from the suspicious "truepenny" to the word that has a cash value of
"a thousand pound."

Hamlet's last speech is the clearest instance of the ghostly succession I have traced:

> O, I die, Horatio,
> The potent poison quite o'ercrows my spirit.
> I cannot live to hear the news from England,
> But I do prophesy th'election lights
> On Fortinbras, he has my dying voice.
>
> (V.v.352–56)

Like the Ghost, Hamlet narrates his own death from poison; like the
Ghost he seeks to mandate the political organization of Denmark
from beyond the grave. The Ghost, too, is "o'ercrowed": when the
cock crows, the Ghost can no longer speak, but must return to its
place in purgatory. But there is also, as in the Ghost's bequest,
something disturbing, something troubling in Hamlet's leaving
Fortinbras—as in a will—his "dying voice," an implication that
Fortinbras's voice will be not his own, but Hamlet's. *Hamlet* is insistently about such difficult bequests. The opening act is about the
Ghost's word, about making the Ghost talk, and about then deciding
how to act on this information; the end of the play is about Hamlet's
word, about the ghostly authority he claims with his "dying voice"
(V.v.356). This "dying voice" is like the Ghost's, an undead man's
authoritative speech. Moving out from the haunted and theatrical
nexus of the cellarage scene shows that Hamlet's materialization of
supernatural authority, his linking it to coins and to the mine, sets an
example for the play as a whole. *Hamlet*, in short, investigates a

---

[35] This passage recalls Hamlet's speech after his first encounter with the Ghost
when he vows that the Ghost's "commandement all alone shall live/Within the
book and volume of my brain,/Unmix'd with baser matter" (I.v.102–4).

group of questions. What gives a ghost authority? What gives value to money? How can one test the supernatural? These are versions of the same central question: How is Hamlet supposed to respond to the Ghost? *Hamlet*'s phantasmagorical axis represents the oldest form of authority—the force of the Ghost's word—in terms of the nascent forms of commodity exchange. These enchanted terms, as the play unfolds, attach themselves to Hamlet. Hamlet's response to the Ghost is to become like the Ghost. The phantasmagoric inheritance is not only Fortinbras's, but that of the audience of *Hamlet*.

"SHAKSPEARIZED," OR, BACK TO
THE BRUMAIRE

Hamlet has become an emblem of modernity. This chapter's "historical allegory," to use Halpern's term, does not assert that this reading of the play and its central character as modernity's icons is wrong, but that these icons need rethinking. *Hamlet* is an image of reenchanted modernity. By focusing on the entanglement of the Ghost and the mine, a different *Hamlet* becomes visible, one that locates a troubled nexus at the heart of modernity—the phantasmagorical intersection of antiquated but powerful authority, the supernatural, and, in the mines, the material base of a commodity culture. Small wonder the nineteenth century embraced *Hamlet* as its own. Emerson writes of "Shakspeare":

> It was not until the nineteenth century, whose speculative genius is a sort of living Hamlet, that the tragedy of Hamlet could find such wondering readers. Now, literature, philosophy and thought are Shakspearized. His mind is the horizon beyond which, at present, we do not see.[36]

According to Emerson, the nineteenth century has just caught up with Shakespeare: "Shakspeare" is coterminous with the spirit of the times. Empson, in 1953, had only somewhat less grandiose claims for *Hamlet* when he wrote that with it ". . . Shakespeare created a new epoch and opened a new territory to the human mind." As Francis Barker writes of Romantic criticism of *Hamlet* and its inheritors,

[36] Ralph Waldo Emerson, "Shakspeare; Or, the Poet," p. 204.

"The startling effect has been to reproduce the text as the great trag-edy of *bourgeois* culture."[37] *Hamlet*, if we are to take these claims seri-ously, both opened up and constitutes modernity. Certainly it is clear that the end to similar claims about *Hamlet* is not in sight.[38] It is commonplace still to associate *Hamlet* with the "spirit" of moder-nity.

On the one hand there is the matter of the play as a signal event for modernity, or a signal event in the history of the modern. On the other hand there is the problem of the archaic Ghost, which, it seems, is a relic of the pre-modern. *Hamlet*, an extraordinary symp-tom of the modern, contains within it an element without which it would be unimaginable, the Ghost, a symptom of the very antithesis of the modern. Indeed, it is precisely the archaic spirit's call for re-venge that initiates the modernity of *Hamlet*. According to this schema, the Ghost's demand—"Revenge his foul and most unnatu-ral murther" (I.v.25)—is part of a larger cultural past; Hamlet's re-sponse, on the other hand, is that of an individual subject, a subject tied only to personal mandates following his discovery of himself. Hamlet's response may be typical of modernity, so goes this argu-ment, but only insofar as modernity allows the subject freedom, making way for the "speculative genius" of the soliloquies, to use Emerson's phrase. In that case, one may read *Hamlet* as the plot of a historical regression. Once Hamlet gives in to the call to revenge, he has abandoned his claim to modernity, and the play returns to the haunted precincts of revenge tragedy.[39]

John Dover Wilson clearly states this contradiction at the heart of the play:

> *Hamlet* is Shakespeare's most realistic, most modern tragedy; the play of all others in which we come closest to the spirit and life of his time,

---

[37] Empson, "*Hamlet*," p. 80; Francis Barker, *The Tremulous Private Body*, p. 38.

[38] See, for instance, Ned Lukacher, *Primal Scenes*, p. 208: "The great critics of *Hamlet*, such as Hegel, Nietzsche, Joyce, Goethe, Coleridge, and Eliot, despite all their differences, agree on the fact that *Hamlet* signals a qualitative transformation in the nature of the human spirit."

[39] Richard Halpern's "*Historica Passio: King Lear's* Fall into Feudalism" has influ-enced my thinking here. See his *The Poetics of Primitive Accumulation*, pp. 215–69.

and he closest to the spirit and life of ours. It is therefore remarkable and perhaps not without a personal significance, that he should have made the supernatural element more prominent here than in any other of his dramas.[40]

According to Dover Wilson, it seems, the "supernatural element" in *Hamlet* stands in contradiction to the prevailing rationalism of our time. Dover Wilson, explaining twentieth-century skepticism about ghosts—more particularly, the dangerous skepticism of W. W. Greg, the critic whose wandering from Shakespearean orthodoxy inspired Dover Wilson's opus—writes: "It is not Shakespeare's fault that ghosts are at a discount in the twentieth century."[41] The *Zeitgeist* of the twentieth century debunks ghosts. Therefore, the mysterious modernity of *Hamlet* needs to be explained despite the Ghost, despite the "supernatural element," despite the fact that the Ghost may be on sale, "at a discount in the twentieth century."

As I have discussed, Dover Wilson's response to this dilemma is to restore value to the discounted Ghost by outlining some of the aspects of the debate about ghosts between Catholics, Protestants, and skeptics in the sixteenth and seventeenth centuries. That our time puts ghosts "at a discount" suggests to Dover Wilson that in order to understand *Hamlet* we need to restore what we have held back; we need to appreciate the Ghost to its full value. But it is precisely *Hamlet*'s figuring a modernity inextricably linked to ghostly injunctions that makes the play so telling an icon of modernity. Dover Wilson's contradiction—that of modernity and the Ghost—is the phantasmagorical contradiction that defines reenchanted modernity.

"Regression" within the modern is the hallmark of the phantasmagoria as Adorno understands it: "Every step forwards is at the same time a step into the remote past." *Hamlet* stages a phantasma-

---

[40] Dover Wilson, *What Happens*, p. 52.

[41] Dover Wilson, *What Happens*, p. 50. The monetarization of the ghostly reappears in Thomas, *Religion and the Decline of Magic*, p. 590: ". . . although men went on seeing ghosts after the Reformation, they were assiduously taught not to take them at their face value." On Dover Wilson's response to Greg, and for a reading of Dover Wilson's project of saving the "objectivity" of the Ghost as a manifestly conservative effort to "save" Shakespeare, see Terence Hawkes's "Telmah." The target that drew Dover Wilson's fire was Greg's essay, "Hamlet's Hallucination."

gorical narrative. The return to the tradition of revenge does not contradict the play's intimations of modernity. The Ghost in the mine is at once the bearer of an archaic summons and the figure of an important subterranean ground to the growing capitalist economy. Marx summons this phantasmagorical *Hamlet*. After *The Eighteenth Brumaire*, this phantasmagorical aspect of nineteenth-century culture becomes only more important to Marx. In his 1856 "Speech at the Anniversary of the *People's Paper*," two of the most powerful pages in his work, Marx declares in tones that recall Carlyle:

> There is one great fact, characteristic of this our nineteenth century, a fact which no party dares deny. On the one hand, there have started into life industrial and scientific forces which no epoch of former human history had ever suspected. On the other hand, there exist symptoms of decay, far surpassing the horrors recorded of the latter times of the Roman empire. In our days everything seems pregnant with its contrary. Machinery, gifted with the wonderful power of shortening and fructifying human labour, we behold starving and overworking it. The new-fangled sources of wealth, by some strange weird spell, are turned into sources of want.[42]

That "strange weird spell" suggests the range of the supernatural in *The Eighteenth Brumaire*. The phantasmagorical conditions of the nineteenth century are now "a fact which no party dares deny." Historical dialectic has become a horror show in which "industrial and scientific forces" contend with "symptoms of decay." Marx stresses, "this antagonism between the productive powers and the social relations of our epoch is a fact, palpable, overwhelming, and not to be controverted." Magic, "some strange weird spell," may be inadequate to the explanation of this "fact," but it emphasizes the resistance of social contradiction to reason.

Marx's "Speech at the Anniversary of the *People's Paper*" has particular importance here because, in it, Marx returns, if in a strange form, to his allusion to *Hamlet*:

[42] Karl Marx, "Speech at the Anniversary of the *People's Paper*," *Surveys from Exile*, p. 299. This two-page speech is in English in the original; all quotations from it are from this edition, pp. 299–300.

On our part, we do not mistake the shape of the shrewd spirit that continues to mark all these contradictions. We know that to work well the newfangled forces of society, they only want to be mastered by newfangled men—and such are the working men. They are as much the invention of modern time as machinery itself. In the signs that bewilder the middle class, the aristocracy and the poor prophets of regression, we do recognize our brave friend, Robin Goodfellow, the old mole that can work in the earth so fast, that worthy pioneer—the Revolution.

Marx adds a bewildering sign of his own. Do "we . . . recognize our brave friend"? That word, "brave," after all, earlier described the labors of the Ghost. Suddenly Marx identifies the "old mole" with Robin Goodfellow, with Puck. One can speculate that in the four years separating the publication of *The Eighteenth Brumaire* in 1852 from that of the "Speech" in 1856 Marx became discontented with the questionable appropriateness of associating the revolution with the feudal Ghost of King Hamlet, and so revised the "old mole" once more. However, his insistence that his audience will recognize "the old mole" from the haunted pages of *The Eighteenth Brumaire* is a clue that Marx imagines the Revolution not as Puck rather than the Ghost but, instead, as some wonderful composite of Puck and the Ghost. Marx's "we" assumes a community able to read the marks and signs of the times: "we do not mistake the shape of the shrewd spirit that continues to mark all of these contradictions." Marx recalls the ghostly being of the mole, and asserts his common membership with a revolutionary group now able to cope with its "questionable shape."

The skeptic might point out that Marx here borrows the sort of superstition he explicitly criticizes elsewhere and harnesses it for his revolution, borrowing the supernatural beliefs of English folk culture for the glorification of the revolution, and hijacking their "self-affirming character."[43] This would echo the argument that Marx's thought in general is a sort of poorly disguised millennial ideology for the industrial age. But what is the precise quality of the utopian impulse here, if indeed it is one? A full accounting of those proleptic

[43] Keith Thomas, *Religion and the Decline of Magic*, p. 614.

moments in Marx where he does indeed gesture towards the post-revolutionary future would have to gather those scant moments and subject them to real scrutiny. The Shakespearean examples from *The Eighteenth Brumaire* and the "Speech at the Anniversary of the *People's Paper*" suggest that Marx's allusions to the future work by deliberate anti-climax. Imagining the revolution as mole or fairy suggests the difficulty in picturing the future, as one can see by looking quickly at the structure of the short speech.

The "Speech at the Anniversary of the *People's Paper*" begins by imagining European history of the nineteenth century as volatile geographical activity: under Europe, the volcano. The "poor incidents" of the revolutions of 1848 were only "small fractures and fissures in the dry crust of European society" and yet "they betrayed oceans of liquid matter, only needing expansion to rend into fragments continents of hard rock." This language sets up a metaphorical chain that goes precisely nowhere; the obvious expectation that Marx will go on to compare the revolution to a volcano remains expectation only. Instead, Marx moves on to other metaphors. Moving from below the earth to the atmosphere above it, he compares bourgeois Europe's failure to feel "the revolutionary atmosphere" before 1858 to the fact that no one registers the "20,000 lb. force" of the atmosphere that bears down on each of us. This turn to scientific discourse cedes to the magical language I have discussed above. This magical language, in turn, has its climax, or, as I have suggested, its anti-climax, in "the signs that bewilder the middle class" of the mid-nineteenth century and a literary critic of the late twentieth, the turn to the enigmatic amalgam of mole and Robin Goodfellow. The speech's imaginative and metaphorical restlessness means this speech has no dominant figure for the future or for anything else.

That it is no comprehensive figure, however, does not mean one should forgo the effort to decipher the conjunction of Puck and mole. Marx has been writing about the "new-fangled forces of society" and how they need to "be mastered by new-fangled men," and this language of the very new contrasts markedly with the use of the figure of Puck. The archaism of Robin Goodfellow, a figure of English folklore long before Shakespeare appropriated him, recalls the linking of the revolution with the archaic ghost.[44] So, as with the ghost, Robin Goodfellow should register as out of place. In particular, Marx oddly links the revolution to the beliefs of the rural countryside that were vanishing in the face of the "progress" of which this speech is so vivid an account. So one might say Marx grants with one hand what he has taken away with the other. Having described irresistible pressures, industrial, political, and social, that are leveling Europe, he associates the revolution with the English countryside which, as Raymond Williams demonstrates so memorably, writers have long described as in the process of vanishing.[45] One might, indeed, mark this combination of mole and Puck as an intimation of the British tradition which stresses the ways Marxism might salvage aspects of the world we have lost, the world we have always been losing. As with the allusion to the mole in *The Eighteenth Brumaire*, Marx alludes to the future via a figure associated with the archaic past. If Marx fosters utopianism, it is a very complex, contradictory utopianism. To examine the constellation surrounding the supernatural allusions to the "old mole" and Robin Goodfellow is to encounter the thoroughness with which Marx made it difficult to imagine a "Marxist" future.

[44] For Robin Goodfellow and English fairy beliefs, see Thomas, *Religion and the Decline of Magic*, p. 606–14.
[45] Raymond Williams, *The Country and the City*, especially pp. 1–8.

PART II

Witchcraft and History

We have all of us become used to finding ourselves sometimes
on the one side of the moon and sometimes on the other,
without knowing what route or journey connects them, related,
apparently, after the fashion of our waking and dreaming lives.
                    John Maynard Keynes, *The General Theory*

                              But at times such as
these late ones, a moaning in copper beeches is heard, of regret,
not for what happened, or even for what conceivably could have
      happened, but
for what never happened and which therefore exists, as dark
and transparent as a dream.
                              John Ashbery, *Flow Chart*

4

John Maynard Keynes and
Reenchantment

PRODUCTIVITY, PRODUCTIVITY, PRODUCTIVITY

Allusive awareness of reenchantment saturates the work of many of
its strongest critics. This was particularly true after World War I. In
the early pages of his analysis of the contradictions of capitalism, *The
Acquisitive Society*, for instance, R. H. Tawney challenges those who
champion production as a panacea for all social ills:

> They may set up a new department, and appoint new officials, and invent
> a new name to express their resolution to effect something more drastic
> than reform, and less disturbing than revolution. But unless they take
> pains, not only to act, but to reflect, they end up effecting nothing. For
> they deliver themselves bound to those who think themselves practical,
> because they take their philosophy so much for granted as to be uncon-
> scious of its implications, and directly they try to act, that philosophy re-
> asserts itself, and serves as an over-ruling force which presses their action
> more deeply into the old channels. "Unhappy man that I am; who shall
> deliver me from the body of this death?"[1]

[1] R. H. Tawney, *The Acquisitive Society*, p. 4. Subsequent references will appear
in parentheses in the text.

This plaintive question is doubly ventriloquized. It is at once Tawney's speech for those caught in the ideology of production he so persuasively sketches, and a paraphrase of Romans 7:24, part of a dense chapter in which Paul discusses the place of sin under the new law of Christ. The aim of Tawney's critique is to disenchant the bureaucratized world—the world of departments, officials, neologisms—and to disrupt it from its "old channels." Where false practicality rules, "unconscious of its implications," there shall thought be.[2] But the economic philosopher's fiat contains within it the allusion to Romans.

Tawney's allusion contributes to the insistent dialogism of the early pages of *The Acquisitive Society*. As in *The Eighteenth Brumaire*, allusion provides a tool for the critique of historical regression; it also enacts such regression. Tawney scatters voices in quotation marks or italics, without introduction, interrupting, throughout the text; these voices speak for an argumentative partner whose "practical" force lies partly in not realizing it has any part in an argument at all. Tawney's description of that "philosophy" of production, which people take "so much for granted as to be unconscious of its implications," implies that the work of quoting these champions of production includes, paradoxically, forcing them into speech for the first time. Tawney must "quote" an antagonist who has never spoken. Quotation, like psychoanalysis, provokes the articulation of that which speaks only in mute symptoms.

Allusion is, then, a counter-symptom, showing the awareness of such unknowing and potentially destructive historical regression. It is precisely to the extent that "philosophy" remains inarticulate that it is at its most powerful and corrosive. ("Philosophy" here seems coterminous with ideology understood as false consciousness.) As long as people live unconscious of the "philosophy" to which they are subject, it's déjà vu all over again:

> When they desire to place their economic life on a better foundation, they repeat, like parrots, the word "Productivity," because that is the

[2] I intend the Freudian echoes here, and am thinking especially of Peter Gay's portrait of Freud as great Enlightenment thinker in his *Freud*.

word that rises first in their minds; regardless of the fact that productivity is the one characteristic achievement of the age before the war, as
religion was of the Middle Ages or art of classical Athens, and that it is
precisely in the century that has seen the greatest increase in productivity since the fall of the Roman Empire that economic discontent has
been most acute. (4–5)

Tawney lays out a dialogue within a dialogue: the voice for productivity that he conjures interrogates itself. The Biblical question: "'Un-
happy man that I am, who shall deliver me from the body of this
death?'" The parroted answer: "'Productivity.'"[3] Recent events inform Tawney's dissatisfaction with this capitalist catechism: World
War I stands as an antidote to unreflective faith in the salvific efficacy
of production. Tawney's phrase, the "age before the war," reveals the
extent to which he considers the time when he writes to be discon-
tinuous with the time before August 1914.

The sense of the years after 1919 as coming after a great historical
break was common enough. Less common was Tawney's sense that
to deliver the post-war "age" to the altar of increased productivity
was to deliver that age to the same force that delivered up the dead
bodies of World War I. More insistent than the note of rupture in
Tawney is the tone of repetition. The strange quotations in *The Acquisitive Society* are symptomatic of his frustrating sense that the prevailing "philosophy," or ideology, barely recognized, will reorganize
society in only the most shallow ways.

As the dialogue continues, the debating partner Tawney imagines
spars again: "'But increased production is important.' Of course it is!
That plenty is good and scarcity evil—it needs no ghost from the
graves of the past five years to tell us that" (5). The Ghost of Hamlet
walks again, and again it haunts a discussion of production. Tawney
echoes Horatio's response to Hamlet's unsatisfying version of the
"news" brought by the Ghost in the first act of *Hamlet*:

[3] The answer of Romans is that the new law of Christ will free one from the
"oldness of the letter" (7:6). Tawney would publish *Religion and the Rise of Capitalism* in 1922; surely the irony of the superimposition of the law of productivity on the
law of the New Testament is not an accident.

> *Ham.*   There's never a villain dwelling in all Denmark
>   But he's an arrant knave.
> *Hor.*   There needs no ghost, my lord, come from the grave
>   To tell us this. (I.v.123–25)

John Dover Wilson comments: "For some reason or other, the War acted as a stimulus for the study of *Hamlet*."[4] For Tawney, on the other hand, *Hamlet* is a stimulus to the study and understanding of the war. In ways that recall *The Eighteenth Brumaire*, an apprehension that history has gone in reverse marks *The Acquisitive Society*. Tawney tries to make sense of this reversal, and to learn from the war. "The events of the last few years," as Tawney writes in a chapter called "The 'Vicious Circle,'" "are a lesson which should need no repetition" (124). What are the ghosts "from the graves of the past five years" good for? Is it not in the nature of lessons that they need to be repeated? In *Hamlet*, the return of ghosts is, among other things, a stimulus to action. Even if the status of the call to revenge remains contested, haunting acts both as supernatural sanction and as ethical compulsion. Tawney reserves this notion, but also leaves open the possibility that the lesson of the ghosts of the First World War will be old news, that "plenty is good and scarcity evil." Ghosts of the battlefields have nothing to say, like the soldiers Benjamin describes: "Was it not noticeable at the end of the war that men returned from the battlefield grown silent—not richer, but poorer in communicable experience?"[5] Tawney's ghosts are surely uncanny, to extend the sense offered by Freud in his study on the subject of 1919: they lead to the all too familiar.

In *The Great War and Modern Memory*, Paul Fussell has demonstrated the self-conscious literary culture that shaped the British experience of the First World War. Here I focus on the work of John Maynard Keynes to demonstrate how his response to the First World War and its aftermath borrowed supernatural elements partly from Shakespeare's plays.[6] In particular, I focus on a constellation that

---

[4] Dover Wilson, *What Happens in Hamlet*, p. 14.

[5] Walter Benjamin, "The Storyteller," in *Illuminations*, p. 84.

[6] All quotations from Keynes in this chapter will cite *The Collected Writings of John Maynard Keynes*; quotations will appear with abbreviations in parentheses in

guides this book. Tawney's allusion to *Hamlet* suggests the ideological work that the "literariness" analyzed by Fussell can perform. The degree zero of allusion lies in the fiction of immediate applicability. General notions of "human nature" and repetition erase historical difference. A certain ahistorical impulse lurks in this sort of invocation by allusion: what was true before, is true still. This fiction can then perform an ideological function, as one reproduces an established or canonical sequence of words without change in a new context and supposes that the truth of these words remains unchanged; everything remains the same because these words mean what they have always meant. This ritual invocation by allusion may function, as I have argued, as a microcosm of the phantasmagoria as Adorno understands it: a disguise under which a culture hides the new.

This formulation, however, problematically assumes that the "new," whatever its allusive, ideological disguises, has come into being. The fear that such an assumption may be groundless motivates Tawney. What haunts Tawney and Keynes alike is the apprehension that the First World War itself will turn out to have been a vast and unprecedented and brutal mass phantasmagoria. They recognized the delusions involved in a historical misprision analyzed by Franco Moretti. Too many critics, Moretti argues, mistake the "crisis" of World War I for the general "Crisis" of liberal capitalism. Such analysis tends to reduce all the tensions of the late nineteenth and early twentieth centuries to the carnage of the war:

> Desirous of moving from the Crisis to the crisis, literary criticism almost always resorts to one single and specific event: the war. There, in the summer of 1914, the break came. There lie the roots of the crisis and the literature of crisis—of *Ulysses* and *The Trial, The Magic Mountain, The Waste Land* and *The Man Without Qualities.* Yet, among the few things these works have in common is exactly the oppo-

---

the text. The volumes I cite include volume II, *The Economic Consequences of the Peace* (ECP); III, *A Revision of the Treaty* (RT); VII, *The General Theory of Employment, Interest, and Money* (GT); IX, *Essays in Persuasion* (EP); X, *Essays in Biography* (EB); and XVII, *Activities 1920–1922: Treaty Revision and Reconstruction* (TRR). The last volume is a very useful collection of miscellaneous writings by Keynes, as well as responses to Keynes, tied together by narrative and introductory material written by the editors.

site certainty: the war is not the *cause* of the crisis, but only its violent and conspicuous manifestation.[7]

Keynes's *The Economic Consequences of the Peace* works on a double axis similar to that evident in Tawney. Intimations that the trauma of the War was only the violent outbreak of a continuing cultural "Crisis" mark Keynes's work. Tawney and Keynes were very much partners in a post-war effort to make sense of capitalism after the dislocations, horrors, and incoherences—even mysteries—of the Great War. Like Tawney, Keynes buttresses his analysis with a supernatural superstructure and, in particular, with allusions to Shakespeare. As in Tawney's allusion to Hamlet, there are signs of the fear that the War has not been something new, but a return, a revenant, a ghost from which the "body of death" will learn nothing.

The question of the manifestations of the "supernatural" around World War I is a large one. Reports of a phantom Russian army marching through London were the stuff of urban legend. *The Strand Magazine* was the site of a debate, dominated by Sir Arthur Conan Doyle, about the possibility of contact with the dead (Conan Doyle came down firmly with the believers). Shakespeare's spirit transmitted poems, many of them about flying aces, to Sarah Taylor Shatford in New Orleans, who wrote them automatically.[8] Virginia Woolf's portrait of Septimus Smith in *Mrs Dalloway*, the shell-shocked veteran who hears voices and receives Shakespearean transmissions, also belongs to this curious constellation; Woolf is an important analyst of this post-war reenchantment. To study the *Eco-*

---

[7] Franco Moretti, "The Long Goodbye: *Ulysses* and the End of Liberal Capitalism," in *Signs Taken for Wonders*, pp. 182–83.

[8] Henry James was one taken in by the "hallucination, misconception, fantastication, or whatever" of the story of the Russian troops. Henry James, *Letters*, vol. 2, p. 404. For Doyle, see, for instance, the culmination of a series in *The Strand Magazine*, a pair of articles by Doyle and Edward Clodd under the shared title, "Is Sir Oliver Lodge Right?" Lodge had written in defense of the notion that the living could communicate with the dead. Doyle agrees; Clodd dissents. Shatford's poems, which suggest that the living Shakespeare was on the whole a better poet than the dead, may be found in *Shakespeare's Revelations by Shakespeare's Spirit*. My introduction mentions Freud's metapsychological essays; they seem to me to belong to this collection of supernatural examples.

nomic Consequences then becomes a case study of a general reenchantment. Each of these examples is worth further consideration, but my claims are local ones and my focus falls on Keynes's writings in the years immediately after the war.

The *Economic Consequences* is the quickly written summary of Keynes's objections to the terms of the Versailles Treaty; he resigned his positions with the British delegation to the Treaty Conference in the spring of 1919, the work first appeared towards the end of that year, and, almost immediately, it had great, even violent, impact.[9] *The Economic Consequences of the Peace* was the first of Keynes's works to gain a wide audience; it was, as an American publisher's flyleaf suggests, an international best-seller, "influencing public opinion throughout the civilized world."[10] The publisher's blurb is especially valuable for the way it establishes one of the key terms of the reception of the *Economic Consequences*: "influence." Robert Skidelsky, for instance, calls the *Economic Consequences* "one of the most influential works of the twentieth century."[11] But such statements may mislead by implying that "influence" is in itself an ac-

[9] "In the closing days of 1919, during holiday celebrations of unparalleled extravagance," writes Raymond Sontag, "there appeared in London a small book which cast a sombre shadow over the gaiety of the season, John Maynard Keynes's *The Economic Consequences of the Peace*." Sontag, *A Broken World*, p. 24. For accounts of the composition and reception of *The Economic Consequences*, see R. F. Harrod, *The Life of John Maynard Keynes*, pp. 195–284; Robert Skidelsky, *Hopes Betrayed*, pp. 376–402; and D. E. Moggridge, *Maynard Keynes*, pp. 319–47. Notes of shock and the language of the front are marked features of contemporary reviews. See, for instance, Allyn A. Young in *The New Republic*, which had serialized three excerpts from the *Economic Consequences*: "His book comes with the impact of a missile. It jolts you out of any inert illusion that the world is just about ready to settle itself comfortably down again in its old grooves." (One thinks of Tawney's "old channels.") Or: "his book is like nothing so much as a fresh breeze coming into a plain where poisonous gases are yet hanging." See Young, "The Economics of the Treaty," pp. 388, 389.

[10] This phrase comes from the flyleaf to the cited edition of Tawney's *Acquisitive Society*. The flyleaf asks: "Have you read *The Economic Consequences of the Peace* By John Maynard Keynes, which is now in its fiftieth thousand, which has been translated into nine languages, and which is influencing public opinion throughout the civilized world?"

[11] Skidelsky, *Hopes Betrayed*, p. 384.

complishment. Keynes's work interrogates the very quality for which his biographer lauds it. Influence is a *problem* for Keynes, especially because of its relationship to the supernatural.

In the *Economic Consequences*, Skidelsky argues, "Keynes was staking the claim of the economist to be Prince. All other forms of rule were bankrupt. The economist's vision of welfare, conjoined to a new standard of technical excellence, were the last barriers to chaos, madness and retrogression."[12] In Skidelsky's paradigm, the Economist Prince dethrones Plato's Philosopher King.[13] (Or is Skidelsky thinking of Machiavelli?) Keynes's rationalist fervor—his hope that European opinion might be susceptible to reason—is indeed unmistakable. The focus of this chapter, however, lies elsewhere. Skidelsky's description misses the *Economic Consequences'* reliance on supernatural rhetoric. Keynes troublingly imagines his own influence as an engagement with supernatural modes.

QUOTATION AND HAUNTED SPHERES

OF INFLUENCE

In 1922, Keynes and David Hunter Miller, who had been a member of the American delegation to the Treaty Conference, waged a newspaper battle over the issue that most exercised Keynes and a large part of public opinion in the years following the war: the question of the terms of the Peace. Miller wrote a review of *A Revision of the Treaty*, Keynes's sequel to the *Economic Consequences*, in the *New York Times Book Review and Magazine*; Keynes responded in a letter in those pages; Miller in turn replied to Keynes's letter. The debate between Keynes and Miller has a special interest here. It includes a skirmish over the function of quotation from Shakespeare, of the scare quote. "In its relation to the Treaty of Versailles," writes Miller dismissively in 1922, summing up his argument, "any question of Shakespearean learning is of little importance" (TRR, 302). Keynes defends the

---

[12] Skidelsky, *Hopes Betrayed*, p. 38.
[13] See, however, Keynes: "No! The economist is not king; quite true. But he ought to be!" (TRR, p. 432).

value of his allusions; this defense opens up the question of the importance of the scare quote in Keynes.

In his initial review, Miller takes Keynes to task for a metaphor in the following paragraph of *A Revision of the Treaty*:

> The deeper and the fouler the bogs into which Mr Lloyd George leads us, the more credit is his for getting us out. He leads us in to satisfy our desires; he leads us out to save our souls. He hands us down the primrose path and puts out the bonfire just in time. Who, ever before, enjoyed the best of heaven and hell as we do? (RT, 115)

This is one of a number of places where Keynes alludes to *Macbeth* in his discussions of the crises of post-war Europe. Keynes quotes the words of the porter, who speaks of letting in "some of all professions that go the primrose way to th' everlasting bonfire" (II.iii.18–19). Where others, like Tawney, turn to *Hamlet*, *Macbeth* is the play against which Keynes imagines the machinations surrounding the attempts to establish a post-war peace.[14]

Miller's rejection of the relevance of "Shakespearean learning" stemmed from Keynes's barbed letter in response to Miller's original review. Keynes wrote:

> Let me quote from his review one other passage for its own sake:
>
>> In his excitement on this subject, Mr Keynes goes so far as to speak of Mr Lloyd George handing us 'down the primrose path,' and then putting out the bonfire. We do not have primrose paths in America, but I should think that the sight of one with a bonfire down it would be rather queer even in England. Politics makes strange metaphors.
>
> No! Not politics, poetry. Even in his literary cavillings Mr Miller has no luck. For, as there are no primrose paths in America, how was he to know that I was echoing the words of a porter (or *commissionaire*) who in a play *Macbeth*, by an author well known in England, speaks of those 'that go the primrose way to the everlasting bonfire'? (In writing '*path*' instead of '*way*,' I was vaguely influenced, through the mixed complex of association which makes the atmosphere of a word, by another passage where Ophelia describes the moralist who:

[14] It will be clear below, however, that *Hamlet* too echoes in Keynes's allusion.

> Himself the primrose path of dalliance treads
> And recks not his own rede.

What explanations, in these days, a poor author has to make! And what a waste of words it is! (TRR, 300–301)

Keynes closes his letter: "I am not quite sure that there may not be, after all, some 'primrose paths in America'—and bonfires down them" (TRR, 301). "Shakespearean learning" may, after all, have something to do with the Treaty of Versailles. Keynes's strained pun insinuates that Miller, a member of the American commission to the treaty conference—or *commissionaire*—is like the porter in welcoming people who have walked the "primrose path" to hell; Miller's failure to recognize the quotation implies that he knows not what he does. If there is a purely "rhetorical" maneuver in this passage, it is where Keynes claims that he quotes the passage from Miller's review "for its own sake": Keynes implies with his letter's closing that Miller's failure to recognize the Shakespearean provenance of his phrase is equivalent to other sorts of interpretative failures, political as well as poetic. Miller's blindness to the source in *Macbeth*—his failure to understand what a "primrose path" might be and that there might be such a thing in America even—figures an interpretative failure with deep and lasting political consequences.[15] (Keynes even offers something like a theory of allusion when he describes the "mixed complex of association which make the atmosphere of a word": the self-consciousness with which Keynes employs Shakespearean language is an antidote to any suggestion that the language is simply a kind of unimportant ornament.) Keynes's scare quote not only locates a blind spot in Miller's appreciation of the significance of the Peace Treaty,

---

[15] When Miller replies to Keynes's response, he hazards a scare quote of his own—immediately after he has assured the reader that "any question of Shakespearean learning is of little importance": "In my review I smiled at the idea of Mr Lloyd George putting out the bonfire, an idea which hardly seems to me to echo the metaphor of 'the everlasting bonfire'; but I shall not waste words on literary differences or distinctions which in a discussion of grave issues are trifles light as air" (TRR, 302). One might imagine Keynes's haughty response to this allusion to *Othello*: those "trifles light as air/Are to the jealous confirmations strong/As proofs of holy writ" (III.iii.322–24). This is exactly the problem Keynes thinks he is investigating: the way words of no substance can become sacred truths that guide policy.

but also illustrates Keynes's tendency to represent successful political manipulation as supernatural activity. The scare quote names this magic: Lloyd George's national sleight-of-hand by which he delivers England from the hell to which he almost leads it, putting "out the bonfire just in time."

Keynes's portrait of Lloyd George leading England down the primrose path to near-perdition links *Macbeth* to questions of political influence and manipulation. *Macbeth* gives Keynes a core for his meditations on the use and abuse of influence. The scare quotes to *Macbeth* locate a troubling nexus for Keynes, where rational structures of influence and persuasion give way to ones that occupy supernatural margins. His own strategies to gain influence at once establish distance from any taint of the supernatural and, at the same time, remain indebted to it. Keynes rejects supernatural influence and yet appears unable to imagine influence apart from occult communication, indicating the double gesture that occupies the core of this chapter: the movement by which Keynes at once censors the supernatural and claims a different and redeemed supernatural power of his own.

To understand Keynes's recourse to the supernatural, one needs to appreciate how thoroughly he imagines the world in which he might have influence as enchanted. Keynes claims occult agency in the face of an occulted world. The Paris of the *Economic Consequences*, the capital of a haunted Europe and the site of most of the Treaty negotiations, recalls that of the *Eighteenth Brumaire*, with its competing sorcerers, ghosts, and spooks:

> an Englishman who took part in the Conference of Paris and was during those months a member of the Supreme Economic Council of the Allied Powers, was bound to become—for him a new experience—a European in his cares and outlook. There, at the nerve centre of the European system, his British preoccupations must largely fall away and he must be haunted by other and more dreadful spectres. (ECP, 2)

This separation from "British preoccupations"—which are themselves "spectres," only not so dreadful as those that haunt the European—lays the ground for a whole series of disconnections in Paris and Europe. The negotiators, Keynes argues, are willfully disconnected from the crises afflicting post-war Europe. Such disconnections, in Keynes's logic of reenchantment, provide opportunities for supernatural work.

The *Economic Consequences* reports a failure to respond to the exigencies of those forces that were at work in post-war Europe:

> one felt most strongly the impression, described by Tolstoy in *War and Peace* or by Hardy in *The Dynasts*, of events marching on to their fated conclusion uninfluenced and unaffected by the cerebrations of statesmen in council:

> ### Spirit of the Years
> Observe that all wide sight and self-command
> Deserts these throngs now driven to demonry
> By the Immanent Unrecking. Nought remains
> But vindictiveness here amid the strong,
> And there amid the weak an impotent rage.

> ### Spirit of the Pities
> Why prompts the Will so senseless-shaped a doing?

> ### Spirit of the Years
> I have told thee It works unwittingly,
> As one possessed not judging. (ECP, 3)

Keynes does not comment on these lines from Hardy's *The Dynasts*, his "Epic-Drama Of The War With Napoleon." One might say the lines speak for themselves. But that is just what they do not do. In a gesture that is typical of the works examined in this study, the *Economic Consequences* introduces the supernatural through quotation. The quotation supplies an authoritative voice for a supernatural discourse Keynes at once acknowledges and disowns. The supernatural falls in quotation; it becomes a scare quote.[16] The critic of reenchantment simultaneously disowns investment in the supernatural and projects it as the construction of another. Keynes's analysis of "events" proceeding independent of human intervention culminates

---

[16] Fussell argues that Hardy was especially important in anticipating the language of the Great War. One might argue that, for Keynes, Hardy equally powerfully imagined a language for the aftermath of World War I. See Paul Fussell, *The Great War*, especially chapter one.

here in a quotation that attributes the "demonry" of "throngs" to capitalized agencies, variously called "Immanent Unrecking," "the Will," and "It." Where there is a disconnection between the work of "statesmen" and the states they represent, the supernatural offers an explanatory language. Keynes's text oscillates in a way one cannot call dialectical between faith in the power of the diplomat, politician, or economist—faith, that is, that those "trained" to do so may rationally reorganize Europe—and the contradictory conviction that such faith is groundless: events march on without any relationship to the "cerebrations of statesmen in council."[17]

The haunted Parisian "nerve centre" of the *Economic Consequences* has a parallel in a text published only posthumously, the compelling "Dr Melchior: A Defeated Enemy," which Keynes "first read to Bloomsbury's Memoir Club in February 1920, where it greatly impressed Virginia Woolf with its 'method of character drawing.'"[18] Like the *Economic Consequences*, "Dr Melchior" treats incidents surrounding the treaty conference, specifically a series of negotiations involving German concessions in exchange for Allied shipments of food to post-war Germany and Keynes's relationship—indeed, his love affair—with one of the negotiators, the Dr. Melchior of the title.[19] Some of these negotiations take place in the Belgian town of Spa, which "had been in the later stages of the war the Grand Headquarters of the German Army."

[17] Indeed, Keynes's term here, the odd "cerebrations," is itself part of this matrix of the intended and the unintended. Dr. W. Carpenter coined the term "*unconscious cerebration*," according to the *OED*, to indicate "that action of the brain which, though unaccompanied by consciousness, produced results which might have been produced by thought." The basis of Keynes's critique of the Treaty of Versailles is that it "might have been produced by thought," but became, under occult influences, the product of irrational forces.

[18] Skidelsky, *Hopes Betrayed*, p. 359. For a brief but incisive essay on Keynes and Bloomsbury, see Raymond Williams, "The Significance of 'Bloomsbury' as a Social and Cultural Group."

[19] Carl Melchior was a German Jewish banker from Hamburg, whom Keynes found uniquely sympathetic among the German negotiators. Melchior, Keynes, and others negotiated in secret; in these secret negotiations, Melchior and Keynes developed what Keynes calls "one of the most curious intimacies in the world . . .": "In a sort of way I was in love with him" (EB, p. 395, p. 415).

Spa is the *locus classicus* of Keynes's reenchanted Europe. When Keynes was there, the villa of the former German general (and future Nazi) Ludendorff had become the lodging of General Haking, the English representative to the Armistice Commission meeting in Spa:

> Up on one side of the semicircle of pine-clad hills which surround the watering place, the lords of Germany had suffered, in physical seclusion, the decisions of fate. A few steps away was the Kaiser's villa and a little farther up the hill Hindenburg's. There, far from the guns and armies, away from the mechanism of Berlin, far also from the starved cities and growling mob, the three despots had dwelt in a surrounding network of telephones. It was not merely sentimental to feel that the ground was haunted. The air was still charged with the emotions of that vast collapse. The spot was melancholy with the theatrical Teutonic melancholy of black pinewoods. As one walked on the villa's terrace the horizon was bounded by the black line of woods, the sun sank behind them, and the trees behind the house sighed like a love-sick Prussian. When Ludendorff's nerves began to break, he got no comfort from nature, and the buzz of the telephones in the back room off the hall mingled with the voice of the trees to suggest to him the conventional symbols of a German's despair. (EB, 410–11)

Spa occupies, like Paris, the center of a now empty "network." "Air," it seems, is where the supernatural survives, where it dwells: trees sigh and have voices, while telephones only "buzz." If it "was not merely sentimental to feel that the ground was haunted," what was it? Jay Dickson has pointed out how troubling modernists, and especially those of Bloomsbury, found the matter of sentimentality, and his work helps us hear a self-defensive reflex in Keynes's rejection of the idea that to perceive haunting would be "merely sentimental."[20] Haunting, here, is connected with the absence of power, but this absence has its own supernatural charge. The "charged" air replaces the "network of telephones" by which the three German leaders conducted war from a distance.

Leo Spitzer suggestively charts the symptomatic history of the words "milieu," "ambiance," and related terms—"background," "at-

---

[20] Jay Dickson, "Modernism Post-Mortem."

mosphere," "environment," and so on—in an essay which illuminates the problem Keynes faces here. Spitzer charts a simple but resonant change. "Milieu" and these related terms begin, with classical authors, as descriptions of a surrounding world that almost lovingly embraces its inhabitants. Spitzer shows, for instance, that the ancients had a notion of "air"—to use a term that appears in Keynes—that made it not only the medium of our own perception but also an element that was perceptive in its own right; ". . . Cicero has expressed the theory that air is not only that by means of which we see and hear, but that which sees and hears with us . . ."[21] This rather lyrical and perhaps idealized notion of the relationship between world and people gives way, slowly and inexorably, to the modern sense that people are victims of their milieu: "The world-embracing, metaphysical, cupola that once enfolded mankind has disappeared . . ."[22] Spitzer's essay illuminates a particular mode of reenchantment, the sense that, in modern culture, networks, the atmosphere, and even the surrounding natural world and the air itself are in some strange and estranging league against us. Ludendorff, abandoned by nature, breathing air electric with the collapse he survived, is also the intimation of a response to this alienation that Spitzer's essay identifies as peculiarly German—the need to lash out against the loss of a reassuring, embracing *Umwelt* by claiming *Lebensraum* through conquest.[23] Part of Keynes's work against reenchantment is to empty these atmospheric zones of their strange power.

Following his theatrical description of Ludendorff's predicament, Keynes's diagnosis of one of the causes of the war comes as no surprise:

> One can believe sometimes that no greater responsibility for the war lies on any one man than on Wagner. Evidently the Kaiser's conception of himself was so moulded. And what was Hindenburg but the

[21] Leo Spitzer, "Milieu and Ambiance," p. 4.

[22] Spitzer, "Milieu and Ambiance," p. 195 n66.

[23] Spitzer, "Milieu and Ambiance," pp. 215–16. Spitzer follows this point with a trenchant critique of Heidegger, "now a Nazi philosopher," which anticipates many recent discussions of the matter of Heidegger's politics (pp. 216–17). Spitzer also has a telling description of Hitler's rhetoric of the "air" of spring (p. 191 n61).

bass and Ludendorff but the fat tenor of third-rate Wagnerian opera? How else did they see themselves in their dreams and in their bath? And what else had planted them in their villas at Spa but that these were the likest the neighbourhood could furnish to third-rate operatic scenery? (EB, 411)[24]

Behind this satirical portrait of German leaders, opera, and the Wagnerian self-fashioning that inspires them lies a serious consideration linked to the question of influence. What if it is not mere sentimentality to imagine that Wagner is as important as any political or economic factor to the actions of the German troika? Clearly the mission of the Economist Prince becomes more difficult when those haunted precincts he now occupies take their cues from Bayreuth.[25] Keynes, to use the language of Spitzer's essay, is constantly alert to the ways the figures he analyzes imagine the milieux that have formed them.

Spa, hub of a network of telephones, repeats Keynes's Paris, not so much a "nerve centre" as a place where nerves are broken, traversed only by supernatural transmissions causing a ghostly "buzz of the telephones." The isolated Germans in Spa are not so different from the *commissionaires* in Paris, whose work lacks connection to real events. The statesmen may just as well destroy Europe as save it, as

[24] Keynes goes on to describe the simultaneous disenchantment and anglicizing of this most German landscape: "*The Times* arrived regularly and in good time; and the sporting A.D.C. had clubbed together with his brother subalterns to import a pack of hounds and was hunting the country as usual eight weeks after his arrival there. But outside on the terrace I could hear Ludendorff unbuckling his bright breast-plate and calling in thick voice on the trees to strike up with their soughings to prelude his passing monody. Miss Bates had vanquished Brünnhilde, and Mr Weston's foot was firmly planted on the neck of Wotan" (EB, 412).

[25] This is not the only place in "Dr Melchior" that Keynes speculates on the causes of the war in a way that is, to say the least, surprising. Keynes describes the Germans among whom Melchior was the humane exception: "Erzberger, fat and disgusting in a fur coat, walked down the platform to the Marshal's saloon. With him were a General and a Sea-Captain with an iron cross round his neck and an extraordinary resemblance of face and figure to the pig in *Alice in Wonderland*. They satisfied wonderfully, as a group, the popular conception of the Huns. The personal appearance of that race is really extraordinarily against them. Who knows but that it was the real cause of the war!" (EB, 394–95).

Keynes argues in a passage where he returns to the rhetoric of Hardy:

> Perhaps it is historically true that no order of society ever perishes save by its own hand. In the complexer world of Western Europe the Immanent Will may achieve its ends more subtly and bring in the revolution no less inevitably through a Klotz or a George than by the intellectualisms, too ruthless and self-conscious for us, of the bloodthirsty philosophers of Russia. (ECP, 150)

Keynes has a very particular "bloodthirsty" philosopher in mind here: "Lenin is said to have declared that the best way to destroy the capitalist system was to debauch the currency" (ECP, 148). The construction is a give-away: "Lenin is said to have declared. . ." We are in the territory of the scare quote. (Recall Marx: "Hegel remarks somewhere . . .") In fact, there is no evidence that Lenin ever said anything along these lines. One of the most-quoted lessons of the *Economic Consequences*, which poses as a quotation, may well be an invention. As Frank Whitson Fetter reports,

> A remark so quotable will not die simply for lack of historical credentials. But it is in order to put on notice any economists, bank presidents and politicians who think they are quoting Lenin on inflation as a threat to capitalism that they are really quoting Keynes.[26]

Hans Hellwig wryly observes: "It is almost a ritual, on the occasion of the required tributes to a stable monetary standard, to quote Lenin as a bogeyman [*Schreck und Scheuche*]."[27] And so Keynes's scare quote becomes a monster: Keynes invents the demonic and "bloodthirsty" philosophy of the menacing Bolshevik, gives it startling and sexualized form—the currency is "debauched"— and distances himself from the form, after which the phrase has its haunting afterlife.

KEYNES'S 'MACBETH'

Words become monsters. Keynes fights the misperception that once words have become monsters, they remain mere words: "The im-

---

[26] Frank Whitson Fetter, "Lenin, Keynes, and Inflation," p. 80.

[27] Hans Hellwig, "Lenin als Inflationspropanz," *Das Profil* (Apr. 1967) 28, qtd. in Fetter, "Lenin, Keynes," p. 79.

practicality of the treaty became, in some months, its main beauty; mythical monsters cannot devour real children . . ." (TRR, 28). In the letter to the *Times* Keynes accuses Miller, who was a "participant in a crime" in Paris: "The subtleties of his intelligence are unconsciously directed to proving that the treaty's words are other than what they are, and that really, rightly understood, it was quite an innocent affair" (TRR, 301). *Macbeth*, with its focus on the understanding of language, on what the play identifies quite exactly as equivocation— "which allowed the faithful to say one thing while holding (but not uttering) mental reservations"[28]—provides a valuable template for the interpretative chicanery that is foremost among Keynes's targets in his post-war writings. Equivocal interpretation of the Treaty becomes malign supernatural intervention.

Disconnections between places have an equivalent in linguistic disconnections. This leads to a large issue, in Keynes's eyes, *the* issue of the debate about Germany's reparations. Many granted Keynes's central point in the *Economic Consequences* that Germany could not possibly pay the reparations demanded by the Treaty. The question then became: Did this matter? Could one disregard the language of the Treaty, knowing full well that it bore no relation to the real capability of Germany to pay? Would there be some sort of diplomatic gentlemen's agreement by which parties to the Treaty agreed to pretend they were complying with the language of the Treaty, while all knowing they were not? As Keynes wrote in some "pencilled notes" for a "gathering" at the House of Commons on February 17, 1921: "As long as lies and humbug lead only to words, it is one thing. But if they show a tendency to plunge Europe into war, the veils must be pulled down" (TRR, 218). Keynes saw dangers in equivocation, and tended to emphasize the importance of putting the possible, rather than the desired but impossible, into the language of the Treaty.

Keynes is unwilling to grant that devaluation of language in the formula that implies that one can ignore that which leads "only to words." This is perhaps clearest in a review article about Bernard Baruch's *The Making of the Reparation and the Economic Sections of*

---

[28] The succinct formulation is that of G. K. Hunter in his introduction to the New Penguin edition of *Macbeth*, p. 40.

the Treaty. On the one hand Keynes praises the volume's lack of rhetorical flourishes, its "business man's lack of easy penmanship": "If it were written with more art, it would tell less" (TRR, 91, 96). On the other hand, it is precisely on this issue of language that Keynes reserves his strongest criticism of Baruch. Those who ruled from Spa now occupy Paris despite their defeat:

> It is dangerous to treat the living word as dead. Words live not less than acts and sometimes longer. The war, it may almost be said, was fought for words. Our victory raised the prestige of words, and the terms we promised enthroned them. But it was as though with the expiring breath of Germany the curse which had destroyed her was inhaled by those who stood over her. The realism which taught that words were the tools of emperors, not their masters, has won after all, and the spirit which invaded Belgium triumphed in Paris. (TRR, 97–98)

Keynes is acutely aware of the material effects of words.[29] If there is the influence of rational persuasion, there is also the supernatural influence of words heard "in the air." Keynes may grant the relative harmlessness of "lies and humbug" that lead "only to words," but he also conceives of a strange fatal language with its special "prestige."[30]

Paris, which should be the nexus of historical happenings, the "nerve centre" of Europe, has become a theatrical setting; it has become, to use Dircks's term, a spectre stage:

[29] Thorstein Veblen, for one, accused Keynes of making errors *because* he shared the "attitude of men accustomed to take political documents at face value"; Keynes, he argues, missed the "unrecorded clause by which the governments of the Great Powers are banded together for the suppression of Soviet Russia . . . [T]his compact for the reduction of Soviet Russia was not written into the text of the Treaty; it may rather be said to have been the parchment upon which the text was written." See Veblen's review of the *Economic Consequences*, pp. 467, 468.

[30] Keynes's friend James Strachey encountered this word when translating Freud's *Group Psychology and the Analysis of the Ego* at about the same time. (The first publication of Strachey's translation was 1922.) Freud, discussing the analysis of Le Bon, recovers the magical roots of "prestige" latent in its etymology: "Prestige is a sort of domination exercised over us by the individual, a work, or an idea. . . . Personal prestige is attached to a few people, who become leaders by means of it, and it has the effect of making everyone obey them as though by the operation of some magnetic magic." Freud, *Group Psychology*, p. 13.

Paris was a nightmare, and every one there was morbid. A sense of impending catastrophe overhung the frivolous scene; the futility and smallness of man before the great events confronting him; the mingled significance and unreality of the decisions; levity, blindness, insolence, confused cries from without—all the elements of ancient tragedy were there. Seated indeed amid the theatrical trappings of the French saloons of state, one could wonder if the extraordinary visages of Wilson and of Clemenceau, with their fixed hue and unchanging characterisation, were really faces at all and not the tragic-comic masks of some strange drama or puppet-show. (ECP, 2–3)

If the *Economic Consequences* charts disjunctions—between "great events" and unreal decisions, between futility and catastrophe, between words and expectations—it is in part to suggest that these disjunctions can be made whole. To identify the "unreal" decisions of Paris, for example, is to suggest that somewhere else there is a "real" decision to be made.[31] The theatrical illusion of an offstage where things continue to happen becomes a political conviction that the "theatrical trappings" of the "nerve centre" conceal those "hidden psychic and economic bonds" it is the project of the *Economic Consequences* to uncover. Keynes's sense that the real "events" are happening "uninfluenced and unaffected by the cerebrations of the statesmen in council" has its complement in his representation of that Council itself as shaped by forces outside of itself, by dramatists and puppet-masters. As ones "possessed not judging," to use Hardy's phrase, the negotiators lack the influence they should exert. Instead, they are victims of influence.

It is in this context of disconnections that one of two significant allusions to *Macbeth* in the *Economic Consequences* surfaces:

[31] The rhetoric of disconnections and the stress on unreality recall *The Waste Land*, with its list of "unreal" cities and its lament, "On Margate Sands/I can connect/Nothing with nothing." On February 21, 1920, Eliot wrote to his mother that as part of his duties working for Lloyd's Bank he was "trying to elucidate knotty points in that appalling document the Peace Treaty." Surely in this process Eliot became familiar with *The Economic Consequences*. Qtd. in Valerie Eliot's introduction, *The Waste Land: A Facsimile*, p. xviii. I quote the lines from the poem from the reprint of the first edition in the same volume (143).

My last and most vivid impression is of such a scene—the President and the Prime Minister as the centre of a surging mob and babel of sound, a welter of eager, impromptu compromises and counter-compromises, all sound and fury signifying nothing, on what was an unreal question anyhow, the great issues of the morning's meeting forgotten and neglected; and Clemenceau, silent and aloof on the outskirts—for nothing which touched the security of France was forward—throned, in his grey gloves, on the brocade chair, dry in soul and empty of hope, very old and tired, but surveying the scene with a cynical and almost impish air; and when at last silence was restored and the company had returned to their places, it was to discover that he had disappeared. (ECP, 20)[32]

The allusion to *Macbeth* has dramaturgical force. It alludes to a statement of extreme futility in Shakespeare and buttresses Keynes's representation of the Paris of the conference as an "unreal" city devoted to the disputation of "unreal" questions. It also remembers a meta-theatrical moment in Shakespeare:

> Life's but a walking shadow, a poor player,
> That struts and frets his hour upon the stage,
> And then is heard no more. It is a tale
> Told by an idiot, full of sound and fury,
> Signifying nothing. (V.v.24–28)

This passage suggests that life is coterminous with the time spent onstage, but the irony of the moment is that—as in Paris—the determining action is offstage: at the end of the previous scene, Malcolm's troops, under cover of branches of Birnan Wood, "*Exeunt marching.*" Macbeth's despairing picture of life as a brief onstage fling is at the same time an exercise in wish-fulfillment; the negation of what is offstage empties out the threat of those forces slowly amassing around Dunsinane. Such a scene of an isolated and falling monarch onstage while the world around is echoing with "confused cries from without" is not unique to *Macbeth*—one can think of

[32] Clemenceau's disappearing act is the perfect emblem for the way in which Keynes stages the treaty conference. Keynes's Clemenceau cynically knows that the real business of rearranging Europe is happening somewhere else. His unnoticed vanishing offers a model for Keynes's own disappearance from the scene.

Richard III calling for his horse—and this sense of "ancient" Shakespearean tragedy informs Keynes's picture of a haunted Paris busy ignoring the "rumblings" of the outside world (ECP, 2).

The most important inheritance Keynes takes from *Macbeth*, however, is the group of witches. The linguistic lesson Keynes reads in Baruch might well be a lesson from *Macbeth*: the perseverance of words, the way in which language takes on a sort of destructive double life, structures the play. (The question of the relationship of such language to allusion is the subject of the next chapter.) Indeed, the language of witchcraft surrounds *The Economic Consequences of the Peace* and its reception. The historian René Albrecht-Carrié, for instance, writes of the work:

> Keynes' critique was a prescient one, though the acerbity of his pen, if it helped the success of his book, had also the effect of giving widespread vogue to other, less helpful myths where the general nature of the peace was concerned. The Four were *not* so many witches concocting an unholy brew in their cauldron.[33]

The very need for the denial in this last sentence suggests the strange, supernatural valence of Keynes's influence. Albrecht-Carrié blames the *Economic Consequences* for a tendency to treat statecraft as witchcraft, and his picture of the four leaders of the Allied Powers as so many witches around a cauldron conjures an image the most memorable version of which surely appears in *Macbeth*. Keynes, however, is not as general in his accusations of witchcraft as Albrecht-Carrié suggests. In fact, witchcraft in the *Economic Consequences* does refer to *Macbeth*, but Keynes appropriates the play because of his more specific concerns with language and interpretation.

Keynes reserves particularly harsh and pointed rhetoric for his analysis of President Wilson. The *Economic Consequences* paints Wilson as simultaneously the victim of dogmatism and of that great problematic in *Macbeth*, equivocation:

[33] René Albrecht-Carrié, *The Meaning of the First World War*, 114. Compare R. C. K. Ensor, in 1945, on the influence of the *Economic Consequences*: ". . . it has become the influence, not of living thought, but of a dead hand." Ensor, introduction to Étienne Mantoux, *The Carthaginian Peace*, p. v.

. . . without any abatement of the verbal inspiration of the Fourteen Points, they became a document for gloss and interpretation and for all the intellectual apparatus of self-deception by which, I daresay, the President's forefathers had persuaded themselves that the course they thought it necessary to take was consistent with every syllable of the Pentateuch. (ECP, 32)

As Keynes represents it, one of the tasks of the crafty negotiators at the conference was to forge a document that seemed consistent with the Fourteen Points, Wilson's list of the unbreakable principles by which he felt the Treaty had to abide, while in fact serving the different sectarian interests of the nations represented. The Treaty's insistence on Germany's responsibility for pensions was, Keynes thought, crucial: "It makes the difference," he writes in *A Revision of the Treaty*, "between a demand which can be met and a demand which cannot be met" (RT, 93). Keynes's analysis of the efforts to make the Treaty seem consistent with the Fourteen Points includes an important scare quote from *Macbeth*, in which Keynes aligns interpreters of the Treaty with witches:

The President's attitude to his colleagues had now become: I want to meet you so far as I can; I see your difficulties and I should like to be able to agree to what you propose; but I can do nothing that is not just and right, and you must first of all show me that what you want does really fall within the words of the pronouncements which are binding on me. Then began the weaving of that web of sophistry and Jesuitical exegesis that was finally to clothe with insincerity the language and substance of the whole Treaty. The word was issued to the witches of all Paris:

Fair is foul, and foul is fair,
Hover through the fog and filthy air.

The subtlest sophisters and most hypocritical draftsmen were set to work, and produced many ingenious exercises which might have deceived for more than an hour a cleverer man than the President. (ECP, 32)

Rather than Wilson's being one of four witches hovering around a cauldron, as Albrecht-Carrié suggests, Keynes represents Wilson as the chief victim of Parisian witchcraft. Like Macbeth, Wilson consults witches to his peril. *Macbeth* provides Keynes with a template for his analysis of Wilson's falling prey to those he calls "subtle and dangerous spellbinders" (ECP, 25). The dilemma this spellbinding poses is not simply a matter of its being, in Keynes's fine phrase, "harder to de-bamboozle this old Presbyterian than it had been to bamboozle him"; it is not simply a matter of Wilson's being gullible or easily led astray (ECP, 34).[34] The combination of witchcraft and "Jesuitical exegesis" locates precisely a conflict in *Macbeth*. Words with a manifest, binding power hover over a crisis; the prophecies of the witches in *Macbeth*, like the Treaty, set the terms of the future. This power, however, is negotiable, uncertain, in short, a matter of potential equivocation.

In "Mr Lloyd George: A Fragment"—concluding pages to the third chapter of the *Economic Consequences*, which were only published later in the *Essays in Biography*—witchcraft is most explicitly at issue in Keynes's post-war writings. Lloyd George, in Keynes's portrait, is a near relative of those sophistical "witches" presented above. Challenged to show what part the Prime Minister played, Keynes asks, ". . . who shall paint the chameleon, who can tether a broomstick?" (EB, 20). Asking why George and Wilson could not manage between them to "give us the Good Peace," Keynes responds:

> The answer is to be sought more in those intimate workings of the heart and character which make the tragedies and comedies of the domestic hearthrug than in the supposed ambitions of empires or philosophies of statesmen. The President, the Tiger [Clemenceau], and the Welsh witch were shut up in a room together for six months and the Treaty was what came out. Yes, the Welsh *witch*—for the British Prime Minister contributed the female element to this triangular intrigue. . . . Let the reader figure Mr Lloyd George as a *femme fatale*. (EB, 22)

[34] Étienne Mantoux criticizes Keynes's account of Wilson, and quotes General Smuts, who had been important in urging Keynes to write his work: "'I did not expect him to turn Wilson into a figure of fun. . . . Every paper I saw,' added the General, 'quoted the part about Wilson's bamboozlement. Wilson was already going down in America. In their hearts, the Americans wanted him to go down: they wanted to evade the duties he imposed on them. The book was absolutely to their purpose. It helped to finish Wilson, and it strengthened the Americans against the League.'" Mantoux, *The Carthaginian Peace*, p. 10. This notion of the powerful and destructive influence of the *Economic Consequences* is part of the subject of the last section of this chapter.

Witchcraft figures not only the interpretation of the Fourteen Points and the shaping of them, but also Lloyd George's magical seduction of and persuasive hold over Wilson. The deliberations become a sort of drawing-room tragedy in which the supernatural diplomat in drag, Lloyd George, "a vampire and a medium in one," seduces and destroys Wilson (EB, 24).

This eroticization of the relationship between George and Wilson in "Mr Lloyd George" climaxes in a Wagnerian fairy-tale, in which Wilson plays prince, Clemenceau king, and George enchantress:

> Prince Wilson sailing out from the West in his barque *George Washington* sets foot in the enchanted castle of Paris to free from chains and oppression and an ancient curse the maid Europe, of eternal youth and beauty, his mother and bride in one. There in the castle is the King with yellow parchment face, a million years old, and with him an enchantress with a harp singing the Prince's own words to a magical tune. If only the Prince could cast off the paralysis which creeps on him and, crying to heaven, could make the Sign of the Cross, with a sound of thunder and crashing glass the castle would dissolve, the magicians vanish, and Europe leap to his arms. But in this fairy-tale the forces of the half-world win and the soul of Man is subordinated to the spirits of the earth. (EB, 23–24)

Keynes's fairy-tale reinforces the connection between interpretation of the Fourteen Points and witchcraft. The peculiarity of the song of Lloyd George, the enchantress, is that s/he sings "the Prince's own words to a magic tune." The repetition and subsequent alienation of Wilson's formulas suggests the pattern characteristic of *Macbeth* and Macbeth's dilemma: the words that should ensure his history turn equivocal and are turned against him, and he recognizes the enchantment behind them only too late. At the crucial moment in this fairy-tale, Wilson fails to make "the Sign of the Cross," and Europe falls again under the enchanted domination of "the spirits of the earth."

It is worth concentrating on one of the odder images here: Europe leaps into Wilson's arms. Such massive and athletic continental shift, one would think, seldom occurs in a reader's lifetime. A continent jumps? But Marx's Europe, too, jumps when the mole breaks through: ". . . all Europe leaps up, and cries, 'Well grubbed, old mole!'" Marx's jubilant Europe leaps, welcoming revolution; Keynes, as if rewriting Marx's rewriting of Hegel, imagines a Europe that never gets its chance. We return to Hegel: the mole doesn't emerge, the spell is not broken, Europe stays put. What is Keynes's fairy-tale, but a fable of reenchantment?

THE FANTASY OF DEFERRED HISTORY

> In fact the dominion that "Bloomsbury" exercises over the sane & the insane alike seems to be sufficient to turn the brains of the most robust. Happily, I'm "Bloomsbury" myself, & thus immune; but I'm not altogether ignorant of what they mean. & its a hypnotism very difficult to shake off, because there's some foundation for it. Oddly, though, Maynard seems to be the chief fount of the magic spirit.
>
> Virginia Woolf, *Diaries*, 14 Jan. 1918

> A prophet runs considerable risks; so perhaps he is entitled to boast when fortune smiles on him.
>
> Keynes, *Activities 1920–1922: Treaty Revision and Reconstruction*

One can situate Keynes's dilemma by examining similar constructions in a later work. The issue of the intermingling of political and supernatural influence figured by *Macbeth* still concerned Keynes in the last paragraph of his *The General Theory of Employment, Interest, and Money*, where he offers a resonant reflection on philosophy, influence, and authority that recalls Tawney's critique of "those who think themselves practical":

> the ideas of economists and political philosophers, both when they are right and when they are wrong, are more powerful than is commonly understood. Indeed the world is ruled by little else. Practical men, who believe themselves to be quite exempt from any intellectual influences, are usually the slaves of some defunct economist. Madmen in authority, who hear voices in the air, are distilling their frenzy from some academic scribbler of a few years back. (GT, 383)

Keynes, writing here in 1936, implicitly indicts both the makeshift economic policies of Britain, devised by "practical men," and the charismatic economic spoutings of Hitler and Mussolini. His two models, the unconscious "practical men," who do not realize that they are "the slaves of some defunct economist" and "Madmen in authority, who hear voices in the air," imply that influence has effects either as an untraceable and nevertheless organizing force—one can recall Smith's "invisible hand"—or as malignant magic, a "frenzy" with a supernatural aura that disguises its source in the crazed moonshine distilleries of academia. What these "Madmen" take to be supernatural soliciting is in fact the distillation of the work of some "academic scribbler."

As Keynes closes the *General Theory*, his emphasis shifts to questions of time, and to the unfolding of influence over time:

> I am sure that the power of vested interests is vastly exaggerated compared with the gradual encroachment of ideas. Not, indeed, immediately, but after a certain interval; for in the field of economic and political philosophy there are not many who are influenced by new theories after they are twenty-five or thirty years of age, so the ideas which civil servants and politicians and even agitators apply to current events are not likely to be the newest. But, soon or late, it is ideas, not vested interests, which are dangerous for good or evil. (GT, 383–84)

This closing passage sounds rather uncontroversial. Keynes offers an inertial theory of ideas according to which slow dissemination, rather than rapid diffusion, is the rule. Another target is probably the Marxist emphasis on economic determinism. Informing this argument about the power of ideas, however, are the problems of influence surrounding *The Economic Consequences of the Peace*. The reader of the *Economic Consequences* and its reception must face a challenge to the inertial scenario of the *General Theory*. What happens when ideas encroach too gradually, when influence is not "in time"? The slow accretion of influence that Keynes recuperates as standard in the closing pages of the *General Theory* marks the reception of the *Economic Consequences* as traumatic. The "influence" of the *Economic Consequences* simply came too late. By 1936, when the *General Theory* appeared, Keynes had long grappled with the difficulty of extracting pure, disenchanted influence from supernatural intervention.

The problems of Europe, according to Keynes, are partly problems of language. The language of the Treaty of Versailles is surrounded by malignant magic: whether the inheritance of a German curse, as Keynes describes it in his criticism of Baruch, or a kind of witchcraft, an equivocal language which tricks its listeners, Keynes is determined to emphasize the importance and power of words. His answer to the falsely prophetic language of the witches is to attempt the invention of a mode of disenchanted prophecy. The problem of such a capture of prophetic influence is that it involves Keynes in the very supernatural structures he might disown as forms of unwitting possession. Keynes masquerades as Lenin, for example, and becomes a bogey-man.

It is around prophecy that some of the most disturbing, unresolved tensions of Keynes's work and its reception cluster. Considering the alternative threats to Europe of potential German "Sparticism" or "reaction," for example, Keynes writes of the latter:

> a victory of reaction in Germany would be regarded by everyone as a
> threat to the security of Europe, and as endangering the fruits of victory
> and the basis of the peace. Besides, a new military power establishing it-
> self in the East, with its spiritual home in Brandenburg, drawing to itself
> all the military talent and all the military adventurers, all those who regret
> emperors and hate democracy, in the whole of Eastern and Central and
> south-eastern Europe, a power which would be geographically inaccessi-
> ble to the military forces of the Allies, might well found, at least in the
> anticipations of the timid, a new Napoleonic domination, rising, as a
> phoenix, from the ashes of cosmopolitan militarism. (ECP, 184)

That one can say that the "anticipations of the timid" were themselves too timid points to a peculiar dilemma of reading the *Economic Consequences* and of understanding the prophetic strains in it. Keynes's seeming anticipation of subsequent historical events is startling; but then one recalls that that predictive force was—or is—in many ways flawed. To the extent that the text is legible as successful prediction, it is, at the same time, legible as a colossal failure. The value of the predictions in the *Economic Consequences* lies in their

being taken as a warning; action against what they predict should in
the end nullify the predictions themselves. But the time in which
such action could have been taken is long gone. To the degree that
the "new Napoleonic domination" now has a name and a history—
Nazism—there is no way to "read" the *Economic Consequences* any-
more, if one understands reading as including an adequate response
to the text's imperatives.

The problem of reading the *Economic Consequences*, while still
powerfully palpable, had a disturbing and tangled history between
the wars. The reception of the *Economic Consequences* is notable not
only for the suggestion that Keynes showed remarkable foresight in
predicting what might be the outcome of the Versailles Treaty but
for another, equally powerful note. Such was Keynes's influence,
some argue, that his work became a key component in the policy of
appeasement that encouraged Nazi aggression.[35] By making so effec-
tive an argument against the terms of the war reparations, the argument runs, Keynes legitimized those who were willing to ignore or
excuse the increasingly outrageous actions of the Nazis in the 1930s;
indeed, accusations of a pro-German bias had dogged Keynes from
the moment of publication. The *Economic Consequences*, then, is
marked by a history of extraordinarily contradictory attributions of
powerful agency. On the one hand, the work appears as a prophetic
warning that, if heeded, might have helped prevent the Nazi rise to
power. On the other hand, it is read as fuel for appeasement, as a
cause of that very rise.

Keynes reflects on his difficult position and problematic influence
in the Preface to his *Essays in Persuasion* of 1931:

> Here are collected the croakings of twelve years—the croakings of a
> Cassandra who could never influence the course of events in time. The
> volume might have been entitled 'Essays in Prophecy and Persuasion,'
> for the *Prophecy*, unfortunately, has been more successful than the *Per-
> suasion*. But it was in a spirit of persuasion that most of these essays
> were written, in an attempt to influence opinion. (EP, xvii)

[35] This argument has perhaps its fullest expression in Étienne Mantoux's *The
Carthaginian Peace*.

One can translate the terms of the title, *Essays in Persuasion*, as "Attempts in Rhetoric," but it is exactly in the area of rhetoric that they are marked as flawed: ". . . the *Prophecy* has been more successful than the *Persuasion*." The essays have succeeded as prophecy, but prophecy succeeds where persuasive rhetoric fails. The "croakings" of the prophet as Cassandra become intelligible in retrospect, once the time of the prophecy is past, that is to say, once the prophecy has been "fulfilled." But such fulfillment entails the failure of persuasion. One is left with a series of essays that should have been rhetoric, or persuasion, but have become instead something supernatural, that is, have become prophecy. His figure for his essays, the "croakings of Cassandra," suggests Keynes's wry admission of his failure as prophet, but it also points to his resentment over that failure.[36]

The marginal position Keynes imagines as his is not only a place, but also a relationship to time. Keynes writes in the Preface to *Essays in Persuasion* that he "could never influence the course of events in time." It is unclear what this phrase, "in time," means here. It might stand as a recognition of belatedness; Keynes as Cassandra speaks as one who does influence events, but always too late, not "in time."[37] Cassandra is a sort of anti-witch, who cannot find a place for her influence. Or does that influence happen somewhere else, or in some other time, or outside of time? Keynes continues in the Preface, writing of his essays:

> They were regarded at the time, many of them, as extreme and reckless utterances. But I think that the reader, looking through them today, will admit that this was because they often ran directly counter to the over-

---

[36] There is a possible Shakespearean genealogy for the phrase. Thersites, in *Troilus and Cressida*, in which Shakespeare's version of Cassandra appears, vows, "I would croak like a raven; I would bode, I would bode" (V.ii.190–91). The association of "croaking" and foretelling may inform Keynes's ruminations. The roots may go further, to that "croaking raven" that "doth bellow for revenge" in *Hamlet* (III.ii.254), which is itself a quotation, notes tell us, from *The True Tragedy of Richard III*.

[37] This might find confirmation when Keynes writes of some of the *Essays in Persuasion*, including those excerpted from *The Economic Consequences of the Peace*: "In these essays the author was *in a hurry*, desperately anxious to convince his audience in time" (EP, xviii).

whelming weight of contemporary sentiment and opinion, and not because of their character in themselves. On the contrary, I feel—reading
them again, though I am a prejudiced witness—that they contain more
understatement than overstatement, as judged by after-events. (EP, xvii)

Keynes himself confronts the odd condition of reading his work, a
condition particularly acute in encountering the *Economic Consequences*. What may have seemed "extreme and reckless utterances,"
mad rhetoric, appears, "judged by after-events," as "understatement."

The conflict between failed rhetoric and accurate if impotent
prophecy inspires speculation about what might have been had Keynes
been more central, had he not left the Conference because he could not
abide its looming outcome. In a hallucinatory but not atypical passage,
R. F. Harrod, one of Keynes's biographers, writes of this choice:

> Would he as a permanent, and not a temporary, Civil Servant have re-
> signed at Paris in 1919? What would have been the balance of good?
> Rising towards the top of the Treasury in the inter-war period, would
> he have achieved a better conduct of British finances? We can hardly
> doubt that Mr. Churchill, the innocent victim, as Chancellor of the
> Exchequer, in the crucial years (1925–29), of the old orthodox school at
> the Treasury and the Bank of England, would have found in Keynes a
> man after his heart's desire. We may guess that Keynes would have in-
> fluenced the mind of Benjamin Strong of the Federal Reserve Bank of
> New York. Could he and Strong's successors between them have
> availed to mitigate the great slump of 1929–32? Then the Nazis would
> not have come to power. A fascinating speculation! But then, although
> no doubt he would have written books—and possibly on economics—
> they would inevitably have been of a different character. Valuable
> analyses we might have had, but the strong undercurrent of rebellion
> could hardly have been present, and, without that, would his works
> have had comparable influence?[38]

[38] Harrod, *Life of John Maynard Keynes*, pp. 120–21. This reverie begins with
Keynes's having failed to achieve the highest score in an exam for the Civil Service;
had he scored first, he might have gone to the British Treasury rather than the India
Office; had he gone to the Treasury, . . . etc. Skidelsky's *Hopes Betrayed* includes a
similar rumination: "Mantoux attacks Keynes's 'economism'. He points out that it
was the Second World War, not 'economics,' that solved the German problem. Yet
the Second World War came after the Great Depression brought Hitler to power.

Harrod's hagiographic fantasies end in an incredible, even shocking, concession to the virtues of the actual. There is more than a hint that Keynes's written work—the work he did write, with its "strong undercurrent of rebellion"—somehow mitigates the Nazi rise to power. Had he not written from an outsider's position, Harrod suggests, the Nazis could not have taken advantage of the economic crisis of the early 1930s, there would have been peace in our time—but, alas, we wouldn't have had the *General Theory*! Another possibility in the passage above is that Harrod means to grant that Keynes's very marginality gave his writing the rebellious power it possessed, that had he been a permanent functionary he might himself have conformed, and would then have had less "influence" and less rhetorical force. But these contradictory possibilities oblige one to ask again what "influence," in a case such as the *Economic Consequences*, means.

. I do not quote Harrod at such length only to suggest an abyss in one quirky historical imagination. The powerful fantasy at work in Harrod works elsewhere also, in less blaring manifestations. The representation of doubled history may take the form of repetition, as in *The Eighteenth Brumaire*; it may, on the other hand, take a form marked at once by a peculiar ghostliness and a kind of ideality. Beside the actual events of history, many people conjure other, shadow histories, supernatural histories. At the core of these histories, as in Harrod's fantasy, is the question of a deferred, or lost, but at the same time recoverable, even redeemable, influence. The fantasy of a Keynesian intervention that did not happen—a Keynesian intervention that might, even, have forestalled the economic crisis of the late twenties and early thirties and thus thwarted the Nazis—suggests, I think, a powerful stratum of twentieth-century supernaturalism. One can call it the fantasy of deferred history. The nature of this fantasy is not simply a matter of historical melancholia, a sense of tragically missed opportunities. The fantasy of deferred history insists on a layered history which leaves something in reserve. Keynes's intention may still be redeemed, even if not "in time."

The Great Depression in turn was brought about by the failure of economic leadership in the early 1920s. Had Keynes's 1919 programme been carried out it is unlikely that Hitler would have become German chancellor" (399).

5

Macbeth, Scare Quotes, and Supernatural History

JAMES AND THE "HORRID SPHERE"

OF WITCHCRAFT

In 1913, a stranger, William Roughead, sent Henry James "a publication of the Juridical Society of Edinburgh, dealing with trials of witches in the time of James I." It was a welcome, if unsettling, gift. James responded in a letter: "I succumbed to your Witchery, that is I read your brave pages, the very day they swam into my ken..."[1] "Witchery," here, might be many things: it might describe James's guilty sense of the glamour of a book that lures him from his writing, and this is, surely, a typically busy and elegant, Jamesian way of conveying thanks for an unexpected gift. But there is also a certain apprehension behind these elaborate thanks, as if James is surprised by the extent of his own fascination: *reading* accounts of witchcraft itself has become succumbing to "Witchery" in James's reply. The letter,

---

[1] "To William Roughead, W. S.," *Letters of Henry James*, vol. 2; all quotations from this letter are from pp. 327–28 of this edition; the description of the volume sent by Roughead, quoted above, is that of the *Letters'* editor, Percy Lubbock.

however, also shows an uncertainty about how to respond, an un-
willingness to submit, even an inability to know what such "succumbing" would entail. These problems of response to James I's
witchcraft persecutions are Henry James's main worry in this remarkable letter to a stranger:

> Of a horrible interest and a most ingenious vividness of presentation is
> all that hideous business in your hands—with the unspeakable King's
> figure looming through the caldron-smoke he kicks up to more abomi-
> nable effect than the worst witch images into which he so fondly seeks
> to convert other people. He was truly a precious case and quite the sort
> of one that makes us ask how the time and place could at all stagger
> under him or successfully stomach him. But the whole, the collective,
> state of mind and tissue of horrors somehow fall outside of our measure
> and sense and exceed our comprehension.

The question at the heart of James's letter also occupies the heart of this
chapter: what is "our" relationship to witchcraft? What are the conditions of the understanding of witchcraft? James's feeling that the meaning of "the whole" escapes "our measure and sense" itself marks a historical moment. James strangely anticipates a notion that many have
held: World War I becomes oddly entangled with the history of witchcraft. Historians of witchcraft and historians of World War I alike, as I
will show, have seen the moment of the Great War as a troubling
juncture, a moment where many realize again the extent of their close-
ness to witchcraft and the aspects of witchcraft no one will master.

This letter comes before the outbreak of the War, before James's
enthusiastic letters about the War as "a kind of invaluable, a really
cherishable, 'race' experience," also before a later letter in which the
War seems to have deranged and damaged not only the present, but
also the past. James writes then of being "under that violence of
rupture with the past which makes me ask myself what will have become of all that material we were taking for granted, and which now
lies behind us like some vast damaged cargo dumped upon a dock
and unfit for human purchase or consumption."[2] James now realizes

[2] Henry James, "To Mrs. T. S. Perry"; "To Compton Mackenzie," *Letters of Henry
James*, vol. 2, pp. 428, 476.

with painful conviction, to quote Keynes, "the intensely unusual, unstable, complicated, unreliable, temporary nature of the economic organization by which Western Europe has lived for the last half century" (ECP, 1); the War transforms "the past" into a pile of useless commodities. Among the damaged goods left by the wake of the War is the sense of distance from witchcraft.

For the moment, one can put James in the intellectual company of the "nineteenth-century liberal historians" of witchcraft of whom H. R. Trevor-Roper writes: "Their philosophy was formed in the happy years before 1914, when men could look back on the continuous progress, since the seventeenth century, of 'reason,' toleration, humanity, and see the constant improvement of society as the effect of the constant progress of liberal ideas." Consequently, these historians saw "the witch-craze of the past . . . as a residue of mere obscurantism which growing enlightenment had gradually dispelled, and which would now never return." "Unfortunately," writes Trevor-Roper, "we have seen them return." He has the Holocaust in mind: "Faced by the recrudescence, even in civilized societies, of barbarous fantasies in no way less bizarre and far more murderous than the witch-craze, we have been forced to think again, and thinking, to devalue the power of mere thought." With his refusal to concede that "thought" might be complicit with "barbarous fantasies," Trevor-Roper may reveal himself to be partially the heir of those liberal historians he somewhat nostalgically criticizes, but on the whole his essay is powerfully aware of reenchantment.[3] That earlier liberal construction of a progressive history has no room for the phantasmagorical. Witchcraft occupies the outer limits of the archaic; the potential for its return lies beyond the scope of this liberal imagination. "1914," for Trevor-Roper, offers a talismanic date, an eruption of the irrational, after which witchcraft has again become comprehensible.

It is important to note that James does not simply dismiss witchcraft in the manner of the historians Trevor-Roper describes: witchcraft *exceeds* "our comprehension." Witchcraft is not simply an occult and progressively vanishing residue, but a problem. The strange-

---

[3] H. R. Trevor-Roper, *The European Witch-Craze*, p. 100.

ness of James I's witchcraft persecutions, however, is such that the
moment offers no analogue to witchcraft.[4] For Henry James, in 1913,
the problem witchcraft poses is one of identifying continuities, and
he pursues "the wonder of what their types and characters would at
all 'rhyme with' among ourselves today . . ."

> That is the flaw in respect to interest—that the "psychology" of the
> matter fails for want of more intimate light in the given, in *any* in-
> stance. It doesn't seem enough to say that the wretched people were
> amenable just to torture, or their torturers to a hideous sincerity of fear;
> for the selectability of the former must have rested on some aspects or
> qualities that elude us, and the question of what could pass for the lat-
> ter as valid appearances, as verifications of the imputed thing, is too
> dismal. And the psychology of the loathsome James . . . is of no use in
> mere glimpses of his "cruelty," which explains nothing, or unless we get
> it *all* and really enter the horrid sphere. However, I don't want to do
> that in truth . . .[5]

James modifies his earlier position in his letter. The problem of the
King's prosecution of witchcraft is not necessarily that it cannot be
understood, but that James is unwilling to enter the "horrid sphere,"
unwilling to occupy the place of witchcraft; James, so to speak, does
not want to find a "rhyme." (And he ignores the one perfect rhyme
here, that of James with James.) He does not want to know what
sorts of signs might have counted as guilt for accused witches.
James's pulling back from the "horrid sphere" is at once a vivid recognition of the allure of witchcraft and an equally vivid emblem of
the pre-War propensity to repress or dismiss that allure.[6]

---

[4] A. C. Bradley, in 1903, lecturing on *Macbeth*, offers this debunking contemporary comparison between witches and spiritualists: "The Witches nowadays take
a room in Bond Street and charge a guinea . . ." Bradley, *Shakespearean Tragedy*, p.
275.

[5] The reason Henry James gives for not wanting to pursue the psychology of the
King is, perhaps, amenable to psychological investigations itself: "the wretched aspects of the creature do a disservice somehow to the so interesting and on the whole
so sympathetic appearance of his wondrous mother."

[6] There may be a certain reluctance in James to think about the often sexually
suggestive location of witches' marks that is a remarkable feature of James I's writings on witchcraft, as of early modern witchcraft persecutions in general. I have

James's response to World War I is typical in that it registers not continuity but a rupture so violent that even the proliferation of commodities of the pre-War period, the profusion of things—a category which clearly includes James's own work—becomes "unfit for human purchase or consumption." In Moretti's formula, James elevates the long Crisis of liberal capitalism to the sudden, abrupt crisis. Keynes's counter-history insists, on the other hand, on the transitoriness of what was taken for granted. More disturbingly, Keynes implies that the document that should bring an end to the War and its outburst of the irrational—the Peace Treaty—is itself the product of witchcraft. The thing that should guarantee an end to the haunted conditions of wartime is the product of the interpretive intervention of witches.

Keynes's witches—Lloyd George and the bamboozling interpreters of the Versailles Treaty—are demonic diplomats. Their skills lie in their abilities to make documents seem to mean what they patently do not mean. Such an ability to misinterpret willfully is not necessarily supernatural; what makes it so in Keynes's account is its persuasive force. This helps to explain, perhaps, the contradictory admiration Keynes expresses for the witches: where he remains Cassandra, unable to convince anyone to believe his frightening prognostications, these witches are successful in their persuasive work.

Macbeth, so important to Keynes's imagination of the Peace Conference, is a sort of negative image of the problem of Cassandra. If the problem of Keynes's playing Cassandra is that belief in his prophecies is always belated, never "in time," the problem of *Macbeth* is hasty belief. The temporality of the play, so famously askew, is marked more by anticipation than belatedness: "Time, thou anticipat'st my dread exploits . . ." (IV.i.144). The witches—and, more particularly, the language of the witches—form the supernatural nexus where questions of "historical" causation and the "natural" meet. To read Keynes is to see *Macbeth* as an allegory of the scare quote; Keynes appropriates a play the thematic core of which is the unfolding of words and influence "in time" that so troubles his work.

---

benefited from Christopher Pye's discussion of the allure of witchcraft in "Froth in the Mirror."

Macbeth returns this question of the scare quote to the "natural"; it is the problem of the relationship of history to nature in *Macbeth* that occupies the following section.

SEEDS, SECOND NATURE, CAMOUFLAGE

Stanley Cavell asks of *Macbeth*: ". . . What does Shakespeare think history is?" Cavell sharpens his question: ". . . How does Shakespeare think things happen?—is it in the way science thinks, in the way magic thinks, or religion, or politics, or perhaps in the way works of art, for example, works of poetic drama think?"[7] There is a sort of vertigo in the progression of Cavell's questions, where the last of his examples might be rephrased: Does Shakespeare think things happen in the way in which plays like *Macbeth* "think" things happen?

I modify Cavell: the question *Macbeth* poses is not so much how things *do* happen, as how things *will* happen. One of the oldest questions about the play—whether the words of the witches cause its events, or "merely" predict them—is also one of the most telling. "History" in *Macbeth* defines not so much a privileged relationship to the way things have happened in the past as a privileged relationship to the future: the Weïrd Sisters, most significantly, figure the "historical" in the play.[8] *Macbeth* may have its privileged place as an object for considering Shakespeare's sense of historical causality because the play itself so insistently works through this very problem.[9] The climactic Show of Kings, in which Macbeth witnesses the phantasmal line of Banquo stretching to the "crack of doom" (IV.i.117), is emblematic not only of a certain glorification of the Tudor line but also of the play's consistent emphasis on the future. The problem that seemingly demonic forces stage the Show of Kings points toward the crux of this chapter. The privileged, sovereign

---

[7] Stanley Cavell, "Macbeth Appalled (I)," pp. 4–5.

[8] Recognizing that the play occupies a moment when the concept of "history" was only in transition, I use the word with caution—but I do believe that something resembling a sense of "history" is at work in the play, even if in a very troubled and troubling form.

[9] See, for two recent discussions, David Norbrook, "*Macbeth* and the Politics of Historiography" and Michael Hawkins, "History, Politics and *Macbeth*."

history has its roots—I use the metaphor advisedly—in the representations of the Weïrd Sisters. The witches, at once part of nature
and foreign to it, are at the heart of *Macbeth*'s contradictory construction of the historical. *Macbeth* represents the creation of historical second nature out of the supernatural.[10]

Macbeth stages scare quotes in reverse. As I argue in my introduction, the scare quote alludes to a supernatural moment in Shakespeare and reveals a fissure in the armature of second nature; the
words of the witches, on the other hand, are supernatural speech that
buttresses second nature. The supernatural in *Macbeth* is an unstable
fulcrum between nature and history. *Macbeth* consistently ties the
witches' foreknowledge not only to the supernatural, but to the natural, and to the organic. The notion of supernatural knowledge as a
kind of unstable seed, for instance, is part of the rhetoric of the play.
Consider, for instance, Banquo's lines to the witches:

> If you can look into the seeds of time,
> And say which grains will grow, and which will not,
> Speak then to me, who neither beg nor fear
> Your favors nor your hate. (I.iii.58–61)

The ability to tell which "seeds of time . . . will grow, and which will
not" figures prophecy as organic. The phrase implies that among the
"seeds of time" are defective ones: it opens up an abyssal structure,
where what will be has a partner in a fantasy of deferred history, a seed
of time that will not grow. This separation of a deferred, even defective, time from one that "will grow" is an early instance of the play's
division of time between that which has a sovereign sanction and that
which cannot be, that which must remain deferred. Or perhaps it is
an exaggeration to say that the phrase implies that there is something
defective in these seeds at all; perhaps part of the proper "nature" of
time is the reservation of such fragments that do not "grow."[11]

---

[10] My sense of the dialectical interdependence of history and nature in what follows
owes much to Susan Buck-Morss's *The Origin of Negative Dialectics,* esp. pp. 52–57.

[11] Fredric Jameson has recently used Shakespeare's figure of "seeds of time" as the
title of a meditation on related issues of the possible shapes of the future after post-
modernity. See his *Seeds of Time.*

This division of seeds of time in *Macbeth* has a partner in a division in the supernatural. The play imagines the supernatural simultaneously for the purposes of sovereignty, granting it the givenness of second nature, and as an unnatural force to be excluded. Banquo's "seeds" have an echo symptomatic of this division later in the play, in the scene where Macbeth returns to the Weïrd Sisters and receives their equivocal prophecies, the scene which culminates in the spectral Show of Kings. Like Banquo, Macbeth calls to the witches to speak:

> I conjure you, by that which you profess
> (How e'er you came to know it), answer me:
> Though you untie the winds, and let them fight
> Against the churches; though the yesty waves
> Confound and swallow navigation up;
> Though the bladed corn be lodg'd, and trees blown down;
> Though castles topple on their warders' heads;
> Though palaces and pyramids do slope
> Their heads to their foundations; though the treasure
> Of nature's [germains] tumble all together,
> Even till destruction sicken; answer me
> To what I ask you. (IV.i.50–61)

Walter Clyde Curry demonstrates that Banquo's "seeds of time" and Macbeth's "nature's germains" refer to a scholastic notion of seminal structures endowed with a temporal charge. Curry notes Marcus Aurelius's succinct description of "certain seeds of future existences, endowed with productive capacities of realization, change, and phenomenal succession."[12] Both Macbeth and Banquo use this notion, which in its very organic consistency implies a certain supernatural possibility: if time and nature are the products of so many seeds, surely, as in any garden, some seeds will not grow. Macbeth, however, inverts the logic of Banquo's appeal to the Weïrd Sisters. This inversion suggests much about the play's construction of the supernatural and of the natural, and of the relation of these to the "historical."

Banquo's appeal to the witches rests on the notion that there is a

[12] Walter Clyde Curry, *Shakespeare's Philosophical Patterns*, p. 32. Curry devotes a chapter, "Tumbling Nature's Germens," to this issue (pp. 29–49).

certain order in the "seeds of time": some may come to fruition, and some not, but the Weïrd Sisters in any case are able to tell those "which will grow, and which will not . . ." The speech of the witches follows their looking into the "seeds." With Macbeth, on the other hand, the order of speech and prophecy is very different. Macbeth asks the Weïrd Sisters to deliver the knowledge despite its consequences, despite its possibly causing "nature's germains" to "tumble together." In short, for Banquo, the prophetic speech of the witches takes its source from the "seeds of time," while Macbeth imagines a sourceless speech that will itself disorder the "germains."

There may be a certain Coleridgean logic of the organic at work here: Banquo, father of the line of kings that culminates in James I, imagines the "seeds" as a supernatural version of the order that should obtain in the political government of the world. There is an "organic" link between the knowledge of the witches and the metaphysical notions of Banquo. The logic of the supernatural, rather than countering the logic of the state, supports it. This is consistent with the argument that *Macbeth* is an elaborate spectacle dedicated to a particular monarch, James I; Banquo's appeal, then, supports Stuart Clark's argument that "demonism was, logically speaking, one of the presuppositions of the metaphysic of order on which James's political ideas ultimately rested."[13] Macbeth's contrary sense of the supernatural as a source of natural disorder then confirms his own place outside of an order at once political and natural.

[13] Stuart Clark, "King James's *Daemonologie*," pp. 156–57. The question of the relationship between *Macbeth* and James I is a very vexed one. Frank Kermode presents a straightforward version of the argument that IV.i. is part of the play's overall "glorification" of James I: "The glorification of Banquo and of Fleance, founder of the Stuart line, was an essential part of the Stuart political myth . . ." Kermode, introduction to *Macbeth*, p. 1356. Christopher Pye, developing the idea of the interdependence of demonism, order, and spectacle along Lacanian lines, argues that *Macbeth* "conserves and renews the structures of law and transgression upon which absolutist power is grounded." Pye, *The Regal Phantasm*, p. 148. The most extensive argument that the play was written with a court production before the King in mind—for which, as far as I know, there is no conclusive evidence—is in Henry Paul's intriguing study, *The Royal Play of "Macbeth."* For a reading that explicitly counters the argument that *Macbeth* necessarily reinforces the power of James I, see Alan Sinfield, "*Macbeth*: History, Ideology, and Intellectuals."

Such a "metaphysic of order," if, indeed, that is what the play of-
fers, should be at work in the first scene in which Duncan meets
Macbeth and Banquo, and congratulates them for exploits in battle.
Duncan first addresses Macbeth:

> Welcome hither!
> I have begun to plant thee, and will labor
> To make thee full of growing. Noble Banquo,
> That hast no less deserv'd, nor must be known
> No less to have done so, let me infold thee
> And hold thee to my heart.
> *Ban.*   There if I grow,
> The harvest is your own.
> *Dun.*   My plenteous joys,
> Wanton in fullness, seek to hide themselves
> In drops of sorrow. (I.iv.27–35)

Significantly, Duncan echoes Banquo's language of growing in his
appeal to the witches in the previous scene. Macbeth himself becomes a kind of seed cultivated by the husbandry of the sovereign.[14]
If Macbeth echoes the witches' incantation with his first line—"So
foul and fair a day I have not seen" (I.iii.38)—Duncan, when he
speaks to Macbeth, echoes Banquo's appeal to the witches. One can
see here how the language of the scenes with the Weïrd Sisters uneasily saturates the play: Duncan, after all, uses the rhetoric of growth
that seems to have been, for Banquo, part of the demonic.

The temptation to load the burden of the demonic on Macbeth,
to identify him as the play's human partner of the evil witches, is
troubled by the insinuations of a relationship between Duncan and
the witches. One could say that Banquo offers the play's moral when
he warns Macbeth:

> . . . oftentimes, to win us to our harm,
> The instruments of darkness tell us truths,

[14] Harry Berger, Jr., writes: "Note here that Banquo has intercepted and expro-
priated the nature-image meant for Macbeth, and has grafted on an image that
happens to fit his share in the witches' prophecies . . ." Berger, "The Early Scenes
of *Macbeth*," p. 88.

> Win us with honest trifles, to betray's
> In deepest consequence. (I.iii.123–26)

If, however, the movement of the supernatural inevitably progresses from the telling of "truths" to betrayal "In deepest consequence," then the Weïrd Sisters' prophecy of Banquo's rule must also fall under a very questionable shadow. Rather than, so to speak, demonizing the demonic, *Macbeth* provides a vivid image of the simultaneous quarantining and mobilization of the supernatural. There is a split in the supernatural not so different from that in the work of Keynes. On the one hand, the play undoubtedly demonizes Macbeth and suggests that his succumbing to the equivocal suggestions of the witches is evil; on the other hand, there is a naturalization—even, to risk a neologism, a second naturalization—of the supernatural for the aggrandizement of sovereignty. That such a split is unsteady is a problem for the play; how one might understand that unsteadiness is, in some ways, the problem I discuss in the last section of this chapter.

Macbeth's aside on the prophecies of the witches is particularly symptomatic of this split:

> This supernatural soliciting
> Cannot be ill; cannot be good. If ill,
> Why hath it given me earnest of success,
> Commencing in a truth? I am Thane of Cawdor.
> If good, why do I yield to that suggestion
> Whose horrid image doth unfix my hair
> And make my seated heart knock at my ribs,
> Against the use of nature? (I.iii.130–37)

For Macbeth, "supernatural soliciting" elicits a response that is "Against the use of nature." Banquo, on the contrary, naturalizes the supernatural. Typical is his assured response after the witches vanish, where he sounds like an early modern super-naturalist, explaining anomalies in nature: "The earth hath bubbles, as the water has/And these are of them" (I.iii.79–80).[15] The lineaments of the production

[15] It is true, however, that Banquo asks: "Were such things here as we do speak about?/Or have we eaten on the insane root/That takes the reason prisoner?"

of something like what Tillyard called the "Elizabethan World Picture" are visible here. The order of nature is in harmony with the order of the state; it is, indeed, in harmony with the supernatural. Banquo's casual, naturalizing explanation is the image of the appropriation of the supernatural by the state.

Macbeth, on the other hand, marks the death of Nature as he prepares to kill Duncan:

> Now o'er the one half world
> Nature seems dead, and wicked dreams abuse
> The curtain'd sleep; witchcraft celebrates
> Pale Hecat's off'rings . . . (II.i.49–52)

Witchcraft, for Macbeth, disturbs nature. This is clear, for instance, in his appeal to the witches quoted before, where he sees
their prophecy not, like Banquo, in conformity with a natural
process, but as a disruption. But paradoxically it is Macbeth who
stakes his future on what he believes to be natural. The prophecy of
the third apparition—"Macbeth shall never vanquish'd be un-
til/Great Birnan wood to high Dunsinane hill/Shall come against
him"—gives him hope:

> That will never be.
> Who can impress the forest, bid the tree
> Unfix his earth-bound root? Sweet bodements! good!
> Rebellious dead, rise never till the wood
> Of Birnan rise, and our high-plac'd Macbeth
> Shall live the lease of nature, pay his breath
> To time and mortal custom. (IV.i.94–100)

The militarization of the forest—its impressing—is an apotheosis
and literalization of the language of supernatural seeds and planting
in the play. It is the play's climactic image of the split in the supernatural I have described.

John Holloway points out that it is a "commonplace" that disorder in *Macbeth*

(I.iii.83–85). I hesitate to identify where the hallucinogenic explanation falls in the
division I am charting.

is seen as an infringement of the whole beneficent order of Nature; and that nothing less than that whole beneficent order gears itself, at last, to ending the state of evil . . . That the coming of Birnam Wood to Dunsinane is a vivid emblem of this, a dumbshow of nature overturning anti-nature at the climax of the play, has gone unnoticed.[16]

This "commonplace" may be, for the most part, sound; what it ignores, however, is the way Macbeth, too, imagines his own future as ensured by the impossibility of such natural disorder. Nature seems to Macbeth to guarantee his position. Precisely because nature is orderly, he feels that there is no need to fear what seems to be the impossible migration of forest to castle. For Macbeth, assurances about the impossibility of such a freak of nature lead to assurances about the security of his own position: "Till Birnan wood remove to Dunsinane / I cannot taint with fear" (V.iii.2–3); "I will not be afraid of death and bane, / Till Birnan forest come to Dunsinane" (V.iii.59–60). The repetition of these lines, which virtually frame V.iii, suggest their incantatory value.

Macbeth seemingly ignores the problem that his assurance about the impossibility of a disturbance in nature rests in a magical spectacle arranged for him by supernatural beings. But this is no less a problem for those who oppose Macbeth.[17]

> *Siw.* What wood is this before us?
> *Ment.*   The wood of Birnan.
> *Mal.* Let every soldier hew him down a bough,
> And bear't before him, thereby we shall shadow
> The numbers of our host, and make discovery
> Err in report of us. (V.iv.3–7)

Is this "nature overturning anti-nature"? Holloway makes the intriguing suggestion that a "contemporary audience" would have found the scene "much more familiar and less unnatural" than we

---

[16] John Holloway, *The Story of Night*, p. 65.

[17] Peter Stallybrass succinctly writes that the witches "are constructed so as to manifest their own antithesis": "Cursed witches prophesy the triumph of godly rule. At one level, no doubt, this implies that even evil works providentially." Stallybrass, "*Macbeth* and Witchcraft," p. 199.

do, recognizing in it a version of spring rituals: "The single figure, dressed in his distinctive costume (one should have Macbeth in his war equipment in mind) pursued by a whole company of others carrying green branches, was a familiar sight as a Maying procession, celebrating the triumph of new life over the sere and yellow leaf of winter."[18] Malcolm and company are, then, the ritual allies of nature. I think Holloway is right to recognize a spring ritual behind *Macbeth*, but the question of how this structure works may be more complicated than he suggests. The similar rituals described by Ginzburg in *The Night Battles* come to mind: the *benandanti*, bearing fennel stalks, fight witches to win a good harvest. Ginzburg's account gives one a new sense of what might be at stake in such rituals from the point of view of the participants. There is no easy assurance; the ritual has not yet become a hollow shell, a celebration of inevitable spring: the *benandanti*, indeed, are confident that their activities are essential to bring a good harvest. In other words, Ginzburg describes a ritual that remains a contest, a ritual where the human participants may well lose.

What is most remarkable, however, about the language of the passage where Malcolm commands his troops to cut down branches is its very plainness; there is no overt suggestion of any ritual action at all. Malcolm prepares the moment that clinches the undoing of Macbeth simply as military strategy, as a shadowing of numbers; it is not even camouflage. There is no question of their being mistaken for nature. But that is what Holloway's formulation—"nature overturning anti-nature"—makes of the soldiers, as do other accounts that insist on the restoration of nature at the play's end. We see Malcolm's strategy as a natural event and so participate in the construction of second nature.

When the Messenger reports the "moving grove" to Macbeth (V.v.37), it is as a prodigy, a freak of nature: ". . . I should report that which I say I saw, / But know not how to do't" (V.v.30–31).

[18] Holloway, *Story of Night*, pp. 65–66. On Holloway's reading, see also Harry Berger, Jr., "The Early Scenes of *Macbeth*," pp. 71–72.

> As I did stand my watch upon the hill,
> I look'd toward Birnan, and anon methought
> The wood began to move. (V.v.32–34)

From pure strategy—hiding numbers—to pure and successful camouflage: the strategy does indeed, as Malcolm hopes, "make discovery/Err in report of us," but the error is not simply a mistaking of numbers, but a mistaking of species. This error allows Macbeth to believe that the prophecy of the witches has come true. (Were the Messenger to report a troop of uncertain numbers carrying branches in front of them it might not have the same effect.) So the Messenger's error is in many senses not an error: the play's structure, like Holloway's ritual, encourages one to believe in exactly the prodigious quality of the mobile forest that Malcolm's clear-eyed strategy belies. It fulfills a prophecy, even if a demonic one. In the scene after the Messenger has taken the camouflaged soldiers for a moving wood, Malcolm addresses the soldiers carrying their branches: "Now near enough; your leavy screens throw down,/And show like those you are" (V.vi.1–2). This short scene reads like a reaction to Macbeth's response; Malcolm seems to know that the branches have done far more than shadow the number of his troops, who now must show not only their numbers but "like those [they] are."[19]

The words of the witches prophesize both the ostracized, scapegoated Macbeth and the future hegemony of the line of the mythical Banquo, whose representative in 1603 was James I.[20] So these words perform a function like the "organic" one of quotations in the cultural fantasy of Coleridge, naturalizing the disturbing genesis of the state made possible by Macbeth's murder of Duncan. (Banquo, as

[19] Indeed, there is some foreshadowing of this use of the trees earlier, when, preparing to depart England for battle in Scotland, Malcolm declares: "Macbeth/Is ripe for shaking, and the pow'rs above/Put on their instruments" (IV.iii.237–39). This image of shaking ripe fruit from the tyrannical tree resonates strangely with Macbeth's imagining the "tumbling germains" of nature.

[20] Henry Paul gives credit for the invention of Banquo to Hector Boece in his *History of Scotland* (1526). Paul, *Royal Play*, p. 169.

Harry Berger, Jr., points out, does not warn Duncan, though he clearly has reason for suspicions and might even "have kept Duncan from being killed."[21]) But this odd supernatural genesis is still apparent in the play. One can only naturalize the new regime by forgetting the double function of the words of the witches that lead to Macbeth's violence as well as to the line of kings stretching to the "crack of doom."

Malcolm addresses those assembled after the defeat of Macbeth:

> We shall not spend a large expanse of time
> Before we reckon with your several loves,
> And make us even with you. My thanes and kinsmen,
> Henceforth be earls, the first that ever Scotland
> In such an honor nam'd. What's more to do,
> Which would be planted newly with the time,
> As calling home our exil'd friends abroad
> That fled the snares of watchful tyranny,
> Producing forth the cruel ministers
> Of this dead butcher and his fiend-like queen,
> Who (as 'tis thought) by self and violent hands
> Took off her life; this, and what needful else
> That calls upon us, by the grace of Grace,
> We will perform in measure, time, and place.
>   (V.ix.26–39)

These last lines of the play illustrate what Stallybrass identifies as the function of witchcraft in *Macbeth*: "a form of ideological closure . . ., a returning of the disputed ground of politics to the undisputed ground of 'Nature.'"[22] This echoes the language Duncan uses in greeting Macbeth and Banquo in I.iv; there is the same movement from the slightly anxious concern with the repayment of debt to the rhetoric of planting and of nature. Malcolm reclaims the rhetoric of the natural, but the episode of Birnan Wood is a lesson in how "nature" becomes a stratagem of sovereignty.

Both Macbeth and Malcolm have supernatural sanction. The play marks the transgression of Macbeth by having him engage in his own

[21] Berger, "Early Scenes of *Macbeth*," p. 96–97.
[22] Stallybrass, "*Macbeth* and Witchcraft," pp. 205–6.

"supernatural soliciting": the crucial companion to Duncan's murder is Macbeth's return to the Weïrd Sisters, his active solicitation of their knowledge. The play introduces Edward the Confessor to contrast the demonic Macbeth with the sacred English King, but there is an interesting elision in the description given (of course) by Malcolm of the royal touch, by which the King heals "the evil" (IV.iii.146): "How he solicits heaven, / Himself best knows . . ." (IV.iii.149–50). It is as if there is a prohibition against describing the mode by which sanctioned power "solicits" its supernatural or sacred support; *Macbeth* is nothing if not an object lesson in mystification. What Edward gets for his solicitation is not only the healing royal touch, but also "a heavenly gift of prophecy" (IV.iii.157). In every detail in this short narrative of healing, Edward is the play's anti-witch, if not its *benandante*.[23] Malcolm cannot be shown to be conscious of his complicity with the supernatural, but it is the same demonic prophecy that damns Macbeth that sanctifies Malcolm's stratagem. "Unnatural deeds / Do breed unnatural troubles . . . ," says the Doctor (V.i.71–72). "Natural" deeds with mystified supernatural sanction breed Malcolm's monarchy.

THE LAST SCARE QUOTE

Christopher Hill offers a thought experiment:

> Suppose the little England of the early years of Elizabeth had continued; suppose the outcome of the English Revolution had been a victory for the radicals who so nearly captured control of the army in 1647–49; that in consequence the proletarianization of small masters of industry, the disappearance of the yeomanry, had been very much slowed down; that Leveller opposition to the conquest of Ireland had prevailed in 1649; suppose the author of *Tyranipocrit* (also published in 1649) had persuaded his fellow-countrymen that it was wrong for merchants to 'rob the poor Indians,' to make slaves, or for governments of the rich to fight their battles for them.

This is a specimen of what I have called the fantasy of deferred history. Beside the course of the actual, the fantasy of deferred history

[23] See Deborah Willis, "The Monarch and the Sacred."

conjures another history. Importantly, the fantasy pictures this history not as one which is simply past, but as deferred. There is always some sense that the generative force of the "seeds" in this fantasy remain available to us. If the phantasmagoria summons the old to put a face on the violence of the new, deferred history summons what never was to provide shelter from past violence. They are inverse modes of historical recognition.

Hill concludes: "The worker who in 1530 could earn his yearly bread by fourteen–fifteen weeks of labour might not have had to work fifty-two weeks to earn the same amount two centuries later." Hill's sympathies are with the contemporary worker; this deferred history imagines a world in which "progress" benefits the worker, not the capitalist. There is much to say about Hill's rewriting of history. What is particularly interesting here is that Hill recognizes it as fantasy, that he knows that what he pictures is not only not possible but not even necessarily the best of all possible Englands for the worker or anyone else. The story's redemptive promise is mostly bogus:

> The long-term factors which in England fostered economic growth also brought about the seventeenth-century revolution. This by hindering hindrances to the expansion of capitalism created the conditions for that uniquely favourable balance between population and resources in England from which the Industrial Revolution was to result. We cannot change one variable without affecting all the others. That, in fact, seems to me to be the ultimate lesson to be learnt from history: that fair is foul and foul is fair. 'Perhaps this is that doom which Adam fell into of knowing good and evil, that is to say of knowing good by evil.' History, as Engels once said, is 'about the most cruel of all the goddesses, who drives her triumphal chariot over heaps of the slain.'[24]

Surely it is remarkable for a historian to grant that the penultimate line of the first scene of *Macbeth* already contains "the ultimate lesson to be learnt from history." Historical knowledge appears to be a kind of return to the words of the witches, words which have anticipated the historian. History concludes where *Macbeth* begins. Hill's ap-

[24] Christopher Hill, *Reformation to Industrial Revolution*, pp. 15–16.

propriation of Shakespeare is the scare quote in its purest form: there is no acknowledgment of the Shakespearean source of the "ultimate lesson." The words from the Weïrd Sisters bear comparison with the sentences that follow, where, first, quotation marks acknowledge that Hill has borrowed the sentence about Adam's fall from Milton's *Areopagitica*, and, second, Hill actually acknowledges Engels as source and puts the phrase from Engels in quotation marks.[25] As in Keynes, as in Marx, Hill does not need to name Shakespeare. More particularly, the privileged moment of historical knowledge is at the same time a supernatural moment.

If, in Keynes, the words of the witches figure a corrupting political language, in Hill the intensely shifting, equivocal, unstable language of the witches becomes the truest summary of historical knowledge. This chapter, then, has charted a movement from a history that cannot account for witches, cannot enter what Henry James calls the "horrid sphere" of witchcraft persecutions, to a history that marks the paradoxical formulation of the witches in *Macbeth* as the "ultimate lesson of history." This is surely strange, but that strangeness is partly what this chapter is about: the supernaturalization of historical understanding. The power given to phrases from Shakespeare is not the unquestioning privileging of an authoritative spirit from the past, not the invocation through prosopopeia of a voice that will speak to us from the past, promising a kind of harmony between past and present.[26] Scare quotes, instead, locate lacunae in historical understanding.

[25] The rhetoric of the immediately preceding passage in Milton is remarkably germane here: "Good and evill we know in the field of this World grow up together almost inseparably; and the knowledge of good is so involv'd and interwoven with the knowledge of evill, and in so many cunning resemblances hardly to be discern'd, that those confused seeds which were impos'd on *Psyche* as an incessant labour to cull out, and sort asunder, were not more intermixt. It was from out the rinde of one apple tasted, that the knowledge of good and evill as two twins cleaving together leapt forth into the World." Milton, *Areopagitica*, p. 514.

[26] It is worth noting that occult communication has become a widespread model for "our" undertakings with the Shakespearean text. The example of Stephen Greenblatt's introduction to *Shakespearean Negotiations*, where he writes of his desire to speak with the dead, is somewhat notorious. See discussion of this in Marjorie Garber's "Shakespeare as Fetish"; Pye's "Froth in the Mirror," pp. 171–72; Richard Halpern's *Shakespeare Among the Moderns*, pp. 42–43; and Cavell, "Macbeth Appalled

Macbeth, too, imagines the "ultimate lesson" of history. Though the word "history" is nowhere in the play, a phrase analogous to it does appear in the play's most familiar passage:

> Wherefore was that cry?
> *Sey.*   The Queen, my lord, is dead.
> *Macb.*   She should have died hereafter;
>   There would have been a time for such a word.
>   To-morrow, and to-morrow, and to-morrow,
>   Creeps in this petty pace from day to day,
>   To the last syllable of recorded time;
>   And all our yesterdays have lighted fools
>   The way to dusty death. (V.v.15–23)

When Macbeth speaks of "the last syllable of recorded time," he describes something that sounds like written history. There is a strange movement in the speech from the "word" for which there is no time to the "syllable" that comes at the end of "recorded time." This imagining of history as a matter of language points to the entanglement of language and history in the play, but this entanglement, again, returns one to the beginning of the play and the words of the Weïrd Sisters. In *Macbeth*, the syllables that have had a special purchase on "recorded time" have been the words of the witches. It is as if Macbeth, even before his disillusioned recognition that he has been paltered with "in a double sense" (V.viii.20), senses the snares of equivocation. But, furthermore, in this last speech equivocal speech encapsulates the historical as such. Macbeth's speech is in many ways about the exemplariness of history; if this is a history play, it is, for the moment, about the foolhardiness of taking the historical past for a model: "all our yesterdays have lighted fools/The way to dusty

---

(I)," p. 6. I offer another example of professional seance, from Peter Stallybrass: "What I'm trying to think about, you might say, is what it means to be haunted, to be inhabited by other people, to be composed by those people who have worked with us, upon us, who have transformed us. And so a lot of my present work is about the desire to be haunted." See "Discussion" following Stallybrass's "Shakespeare, the Individual, and the Text," p. 612. Stallybrass's formulation recalls Emily Dickinson's wonderful, aphoristic sentence: "Nature is a Haunted House—but Art—a House that tries to be haunted." Dickinson, *Selected Letters*, p. 236.

death." Imitation of the historical is the foolishness of those who think there is light at the end of the tunnel.

Stuart Clark writes of the need of Christian metaphysics "to give a dualistic account of the imperfections which marred the Creation without extending this to first principles." He describes one of Augustine's solutions to this problem:

> Augustine achieved this by comparing the course of world history with the forms of ancient rhetoric. For him, the *civitas dei* and the *civitas terrena* symbolized an absolute dichotomy between the values and fortunes exhibited by communities in time, but this did not mean that they had independent origins or purposes. For God had 'composed' history as the Romans wrote their poetry, gracing it with 'antithetic figures.' Just as the clash of opposites (*antitheta*) was the most effective form of verbal eloquence, 'so is the world's beauty composed of contrarieties, not in figure, but in nature'.[27]

So *Macbeth*'s tracing a movement from the words of the witches to the natural history of power is an imitation itself, an imitation of the order the word of God has installed in the world—"not in figure, but in nature." The language of the witches is the language of the play, but that language turns out to be sacred. Had there been no witches, early modern Europe would have had to invent them: God's antithetical "nature" requires them. This, in fact, has been the standard interpretation of witchcraft persecutions, suggested by Henry James's phrase, when he writes of "the unspeakable King's figure looming through the caldron-smoke he kicks up to more abominable effect than the worst images into which he seeks to convert other people." Witches are the conversions, the projections of a culture that needs witches.

This suggests the lineaments of a rather conservative *Macbeth*, a

[27] Stuart Clark, *Thinking with Demons*, p. 45. In an earlier version of which this is an elaboration, *Macbeth* offers something like a summarizing case for Clark. See "Inversion, Misrule, and the Meaning of Witchcraft," p. 126. My understanding of the language of *Macbeth* also owes much to Lawrence Danson's chapter, "*Macbeth*," in *Tragic Alphabet*, pp. 122–41, and to Steven Mullaney's "Lying Like Truth." The first part of Clark's massive *Thinking with Demons*, "Language," will be essential to any further writing on the language of early modern witchcraft.

Macbeth that inevitably underwrites the hegemonic assumptions of the culture around it, despite its compelling witches and its protagonist's speech of despair over the potential for meaningful historical action. I think there is much to be said for such a reading. I will, however, read against the grain of this interpretation. It rests on continuities—linguistic, social, political—that are not, I think, necessarily in place in *Macbeth*. The sticking point, it seems to me, lies in the words of the witches, in the play's orientation toward the future, and in the question of nature.

First, a detour into *Hamlet*, and a word on the way in which omens work there. Horatio reads the Ghost as a historical omen:

> A mote it is to trouble the mind's eye.
> In the most high and palmy state of Rome,
> A little ere the mightiest Julius fell,
> The graves stood [tenantless] and the sheeted dead
> Did squeak and gibber in the Roman streets.
>
> (I.i.112–16)

Marcellus's earlier description of the "portentous figure" of the Ghost (I.i.109) and Horatio's historical parallel have an analogue, and perhaps even roots, in the medieval tradition of figural interpretation discussed by Erich Auerbach: "Figural interpretation establishes a connection between two events and persons, the first of which signifies not only itself but also the second, which encompasses or fulfills the first." Such interpretation is distinguished "by the historicity of the sign and what it signifies."[28] This sort of figure is already "portentous"; Marcellus and Horatio, in insisting on the historical ground of the Ghost's appearance, anxiously install the Ghost in an available system of interpretation. As Marjorie Garber writes, "The 'high and palmy state of Rome,' soon to be disrupted by the assassination of its paternal leader, foreshadows a similar development in Denmark."[29]

But there is surely a problem among these similarities, parallels, and figures. If there is a suggestion of the sort of historical interpre-

---

[28] Erich Auerbach, "Figura," p. 53.
[29] Marjorie Garber, *Shakespeare's Ghost Writers*, p. 72.

tation Auerbach analyzes, then *Hamlet* stages the partial obsolescence of such figuration. The figure comes after the event: an assassination, after all, precedes the play, and the Ghost is a belated "figure" of the murder of King Hamlet.[30] And, soon enough, any discussion of "figuration" becomes moot when the Ghost speaks to Hamlet and makes his task clear; a salient difference between *Hamlet* and a play like Kyd's *The Spanish Tragedy* is that in Kyd the ghost of the murdered Don Andrea watches the slowly unfolding spectacle of his revenge without interference. Indeed, one can say that the very need of the Ghost of Hamlet to speak is an indication of the distance between *Hamlet* and the world of figuration Auerbach describes. The understanding of figuration, Auerbach stresses, is a "spiritual act."[31] In *Hamlet*, such spiritual action has become impossible; "we defy augury," claims Hamlet (V.ii.219), but such defiance is partly the necessary counterpoint to the resistance of omens. Augurs defy us. To recognize the figural fulfillment of the first event in the second demands a certain sacred—and lost—legibility to the world, like that suggested by Augustine's antithetical cosmos. The revenge Ghost, replacing the figure with the literal command, substitutes dictation for figural interpretation. "O my prophetic soul!" cries Hamlet (I.v.40), as if he had known the Ghost's news all along. If he did, why didn't he say so? The continuities of figuration assume an accepted sacralization of the world. Hamlet's retrospective divination, under pressure of a command, rescues continuity.[32]

"The people in the plays," writes C. L. Barber, "try to organize

[30] The killing of Claudius is perhaps a development similar to the assassination of Caesar, but the implied parallel between Claudius and Caesar quickly seems untenable.

[31] Auerbach, "Figura," p. 53.

[32] Keith Thomas discusses a type of prophecy of particular interest here, that invented after the event allegedly prophesied: "The truth seems to be that at the heart of the belief in prophecies there lay an urge to believe that even the most revolutionary doings of contemporaries had been foreseen by the sages of the past. . . . This had the effect of disguising any essentially revolutionary step by concealing it under the sanction of past approval. Prophecies, therefore, were not simple morale-boosters: they provided a 'validating charter' (to adopt the anthropologists' phrase) for new enterprises undertaken in the face of strong contemporary prohibitions." Keith Thomas, *Religion and the Decline of Magic*, p. 423.

their lives by pageant and ritual, but the plays are dramatic precisely because the effort fails. This failure drama presents as history and personality; in the largest perspective, as destiny." What binds *Hamlet* and *Macbeth* is something like such a failure. The ritual aspects of the episode of Birnan Wood seem to me especially telling. Barber writes of rituals in Shakespeare that they "are abortive or perverted; or if they succeed, they succeed against the odds or in an unexpected fashion."[33] Certainly the movement of Birnan Wood happens in an unexpected way; it is not a miracle, even if it retains traces of the miraculous. These traces, I think, are the product of the audience's work: the audience, like Hamlet, rescues sacred continuity, making of the plain and strategic act a prophesied, ritual action. The audience, that is, participates in the creation of second nature.

Such participation in the creation of second nature might define the ideological project of the play. But what of Hill's scare quote? His purpose is not to naturalize history by appealing to some supernatural sanction. On the contrary, Hill's scare quote implies just the reverse, that history is best understood in the supernatural words of the witches. One senses, however, that Hill's rejection of one fantasy of deferred history is on behalf of another history, itself deferred. The recognition of the "ultimate lesson" of history in the scare quote could function in a way analogous to the workings of the movement of Birnan Wood. The supernatural sanctions the action in the play, and one could say that the supernatural structures Hill's scare quote, as well, meaning to suggest that the "ultimate lesson" of history is also the last. But the scare quote distances at the same time that it acknowledges. Hill reserves, unwritten, a history not summed up in the witches' words and the crushing "triumphal chariot." Like Marx, Hill alludes to the "future."

[33] C. L. Barber, *Shakespeare's Festive Comedy*, p. 193.

Conclusion

ENDS OF THE SCARE QUOTE

Our revels now are ended.
Samuel Beckett, *Endgame*

Mature economists steal. In 1938, Keynes quoted George Herbert without citing his source, and commented mischievously: "When in *The Economic Consequences of the Peace* I quoted a verse of Shelley without acknowledgement, I was generally believed to be the author. I hope that the same thing will happen this time."[1] This unacknowledged quotation recalls Keynes's dialogue with David Hunter Miller. Hoping that his audience will not recognize Herbert has become part of an erudite, and perhaps snobbish, game. Quotation becomes a code for those in the know:

> Even in his literary cavillings Mr Miller has no luck. For as there are no primrose paths in America, how was he to know that I was echoing the words of a porter (or *commissionaire*) who in a play *Macbeth*, by an author well known in England, speaks of those 'that go the primrose way to the everlasting bonfire'?

[1] John Maynard Keynes, *Social, Political and Literary Writings*, *Collected Writings*, vol. 28, p. 109.

Miller's lack of recognition allows Keynes an opportunity to indulge in an anti-American jab, but there is also something more sympto-matic of Keynes's attitude in the weird non-sequitur of his logic. Be-cause there are no primrose paths in America, Miller does not recog-nize the words of *Macbeth*. Miller had written: "We do not have primrose paths in America, but I should think that the sight of one with a bonfire down it would be rather queer even in England." Miller literalizes a metaphor he does not recognize as quotation. Keynes pretends to follow him in this literalization, as if to suggest that the whole habit of literalization is the error of those who do not recognize quotations—and, at the same time, a particular habit of Americans, who, Keynes pretends, do not know Shakespeare. In-deed, Keynes does the scare quote one better. Not only did he ini-tially feel no need at first to identify the quotation from Shakespeare, but here Shakespeare himself goes unnamed, as "an author well known in England."

I return to this exchange because it is a story of the end of the scare quote. Are scare quotes to Shakespeare still common? I would sug-gest that the answer is, bluntly: No. The long historical moment that allowed for them is past. Institutions that enforced knowledge of Shakespeare are weaker, so the general diffusion of Shakespearean quotation through the bloodstream of the body politic is less general. Shakespeare is no longer essential to education; the sorts of political pressures that nearly mandated recognition of quotation for a large class in England, for instance, are weaker. Nor is Shakespeare the stuff of popular culture as he was in the nineteenth and early twenti-eth century.[2] No one, in short, is likely to follow Austen in imagining Shakespeare's language as part of our "constitution," in any of the senses of that word. Areas in which one can still assume an audience that will recognize tags from Shakespeare remain. But the audience is smaller. Today, quotation from Shakespeare, rather than being allu-sive, is most often quite deliberate. Those who quote Shakespeare carefully frame their quotations with acknowledgment: "As Shake-

[2] See, for instance, Chris Baldick, *The Social Mission of English Criticism*, pp. 59–85; and Lawrence Levine, *Highbrow/Lowbrow*. A recent book that will revise this picture is Richard Halpern's *Shakespeare Among the Moderns*.

speare said, . . ." 1922, when Miller and Keynes engaged in their dialogue in the *Times*, might then stand as a kind of cusp between the period when the scare quote was possible and that which followed; Miller's insistence on the irrelevance of "Shakespearean learning," then, becomes a telling sign of the times, and Keynes's show of erudition a relic. One might even imagine that Miller is stubbornly refusing to play the game of erudition, and sending up the notion that the telling allusion tells us anything at all.

So strict a date as 1922 to mark the scare quote's demise is misleading: the scare quote dies out in different areas at different times, but it strikes me as important to suggest the ways in which the conditions that made possible the phenomenon I have been investigating are no longer present. Indeed, I think part of the reason I took on this project is precisely that I live when the culture of the scare quote is past. A phenomenon that seems so unremarkable in certain contexts, the omnipresence of quotation from and allusion to Shakespeare—"Isn't Shakespeare quoted all the time?"—gains interest as it dies out. As recognition of Shakespearean allusion can be less and less taken for granted, the conditions that made it a given are suddenly more and more susceptible to study. I am sure that at times I have erred in ways not so dissimilar from those who mistake a passage from *Prometheus Unbound* for the work of Keynes: the fear that I have missed significant allusions has shadowed this project. Intertextuality becomes an obsession once the awareness that makes it possible is increasingly rare. The old mole of Minerva burrows only at dusk.

LAST WORDS ON WITCHCRAFT

In closing, however, I turn to an example of an allusion to Shakespeare in the period when scare quotes were common. In 1863, a group in Sible Hedingham, a village in Essex, drove an aged, deaf and dumb Frenchman called "Dummy" to death on suspicion of witchcraft. The death is one of the last recorded in England resulting from such persecution. The story strikingly resembles those in Alan Macfarlane's *Witchcraft in Tudor and Stuart England*, one of the most vivid accounts of the trivial disagreements and rural entangle-

ments that led to serious accusations, and sometimes to brutal pun-
ishment, during the early modern period in England. The tale in Sible Hedingham is a simple one. Emma Smith provides shelter in a
shed to Dummy, a man endowed, many in the town believe, with
supernatural powers. After a few days, she asks him to leave her shelter. Dummy "makes signs," and predicts in writing that Emma will
fall ill in ten days. She does indeed become ill, and he refuses to lift
his curse, even when offered a payment of three sovereigns. Instead,
he threateningly draws his finger across his throat. Emma Smith, in
concert with two men, one named Stammers, "duck" Dummy in a
river. He survives this ordeal by water, but dies later as a result of ex-
posure.

A lead editorial in the *Times* on this case begins:

> The elaborate spiritualism of the nineteenth century has resolved itself
> into a theatrical ghost. In the "terrific spectral illusions" called up every
> night to order on the metropolitan stage we see as impressive and perhaps
> as genuine a phantasm as ever formed the subject of a story. "Mediums"
> are beaten out of the field by enterprising managers, and the art of evok-
> ing spirits can be now acquired from Christian Professors on terms more
> reasonable than those exacted from FAUST. But there is really something
> behind all this. There is an actual and potent reality about Witches and
> Witchcraft which it will not do to overlook. It is nothing supernatural; on
> the contrary, it is only too natural. It is not undreamt of in our philoso-
> phy, but is comprehended as perfectly as any other phenomenon.[3]

This remarkable editorial allows me to review the course of this
book. It begins by referring to the ghost machine of those "Christian
Professors," Pepper and Dircks, alludes to *Hamlet*, and it includes an
intriguing meditation on witchcraft. The allusion illuminates the
editorial's emphasis: we are not Horatios, blinded by our education
or our skepticism, and therefore unable to appreciate the reality of
the supernatural. Our philosophy dreams of witchcraft, and comprehends it "as perfectly as any other phenomenon."

This *Times* editorial is a strange relic of what Trevor-Roper was
able to call "the happy years before 1914, when men could look back

---

[3] *The Times* (Sept. 24, 1863), p. 6. All quotations from this editorial are from this
page. I draw details about the case from this long piece.

on the continuous progress, since the seventeenth century, of 'reason,' toleration, humanity, and see the constant improvement of society as the effect of the constant progress of liberal ideas."[4] On the one hand, it speaks with an enviable confidence of the way "we" are now able to understand witchcraft. On the other hand, the assurance with which the editorial claims that is "only too natural" may seem not at all reassuring. The editorial oddly inverts Hamlet's emphasis:

> *Ham.*   And therefore as a stranger give it welcome.
> There are more things in heaven and earth, Horatio,
> Than are dreamt of in your philosophy.
> (I.v.165–67)

Hamlet's wonderful command to welcome the Ghost as a stranger is hard to read. The crucial phrase—"as a stranger"—is a tantalizing dangling modifier. It may refer to the Ghost, whom one should treat with the hospitality due a stranger. The "stranger" may, instead, name Horatio, who, as a stranger to the world of the ghostly, should welcome that world with cautious openness. Either way, the situation is one of incomplete knowledge. To argue, as the *Times* editorial does, that "philosophy" now comprehends the world of the persecution of Dummy, as of earlier witchcraft persecutions, is to insist that witchcraft has become known. In 1863, there are fewer things, perhaps, indeed, none at all, that are "undreamt of in our philosophy." So the allusion to the strange encounter with the supernatural in *Hamlet* implies that such encounters have passed; we comprehend ghosts now, and are no longer strangers to them. The allusion is, then, not a scare quote in my sense: it does not acknowledge the supernatural, but instead denies the existence of it.

The confidence of the editorial is that we now understand witchcraft as a real mental process; this witchcraft is "as genuine" as the phantasms of the Dircksian phantasmagoria. To explain this process, the writer introduces one of the crucial terms of the last chapters of this book, "influence":

> The superstition or credulity implanted in many minds allows of the exercise of such an influence over them as will produce material results.

[4] H. R. Trevor-Roper, *The European Witch-Craze*, p. 100.

So far as Witchcraft represents this influence, Witchcraft is a reality, and it is only necessary that we should discard the figments of its origin and its functions.

The rhetoric here disguises some difficulties in the argument. It explains susceptibility to influence as the cause of the material effects of witchcraft. But the word for how this "superstition" or "credulity" came to occupy susceptible minds gives the lie to the claim that we have already dreamt of everything. As in *Macbeth*, the language of the organic disguises the creation of a second nature that may be no more manageable than super-nature. This superstition is simply natural, "implanted"—by what force of nature or by what demonic gardener are questions that remain murky. In a telling detail in the narration of the events that led to the death of "Dummy," the writer describes Dummy's being dragged to the stream where Emma Smith and Stammers dunked him "through some instinct or instigation." The alliteration seems designed to smooth over the need to explain the existence of this tenacious "instinct."[5] There is no registration of the difficulties inherent in referring witchcraft to this more natural "origin" in the mind or instinct.

The editorial draws a somewhat surprising conclusion from this reasoning: "The man did bewitch her; not, indeed, by the exercise of power diabolically derived, but by the influence which his threats, combined with his reputation, produced upon her mind." Just as Dircks and Pepper need not sell their souls to Mephistopheles in order to raise spirits, so Dummy needs no pact with the devil to perform the offices of a witch. The reality of his craft, however, is no less real for its having no diabolical underpinnings. Furthermore, the editorial argues, the justice of witch hunts is no more suspect:

[5] This argument leant itself to an implicit comparison between the inhabitants of the Essex village and those of the Sandwich Islands, as the Hawaiian islands were then called. One E.L.C. responded to the editorial: "Sir,—The views expressed in your leader of to-day on the witchcraft case at Sible Hedingham, received a remarkable illustration from the last packet of news sent home by the Mission to the Sandwich Islands. So many people die of being 'prayed to death' that the clergy reckon it as one among the causes of the rapid decrease of the native population." E.L.C., letter, *The Times* (Sept. 26, 1863), p. 11.

We are not disposed to conclude that every witch was unjustly perse-
cuted. In so far as they were condemned to a barbarous death for dealing with the Devil, the proceedings were both shocking and groundless; but if we presume, as we most reasonably may, that many of these
reputed sorcerers did, by their threats and curses, produce in positive
form the results vulgarly ascribed to incantations and charms, we cannot hold them guiltless of crime. They were really evil-doers, though
not of the kind supposed. . . . Their operations were based upon the
influence of imagination over the functions of the physical body, and the
very belief that gave them their reputation also gave them their power.

The *Times* editorial offers this translation of the supernatural to the
psychic as a solution to the mystery of supernatural power. And in 1863
perhaps it passed for many readers as a thorough and complete explanation. This editorial's logic, however, recalls Dircks's confident belief
in the demystifying power of his phantasmagoria: our rational understanding of supernatural effects, whether produced by the phantasmagoria or by the mind, will dissolve the power of the "supernatural."

Terry Castle has linked the phantasmagoria to Freud's grander
attempt to understand unconscious processes. The phantasmagoria,
she argues, contributed to a model for the haunted psyche to which
Freudian theory later gave legitimacy: "the mind itself now seemed a
kind of supernatural space, filled with intrusive spectral presences . . ."
Freud's "project," she writes, "was compromised by the classic rationalist paradox": "Even as he attempted to demystify the uncanny
forces of the psyche, he could not help reinventing in the very theory
of the unconscious itself an essentially daemonic conception of
thought."[6] The *Times* editorial goes about demystifying the uncanny
events that led to the death of Dummy, but without registering ways
this demystification, like Freud's, might provoke yet another mystifying dilemma for thought. The editorial asserts that our philosophy
has left nothing "undreamt," but this assertion may now be legible
only as a scare quote, a veiled acknowledgment of a reenchantment
to which the writer is no stranger.

[6] Terry Castle, "Phantasmagoria and the Metaphorics of Modern Reverie," p. 167.

Reference Matter

Works Cited

Adams, W. Bridges. "Patent Ghosts." *Once a Week* (19 Sept. 1862): 361–62.

Adorno, Theodor W. "The Idea of Natural History," trans. Bob Hullot-Kentor. *Telos* 60 (summer 1984): 97–124.

———. *In Search of Wagner*, trans. Rodney Livingstone. London: NLB, 1981.

Agnew, Jean-Christophe. *Worlds Apart: The Market and Theater in Anglo-American Thought, 1550–1750*. Cambridge: Cambridge University Press, 1988.

Albrecht-Carrié, René. *The Meaning of the First World War*. Englewood Cliffs: Prentice, 1965.

Althusser, Louis. "Ideology and Ideological State Apparatuses." In *Lenin and Philosophy and Other Essays*, trans. Ben Brewster. New York: Monthly Review Press, 1971.

Altick, Richard D. *The Shows of London*. Cambridge: The Belknap Press of Harvard University Press, 1978.

Anderson, Perry. "Nocturnal Enquiry: Carlo Ginzburg." In *A Zone of Engagement*. London: Verso, 1992.

Arac, Jonathan. *Commissioned Spirits: The Shaping of Social Motion in Dickens, Carlyle, Melville, and Hawthorne*. New Brunswick: Rutgers University Press, 1979.

———. "Hamlet, *Little Dorrit*, and the History of Character." In *Critical Conditions: Regarding the Historical Moment*. Ed. Michael Hays. Minneapolis: University of Minnesota Press, 1992.

Auerbach, Erich. "Figura." In *Scenes from the Drama of European Literature*, trans. Ralph Mannheim. Theory and History of Literature, vol. 9. Minneapolis: University of Minnesota Press, 1984.

Austen, Jane. *Mansfield Park*. Harmondsworth: Penguin, 1984.

Bacon, Francis. *The New Organon and Related Writings*, ed. Fulton H. Anderson. Indianapolis: Bobbs, 1960.

Bagehot, Walter. *Letters on the French Coup d'État of 1851*. In *The Impact of the 18th Brumaire*, ed. J. P. Mayer. New York: Arno, 1979.

Baldick, Chris. *The Social Mission of English Criticism 1848–1932*. Oxford: Clarendon, 1983.

Balfour, Ian. "Reversal, Quotation (Benjamin's History)." *MLN* 106 (1991): 622–47.

Barber, C. L. *Shakespeare's Festive Comedy: A Study of Dramatic Form and Its Relation to Social Custom*. Cleveland: Meridian, 1963.

Barker, Clive. "The Audiences of the Britannia Theatre, Hoxton." *Theatre Journal* 9, no. 34 (summer 1979): 27–41.

Barker, Francis. *The Tremulous Private Body: Essays on Subjection*. London: Methuen, 1984.

Barnouw, Erik. *The Magician and the Cinema*. New York: Oxford University Press, 1981.

Bate, Jonathan. *Shakespearean Constitutions: Politics, Theatre, Criticism, 1730–1830*. Oxford: Clarendon, 1989.

Bazin, André. "Theater and Cinema—Part Two." In *What Is Cinema?*, trans. Hugh Gray. Berkeley: University of California Press, 1971.

Benjamin, Walter. "Edward Fuchs, Collector and Historian." In *One Way and Other Writings*, trans. Edmund Jephcott and Kingsley Shorter. London: NLB, 1979.

———. *Illuminations*, trans. Harry Zohn, ed. Hannah Arendt. New York: Schocken, 1969.

———. "Karl Kraus." In *Reflections: Essays, Aphorisms, Autobiographical Writings*, trans. Edmund Jephcott, ed. Peter Demetz. New York: Harcourt, 1978.

———. *The Origin of German Tragic Drama*, trans. John Osborne. London: Verso, 1977.

Bennett, Tony. *Formalism and Marxism*. New York: Methuen, 1979.

Berger, Harry, Jr. "The Early Scenes of *Macbeth*: Preface to a New Interpretation." In *Making Trifles of Terrors: Redistributing Complicities in Shakespeare*. Stanford: Stanford University Press, 1997.

Bloom, Harold. *The Anxiety of Influence: A Theory of Poetry*. London: Oxford University Press, 1973.

Booth, Stephen. "On the Value of *Hamlet*." In *Reinterpretations of Elizabe-than Drama*, ed. Norman Rabkin. Selected Papers from the English In-stitute, 1968. New York: Columbia University Press, 1969.

Bové, Paul. "The Metaphysics of Textuality: Marx's *Eighteenth Brumaire* and Nietzsche's *Use and Abuse of History*." *Dalhousie Review* 64, no. 2 (summer 1984): 401–22.

Bradley, A. C. *Shakespearean Tragedy*. New York: Meridian, 1955.

Brecht, Bertolt. *Brecht on Theatre*, trans. John Willett. New York: Hill and Wang, 1978.

Buck-Morss, Susan. *The Dialectics of Seeing: Walter Benjamin and the Ar-cades Project*. Cambridge: MIT Press, 1981.

———. *The Origin of Negative Dialectics: Theodor W. Adorno, Walter Ben-jamin, and the Frankfurt Institute*. New York: Free Press, 1977.

Burke, Edmund. *Reflections on the Revolution in France*. Ed. Conor Cruise O'Brien. Harmondsworth: Penguin, 1968.

Burke, Kenneth. *A Rhetoric of Motives*. Berkeley: University of California Press, 1969.

Burke, Peter. *Popular Culture in Early Modern Europe*. New York: Harper, 1978.

Cadava, Eduardo. *Words of Light: Theses on the Photography of History*. Princeton: Princeton University Press, 1997.

Carlyle, Thomas. "Count Cagliostro, In Two Flights." In *Critical and Mis-cellaneous Essays*. Vol. 8 of *Carlyle's Complete Works*. New York: John W. Lovell, n.d.

———. *Past and Present*, ed. Edwin Mims. New York: Scribner's, 1918.

Castle, Terry. "Phantasmagoria: Spectral Technology and the Metaphorics of Modern Reverie." In *The Female Thermometer: Eighteenth-Century Culture and the Invention of the Uncanny*. New York: Oxford University Press, 1995.

Cavell, Stanley. "The Avoidance of Love: A Reading of *King Lear*." In *Dis-owning Knowledge in Six Plays of Shakespeare*. Cambridge: Cambridge University Press, 1987.

———. "Macbeth Appalled (I)." *Raritan* 12, no. 2 (fall 1992): 1–15.

———. "Macbeth Appalled (II)." *Raritan* 12, no. 3 (winter 1993): 1–15.

Chaouli, Michel. "Masking and Unmasking: The Ideological Fantasies of the *Eighteenth Brumaire*." *Qui Parle* 3, no. 1 (spring 1989): 53–71.

Clark, Stuart. "Inversion, Misrule, and the Meaning of Witchcraft." *Past and Present* 87 (May 1980): 98–127.

———. "King James's *Daemonologie*: Witchcraft and Kingship." In *The Damned Art: Essays in the Literature of Witchcraft*, ed. Sydney Anglo. London: Routledge & Kegan Paul, 1977.

————. *Thinking with Demons: The Idea of Witchcraft in Early Modern Europe*. Oxford: Clarendon, 1997.

Cohen, Margaret. *Profane Illumination: Walter Benjamin and the Paris of Surreal Revolution*. Berkeley: University of California Press, 1993.

Coleridge, Samuel Taylor. *Lectures and Notes on Shakspere and Other English Poets*. London: George Bell and Sons, 1904.

Curry, Walter Clyde. *Shakespeare's Philosophical Patterns*. Baton Rouge: Louisiana State University Press, 1937.

Danson, Lawrence. *Tragic Alphabet: Shakespeare's Drama of Language*. New Haven: Yale University Press, 1974.

Debord, Guy. *The Society of the Spectacle*. Detroit: Black & Red, 1977.

DeLuca, Diana Macintyre. "The Movements of the Ghost in *Hamlet*." *Shakespeare Quarterly* 24, no. 2 (spring 1973): 147–54.

Demetz, Peter. *Marx, Engels, and the Poets: Origins of Marxist Literary Criticism*, rev. ed., trans. Demetz and Jeffrey L. Sammons. Chicago: University of Chicago Press, 1967.

Derrida, Jacques. *Limited Inc.* Evanston: Northwestern University Press, 1988.

————. *Specters of Marx: The State of the Debt, the Work of Mourning, and the New International*, trans. Peggy Kamuf. New York: Routledge, 1994.

Dickinson, Emily. *Selected Letters*, ed. Thomas H. Johnson. Cambridge: Belknap Press of Harvard University Press, 1986.

Dickson, Jay. "Modernism Post Mortem: Narrative and Sentimental Bereavement after Victoria" Ph.d. diss., Princeton University, 1996.

Dircks, Henry. *The Ghost! As Produced in the Spectre Drama, Popularly Illustrating the Marvellous Optical Illusions Obtained by the Apparatus Called the Dircksian Phantasmagoria: Being a Full Account of Its History, Construction, and Various Adaptations*. London: E. and F. N. Spon, 1863.

————. *Scientific Studies: Practical, in Contrast with Chimerical Pursuits; Exemplified in Two Popular Lectures*. London: E. & F. N. Spon, 1869.

Doran, Madeleine. "That Undiscovered Country: A Problem Concerning the Use of the Supernatural in *Hamlet* and *Macbeth*." *Philological Quarterly* 20, no. 3 (July 1941): 413–27.

Doyle, A. Conan, and Edward Clodd. "Is Sir Oliver Lodge Right?" *The Strand Magazine* 54, no. 319 (July, 1917): 49–54.

During, Simon. "Magical Effects: The Cultural Work of Sleights, Tricks and Illusions 1720–1780." Paper presented to the Department of English, Princeton University, Dec. 1995.

Eagleton, Terry. *Walter Benjamin, or, Towards a Revolutionary Criticism*. London: Verso, 1981.

Eliot, T. S. *The Waste Land: A Facsimile and Transcript of the Original Drafts*, ed. Valerie Eliot. New York: Harvest, 1971.

Emerson, Ralph Waldo. "Shakspeare; Or, the Poet." In *Representative Men*. Boston: Houghton Mifflin, 1903.

Empson, William. *Essays on Shakespeare*, ed. David Pirie. Cambridge: Cambridge University Press, 1986.

E.S. *Spiritualism and Other Signs*. London: Simpkin, Marshall, & Co., 1865.

Ferguson, Margaret. "*Hamlet*: Letters and Spirits." In *Shakespeare and the Question of Theory*, ed. Patricia Parker and Geoffrey Hartman. New York: Methuen, 1985.

Fetter, Frank Whitson. "Lenin, Keynes, and Inflation." *Economica* 44 (Feb. 1977): 77–80.

Freedman, Jonathan. *Professions of Taste: Henry James, British Aestheticism, and Commodity Culture*. Stanford: Stanford University Press, 1990.

Freud, Sigmund. *Group Psychology and the Analysis of the Ego*, trans. James Strachey. New York: Norton, 1959.

———. "The 'Uncanny.'" *Studies in Parapsychology*, trans. Alix Strachey, ed. Philip Rieff. New York: Collier, 1963.

Frye, Roland Mushat. *The Renaissance Hamlet*. Princeton: Princeton University Press, 1984.

Furness, Howard Horace, ed. *Hamlet*. 5th ed. The New Variorum Shakespeare. Philadelphia: J. B. Lippincott, 1877.

Fussell, Paul. *The Great War and Modern Memory*. London: Oxford University Press, 1975.

Gagnier, Regenia. *Idylls of the Marketplace: Oscar Wilde and the Victorian Public*. Stanford: Stanford University Press, 1986.

Garber, Marjorie. "Shakespeare as Fetish." *Shakespeare Quarterly* 41, no. 2 (summer 1990): 242–50.

———. *Shakespeare's Ghost Writers: Literature as Uncanny Causality*. New York: Methuen, 1987.

Gay, Peter. *Freud: A Life for Our Time*. New York: Norton, 1988.

"Ghosts Without Spirit." *Punch, Or the London Charivari* 45 (Oct. 10, 1863): 146.

Ginzburg, Carlo. *Ecstasies: Deciphering the Witches' Sabbath*, trans. Raymond Rosenthal. New York: Penguin, 1992.

———. *The Night Battles: Witchcraft & Agrarian Cults in the Sixteenth & Seventeenth Centuries*, trans. Anne and John Tedeschi. New York: Penguin, 1985.

Glockner, Hermann. *Hegel-Lexikon*. Stuttgart: Frommans, 1957.

Goldfarb, Russell M. and Clare R. *Spiritualism and Nineteenth-Century Letters*. Rutherford: Fairleigh Dickinson University Press, 1978.

Greenblatt, Stephen. *Shakespearean Negotiations: The Circulation of Social Energy in Renaissance England*. Berkeley: University of California Press, 1988.

Greg, W. W. "Hamlet's Hallucination." *The Modern Language Review* 21 (Oct. 1917): 393–421.

Habermas, Jürgen. "The Entwinement of Myth and Enlightenment: Max Horkheimer and Theodor Adorno." In *The Philosophical Discourse of Modernity*, trans. Frederick Lawrence. Cambridge: MIT Press, 1987.

Haill, Catherine. "Spirits and Ghosts That Glide by Night." *Scottish Opera Yearbook* (1985/86): 64–67.

Halpern, Richard. *The Poetics of Primitive Accumulation: English Renaissance Culture and the Genealogy of Capital*. Ithaca: Cornell University Press, 1991.

———. *Shakespeare Among the Moderns*. Ithaca: Cornell University Press, 1997.

Harrod, R. F. *The Life of John Maynard Keynes*. New York: St. Martin's Press, 1966.

Hartman, Geoffrey. *The Fateful Question of Culture*. New York: Columbia University Press, 1997.

"Haunted Hoxton." *All the Year Round* (27 June 1863): 420–24.

Hawkes, Terence. "Telmah." In *Shakespeare and the Question of Theory*, ed. Patricia Parker and Geoffrey Hartman. New York: Methuen, 1985.

Hawkins, Michael. "History, Politics and *Macbeth*." In *Focus on Macbeth*, ed. John Russell Brown. London: Routledge, 1981.

Hegel, Georg Wilhelm Friedrich. *Lectures on the Philosophy of World History. Introduction: Reason in History*, trans. H. B. Nesbit. Cambridge: Cambridge University Press, 1975.

———. *On Tragedy*, ed. Anne and Henry Paolucci. New York: Harper, 1962.

———. *The Philosophy of History*, rev. ed., trans. J. Sibree. New York: Willey, 1900.

———. *Philosophy of Right*, trans. T. M. Knox. London: Oxford University Press, 1967.

Herzen, Alexander. *My Past and Thoughts: The Memoirs of Alexander Herzen*, trans. Constance Garnett, rev. by Humphrey Higgins, ed. Dwight Macdonald. Berkeley: University of California Press, 1982.

Hill, Christopher. *Reformation to Industrial Revolution*. The Pelican Economic History of Britain, vol. 2. Harmondsworth: Penguin, 1969.

Hoffmann, Louise. "War, Revolution, and Psychoanalysis: Freudian Thought Begins to Confront Social Reality." *Journal of the History of the Behavioral Sciences* 17 (1981): 251–69.

Holloway, John. *The Story of Night: Studies in Shakespeare's Major Tragedies*. Lincoln: University of Nebraska Press, 1961.

Hooson, William. *The Miners Dictionary. Explaining Not only the Terms used by Miners, But also Containing The Theory and Practice Of that most Useful Art of Mining* ... Wrexham: Printed for the Author, and T. Payne, Bookseller, 1747.

Horkheimer, Max. "The End of Reason." In *The Essential Frankfurt School Reader*, ed. Andrew Arato and Eike Gebhardt. New York: Continuum, 1982.

Horkheimer, Max and Theodor W. Adorno. *Dialectic of Enlightenment*, trans. John Cumming. New York: Continuum, 1988.

Hughes, Peter. "Painting the Ghost." *NLH* 19, no. 2 (winter 1988): 371–84.

Hunter, G. K. Introduction to *Macbeth*, by William Shakespeare. The New Penguin Shakespeare. Harmondsworth: Penguin, 1967.

The Illustrated London News, 1863.

James, Henry. *The Letters of Henry James*, ed. Percy Lubbock. 2 vols. New York: Scribner's, 1920.

Jameson, Fredric. "Marx's Purloined Letter." *New Left Review* 209 (Jan./Feb. 1995): 75–109.

———. *The Seeds of Time*. New York: Columbia University Press, 1994.

Jenkins, Harold, ed. *Hamlet*. The Arden Shakespeare. London: Methuen, 1982.

Joyce, James. *Ulysses*. New York: Random House, 1946.

Kantorowicz, Ernst H. *The King's Two Bodies: A Study in Mediaeval Political Theology*. Princeton: Princeton University Press, 1957.

Keenan, Thomas, "The Point Is to (Ex)Change It: Reading 'Capital,' Rhetorically." In *Fables of Responsibility: Aberrations and Predicaments in Ethics and Politics*. Stanford: Stanford University Press, 1997.

Kermode, Frank. Introduction to *Macbeth*, by William Shakespeare. In *The Riverside Shakespeare*. 2d ed. Boston: Houghton Mifflin, 1997.

Keynes, John Maynard. *The Collected Writings of John Maynard Keynes*. General eds. Austin Robinson and Donald Moggridge. London: Macmillan, 1971–89.

Krell, David Farrell. "Der Maulwurf: Die philosophische Wühlarbeit bei Kant, Hegel und Nietzsche (The Mole: Philosophical Burrowing in Kant, Hegel, and Nietzsche)." In *Why Nietzsche Now?*, ed. Daniel O'Hara. Bloomington: Indiana University Press, 1985.

Lavater, Ludwig. *Of Ghostes and Spirites Walking by Nyght*, ed. J. Dover Wilson and May Yardley. Oxford: Printed for The Shakespeare Association at the University Press, 1929.

Lears, T. J. Jackson. *No Place of Grace: Antimodernism and the Transformation of American Culture, 1880–1920*. New York: Pantheon, 1981.

Lefebvre, Henri. *Critique of Everyday Life*, vol. I: *Introduction*, trans. John Moore. London: Verso, 1991.

Levine, Lawrence W. *Highbrow/Lowbrow: The Emergence of Cultural Hierarchy in America*. Cambridge: Harvard University Press, 1988.

Lukacher, Ned. *Primal Scenes: Literature, Philosophy, Psychoanalysis*. Ithaca: Cornell University Press, 1986.

Lukács, Georg. "Reification and the Consciousness of the Proletariat." In *History and Class Consciousness: Studies in Marxist Dialectic*, trans. Rodney Livingstone. Cambridge: MIT Press, 1971.

Macfarlane, Alan. *Witchcraft in Tudor and Stuart England: A Regional and Comparative Study*. New York: Harper, 1970.

Mantoux, Étienne. *The Carthaginian Peace: or The Economic Consequences of Mr. Keynes*. Introduction by R. C. K. Ensor. New York: Scribner's, 1952.

Marshall, David. "Exchanging Visions: Reading *A Midsummer Night's Dream*." *ELH* 49, no. 3 (fall 1982): 543–75.

Marx, Karl. *Der Achtzehnte Brumaire des Louis Bonaparte*. In *Werke, Artikel, Entwürfe Juli 1851 bis Dezember 1852*. Part I, vol. 11 (text) of *Karl Marx Friedrich Engels Gesamtausgabe (MEGA)*. Berlin: Dietz Verlag, 1985.

———. *Capital: A Critique of Political Economy*, vol. 1, trans. Ben Fowkes. New York: Vintage Books, 1977.

———. *Early Writings*, trans. T. B. Bottomore. New York: McGraw, 1964.

———. *The Eighteenth Brumaire of Louis Bonaparte*, trans. C. Dutt [?]. New York: International, 1963.

———. *Surveys from Exile. Political Writings*, vol. 2, trans. Ben Fowkes and Paul Jackson, ed. David Fernbach. New York: Random House, 1973.

———. "Vorwort [zur zweiten Ausgabe]," in Marx and Friedrich Engels, *Ausgewählte Werke*, 6 vols. (Berlin: Dietz, 1986), 2: 303–5.

Marx, Karl, and Friedrich Engels. *The Communist Manifesto*. In *The Marx-Engels Reader*, 2nd ed., ed. Robert C. Tucker. New York: Norton, 1978.

———. *The German Ideology, Part One*, ed. C. J. Arthur. New York: International, 1970.

Mazlish, Bruce. "The Tragic Farce of Marx, Hegel, and Engels: A Note." *History and Theory* 11, no. 3 (1972): 335–37.

McLellan, David. *Marx Before Marxism*. 2nd ed. London: Macmillan, 1980.

Mehlman, Jeffrey. *Revolution and Repetition: Marx/Hugo/Balzac.* Berkeley: University of California Press, 1977.

Mehring, Franz. *Karl Marx: The Story of His Life,* trans. Edward Fitzgerald. New York: Covici, Friede, 1935.

Menke, Bettine. "Das Nach-Leben im Zitat: Benjamins Gedächtnis der Texte." In *Gedächtniskunst: Raum—Bild—Schrift: Studien zur Mnemotechnik,* ed. Anselm Haverkamp and Renate Lachmann. Frankfurt: Suhrkamp, 1991.

Menninghaus, Winfried. "Walter Benjamin's Theory of Myth," trans. Gary Smith. In *On Walter Benjamin: Critical Essays and Recollections.* Cambridge: MIT Press, 1988.

Merchant, Carolyn. *The Death of Nature: Women, Ecology, and the Scientific Revolution.* San Francisco: Harper, 1980.

Milton, John. *Areopagitica.* In *Complete Prose Works,* vol. 2. New Haven: Yale University Press, 1959.

Mitchell, W. J. T. *Iconology: Image, Text, Ideology.* Chicago: University of Chicago Press, 1986.

Moggridge, D. E. *Maynard Keynes: An Economist's Biography.* London: Routledge, 1992.

Monléon, José B. *A Specter Is Haunting Europe: A Sociohistorical Approach to the Fantastic.* Princeton: Princeton University Press, 1990.

Moretti, Franco. *Signs Taken for Wonders: Essays in the Sociology of Literary Forms,* trans. Susan Fischer, David Forgacs, and David Miller. London: Verso, 1983.

Mullaney, Steven. "Lying Like Truth: Riddle, Representation and Treason." In *The Place of the Stage: License, Play, and Power in Renaissance England.* Ann Arbor: University of Michigan Press, 1988.

Munro, John, ed. *The Shakspere Allusion-Book: A Collection of Allusions to Shakspere from 1591 to 1700,* vol. 1. New York: Duffield, 1909.

The New-York Daily Tribune, 1863.

The New-York Times, 1863.

Norbrook, David. "*Macbeth* and the Politics of Historiography." In *Politics of Discourse: The Literature and History of Seventeenth-Century England,* ed. Kevin Sharpe and Steven N. Zwicker. Berkeley: University of California Press, 1987.

Nunokawa, Jeff. *The Afterlife of Property: Domestic Security and the Victorian Novel.* Princeton: Princeton University Press, 1994.

Owen, Alex. *The Darkened Room: Women, Power, and Spiritualism in Late Victorian England.* London: Virago, 1989.

Paul, Henry. *The Royal Play of "Macbeth."* New York: Macmillan, 1950.

Pepper, John Henry. *The True History of the Ghost; and All About Metempsychosis.* London: Cassell, 1890.

Petry, Sandy. "The Reality of Representation: Between Marx and Balzac." *Critical Inquiry* 14 (spring 1988): 448–68.

Plancy, Collin de. *Dictionnaire Infernale, ou Bibliothèque Universelle . . .* Paris: A la Librarie Universelle, 1826.

Pöggeler, Otto. "Heidegger, Nietzsche, and Politics." In *The Heidegger Case: On Philosophy and Politics.* Ed. Tom Rockmore and Joseph Margolis. Philadelphia: Temple University Press, 1992.

Prosser, Eleanor. *Hamlet and Revenge,* 2nd. ed. Stanford: Stanford University Press, 1971.

Proudhon, Pierre Joseph. *Selected Writings,* trans. Elizabeth Fraser. New York: Anchor, 1969.

Pye, Christopher. "Froth in the Mirror: Demonism, Sexuality, and the Early Modern Subject." In *Repossessions: Psychoanalysis and the Phantasms of Early Modern Culture.* Ed. Timothy Murray and Alan K. Smith. Minneapolis: University of Minnesota Press, 1998.

———. *The Regal Phantasm: Shakespeare and the Politics of Spectacle.* London: Routledge, 1990.

Rees, Terence and David Wilmore, ed. *British Theatrical Patents 1801–1900.* London: The Society for Theatre Research, 1996.

Robertson, Priscilla. *Revolutions of 1848: A Social History.* New York: Harper Torchbooks, 1960.

Rolleston, James L. "The Politics of Quotation: Walter Benjamin's Arcades Project." *PMLA* 104, no. 1 (Jan. 1989): 13–27.

Rose, Gillian. *The Melancholy Science: An Introduction to the Thought of Theodor W. Adorno.* New York: Columbia University Press, 1978.

Rosenheim, Shawn James. *The Cryptographic Imagination: From Edgar Poe to the Internet.* Baltimore: Johns Hopkins University Press, 1997.

Said, Edward W. "On Repetition." In *The World, The Text, and the Critic.* Cambridge: Harvard University Press, 1983.

Sala, George Augustus. "On Having Seen a Ghost at Hoxton, and the Very Deuce Himself in Paris," "Breakfast in Bed; Or, Philosophy Between the Sheets," no. 10 *Temple Bar* 8 (July 1863): 503–12.

Schlegel, A. W. von, trans. *Hamlet, Prinz von Danemark.* Leipzig: Tempel Verlag, n.d.

Sébillot, Paul. *Les Travaux Publics et les Mines dans les Traditions et les Superstitions de tout les Pays.* Paris: J. Rothschild, 1894.

Shakespeare, William. *The Riverside Shakespeare,* ed. G. Blakemore Evans et al. 2d ed. Boston: Houghton Mifflin, 1997.

Shatford, Sarah Taylor. *Shakespeare's Revelations by Shakespeare's Spirit*. New York: The Torch Press, 1919.

Shklovsky, Victor. "Art as Technique." In *Russian Formalist Criticism: Four Essays*, trans. Lee T. Lemon and Marion J. Reis. Lincoln: University of Nebraska Press, 1965.

Shoreditch Observer, 1863.

Sinfield, Alan. "*Macbeth*: History, Ideology, and Intellectuals." *Faultlines: Cultural Materialism and the Politics of Dissident Reading*. Berkeley: University of California Press, 1992.

Skidelsky, Robert. *Hopes Betrayed: 1883–1920*. Vol. 1 of *John Maynard Keynes*. New York: Viking, 1986.

Smith, Adam. *An Inquiry into the Nature and Causes of the Wealth of Nations*. 2 vols. Indianapolis: Liberty Fund, 1981.

———. *The Theory of Moral Sentiments*. Indianapolis: Liberty Fund, 1984.

Sontag, Raymond. *A Broken World: 1919–1939*. New York: Harper, 1971.

Speaight, George. "Professor Pepper's Ghost." *Theatre Notebook* 43, no. 1 (1989): 16–24.

Spitzer, Leo. "Milieu and Ambiance: An Essay in Historical Semantics," parts 1 and 2. *Philosophy and Phenomenological Research* 3, no. 1 (Sept. 1942): 1–42; no. 2 (Dec. 1942): 169–218.

Stallybrass, Peter. "*Macbeth* and Witchcraft." In *Focus on Macbeth*, ed. John Russell Brown. London: Routledge, 1982.

———. "Marx and Heterogeneity: Thinking the Lumpenproletariat." *Representations* 31 (summer, 1990): 69–95.

———. "Shakespeare, the Individual, and the Text." In *Cultural Studies*, ed. Lawrence Grossberg, Cary Nelson, and Paula A. Treichler. New York: Routledge, 1992.

Table Talk, Or, 'Shreds and Patches' A POPULAR ENTERTAINMENT, Delivered by M. Henry, With the most distinguished success, at the ADELPHI Theatre . . . London: Duncombe, 1825?.

Taussig, Michael T. *The Devil and Commodity Fetishism in South America*. Chapel Hill: University of North Carolina Press, 1980.

Tawney, R. H. *The Acquisitive Society*. New York: Harcourt, Brace, and Howe, 1920.

———. *Religion and the Rise of Capitalism*. New York: Mentor, 1954.

Taylor, Gary. *Reinventing Shakespeare: A Cultural History, From the Restoration to the Present*. New York: Weidenfeld & Nicolson, 1989.

Taylor, Tom. *The Ghost! The Ghost!! The Ghost!!! Or The Late Awful Rise in Spirits, an apropos jeu d'esprit*. London: W. Davey, 1863.

Thomas, Keith. *Religion and the Decline of Magic*. New York: Scribner's, 1971.

Thorndike, Ashley H. "The Relation of *Hamlet* to Contemporary Revenge Plays." *PMLA*, n.s., 10 (1902): 125–220.

Tifft, Stephen. "*Drôle de Guerre*: Renoir, Farce, and the Fall of France." *Representations* 38 (spring 1992): 131–65.

The Times (London), 1863.

Tolles, Winton. *Tom Taylor and the Victorian Drama*. New York: Columbia University Press, 1940.

Trevor-Roper, H. R. *The European Witch-Craze of the Sixteenth and Seventeenth Centuries and Other Essays*. New York: Harper, 1969.

Turner, John. "The Tragic Romances of Feudalism." In *Shakespeare: The Play of History*. By Graham Holderness, Nick Potter, and Turner. Iowa City: University of Iowa Press, 1987.

Veblen, Thorstein. Review of *The Economic Consequences of the Peace*, by John Maynard Keynes. *Political Science Quarterly* 35, no. 3 (Sept. 1920): 467–72.

Walpole, Horace. *The Castle of Otranto*. New York: Collier, 1963.

Weber, Max. *The Protestant Ethic and the Spirit of Capitalism*, trans. Talcott Parsons. New York: Charles Scribner's Sons, 1958.

———. "Science as Vocation." *From Max Weber: Essays in Sociology*, trans. H. H. Gerth and C. Wright Mills. New York: Oxford University Press, 1946.

———. *The Theory of Social and Economic Organization*, trans. A. M. Henderson and Talcott Parsons. New York: The Free Press, 1964.

Wicke, Jennifer. *Advertising Fictions: Literature, Advertisement, and Social Reading*. New York: Columbia University Press, 1988.

Williams, Raymond. "Base and Superstructure in Marxist Cultural Theory." In *Problems in Materialism and Culture: Selected Essays*. London: NLB, 1980.

———. *The Country and the City*. New York: Oxford University Press, 1973.

———. "The Significance of 'Bloomsbury' as a Social and Cultural Group." *Keynes and the Bloomsbury Group*, ed. Derek Crabtree and A. P. Thirlwall. New York: Holmes and Meier, 1980. 40–67.

Williams, Rosalind. *Dream Worlds: Mass Consumption in Late Nineteenth-Century France*. Berkeley: University of California Press, 1982.

Willis, Deborah. "The Monarch and the Sacred: Shakespeare and the Ceremony for the Healing of the King's Evil." In *True Rites and Maimed Rites: Ritual and Anti-Ritual in Shakespeare and His Age*, ed. Linda Woodbridge and Edward Berry. Urbana: University of Illinois Press, 1992.

Wilson, John Dover. *What Happens in Hamlet.* Cambridge: Cambridge University Press, 1960.

Young, Allyn A. "The Economics of the Treaty." *The New Republic* 21, no. 273 (Feb. 25, 1920): 388–89.

Žižek, Slavoj. *The Sublime Object of Ideology.* London: Verso, 1989.

Zola, Émil. *Germinal,* trans. Leonard Tancock. Harmondsworth: Penguin, 1954.

Index

In this index an "f" after a number indicates a separate reference on the next page, and an "ff" indicates separate references on the next two pages. A continuous discussion over two or more pages is indicated by a span of page numbers, e.g., "57–59." *Passim* is used for a cluster of references in close but not consecutive sequence.